Blackwell Publishers
Oxford, UK and Cambridge, USA

ART HISTORY

Journal of the Association of Art Historians

Volume 16 Number 3 September 1993

Art History is published quarterly in March, June, September and December for the **Association of Art Historians** by **Blackwell Publishers**, 108 Cowley Road, Oxford OX4 1JF or 238 Main Street, Cambridge, MA 02142, USA. Registered charity no. 282579

Information for Subscribers: New orders and sample copy requests should be addressed to the Journals Marketing Manager at the publisher's address above. Renewals, claims and all other correspondence relating to subscriptions should be addressed to the Journals Subscriptions Department, Marston Book Services. PO Box 87, Oxford OX2 0DT. Cheques should be made payable to Basil Blackwell Ltd.

SUBSCRIPTION PRICES 1993	UK/EUR	NA*	ROW
Institutions	£73.50	US$151.00	£81.50
Individuals	£44.00	US$ 96.50	£53.50
Single copies (Institutions)	£23.00	US$ 43.00	£23.00
Single copies (Individuals)	£15.00	US$ 29.00	£16.00

*Canadian customers/residents please add 7% for GST

US mailing: Second class postage pending at Newark, New Jersey. Postmaster: send address corrections to Art History, ℅ Virgin Mailing & Distribution Building 150, Newark International Airport, Newark, NJ 07114, USA. (US Mailing Agent).

Articles for consideration to: Marcia Pointon, Editor, *Art History*, Department of History of Art, University of Manchester, Manchester M13 9PL, England.

Articles/Books for review to: Kathy Adler, Reviews Editor, *Art History*, Centre for Extra-Mural Studies, Birkbeck College, University of London, 26 Russell Square, London WC1B 5DQ, England.

Membership of the Association of Art Historians is open to individuals who are art or design historians by profession or avocation and to those otherwise directly concerned in the advancement of the study of the history of art and design. The annual subscription, due on 1 January each year, is £26.00 (UK); £30.00 (Europe); £34.00 or $70.00 (USA and Rest of the World), and includes four issues of both the journal *Art History* and the *Bulletin*. Student rates (UK) are available on application. Applications should be sent to Kate Woodhead, Dog and Partridge House, Byley, Cheshire CW10 9NJ. Tel: 060 835517.

Back Issues: Single issues from the current and previous three volumes are available from Marston Book Services at the current single issue price. Earlier issues may be obtained from Swets & Zeitlinger, Back Sets, Heereweg 347, PO Box 810, 2160 SZ Lisse, Holland

Microform: The journal is available on microfilm (16mm or 35mm) or 105mm microfiche from the Serials Acquisitions Department, University Microfilms Inc, 300 North Zeeb Road, Ann Arbor, MI 48106, USA.

Printed in Great Britain by Hobbs the Printers of Southampton
This journal is printed on acid-free paper

 ISBN 0-631-193-243 ISSN 0141-6790

CONTENTS

'Take Back Your Mink': Lewis Carroll, Child Masquerade and the Age of Consent 369
Lindsay Smith

Iyoba, The Queen Mother of Benin: Images and Ambiguity in Gender and Sex Roles in Court Art 386
Flora Ẹdowaye S. Kaplan

Picturing a Personal History: the Case of Edward Onslow 408
Karen Stanworth

A Canon of Deformity: *Les Demoiselles d'Avignon* and Physical Anthropology 424
David Lomas

Pictures Fit for a Queen: Peter Paul Rubens and the Marie de' Medici Cycle 447
Geraldine A. Johnson

Review Articles

The Woman Who Mistook Her Art for a Hat: *Berthe Morisot's Images of Women* by Anne Higonnet 470
Mary Jacobus

Mute Signs and Blind Alleys: *Pieter Saenredam, The Painter and his Time* by Gary Schwartz and Marten Jan Bok; *Perspectives: Saenredam, and the Architectural Painters of the 17th Century*, exh. cat., with essays by Jeroen Giltaij, J.M. Montias, Walter Liedtke, Rob Rours, catalogue entries by Jeroen Giltaij and Guido Jansen 475
Martin Kemp

Of War, Demons and Negation: *Jackson Pollock: An American Saga* by Steven Naifeh and Gregory White Smith; *Jackson Pollock* by Ellen Landau; *Reconstructing Modernism: Art in New York, Paris and Montreal 1945–1964* edited 479

by Serge Guilbaut; *Abstract Expressionism* by David and Cecile Shapiro; *Abstract Expressionism: Creators and Critics* by Clifford Ross; *Benton, Pollock, and the Politics of Modernism: from Regionalism to Abstract Expressionism* by Erika Doss; *Abstract Expressionism and the Modern Experience* by Stephen Polcari
David Anfam

American Culture Wars: Prisoners of the Past: *Culture Wars: Documents from the Recent Controversies in the Arts* edited by Richard Bolton 485
Francis Frascina

Shorter Reviews

Angelica Kauffman. A Continental Artist in Georgian England edited by Wendy Wassyng Roworth with essays by David Alexander, Malise Forbes Adam & Mary Mauchline, Angela Rosenthal, Wendy Wassyng Roworth 491
Helen Weston

The Female Nude: Art, Obscenity and Sexuality by Lynda Nead 492
Nicola Ward Jouve

Watteau's Painted Conversations: Art, Literature, and Talk in Seventeenth- and Eighteenth-Century France by Mary Vidal 494
Humphrey Wine

Correspondence 495

NOTES FOR CONTRIBUTORS

Art History provides an international forum for original research relating to all aspects of the historical and theoretical study of painting, sculpture, design and other areas of visual imagery. The journal is committed to the publication of innovative, synthetic work which extends understanding of the visual within a well-developed interdisciplinary framework and raises significant issues of interest to those working both within the history of art and in related fields.

(1) *Two copies* of manuscripts should be submitted; the overall word length should not normally exceed 9,000 words. They should be clearly typewritten, *double spaced* with generous margins. The title page of the script should indicate the author's name, institution, address and telephone number, together with accurate estimates of text and footnote wordlengths; subsequent pages should be numbered and should carry an identifying running head. The author should retain an up-to-date copy of the typescript. Photocopies of illustrations should be included with initial submissions and originals supplied only on the editor's request.

(2) English spelling conventions should be followed in the text (e.g. colour, centre); foreign-language citations should be given in translation in the main text, with the original appearing in full in an accompanying footnote. All quotations within the text should be enclosed within *single* inverted commas. More extensive citations should be indented without quotation marks. All new paragraphs should be clearly indicated by indentation.

(3) Footnotes should follow the text and be double spaced. References should be kept to a practical minimum and should avoid unnecessary digression or redundant displays of erudition. Bibliographical references should correspond to the following examples:

> M. Baxandall, *The Limewood Sculptors of Renaissance Germany*, New Haven and London, 1980, pp. 20–1.
> P.F. Brown, 'Painting and History in Renaissance Venice', *Art History*, vol. 7, no. 3, September 1984, pp. 263–95.

Titles in French should follow the capitalisation conventions adopted by the Bibliothèque nationale, Paris, as in the following example:

> J.-C. Chamboredon, 'Production symbolique et formes sociales. De la sociologie de l'art et de la littérature à la sociologie de la culture', *Revue française de sociologie*, vol. 27, no. 3, July–September 1986, pp. 505–30.

(4) Illustrations should be used discriminatingly and should be confined to objects whose discussion forms a substantive part of the text. Good quality black-and-white plates should be provided upon acceptance of an article for publication. These must be clearly labelled and numbered, with accompanying typewritten captions on a separate sheet. Where indicated, measurements should be given in metric form; any details for reproduction from a larger image should be clearly indicated. Illustrations should be referred to as 'plate' in the text. All copyright clearance is the author's responsibility and full acknowledgement of sources should be included where appropriate.

(5) Corrections to accepted scripts should be kept to a strict minimum at proof stage. In view of the costs involved, the editor reserves the right to refuse any extensive alterations to authors' texts in proof. Prompt return of corrected proofs to the editor is essential.

(6) Manuscripts will not be returned to contributors.

Art History Vol. 16 No. 3 September 1993 0141—6790 pp. 369–385

'TAKE BACK YOUR MINK': LEWIS CARROLL, CHILD MASQUERADE AND THE AGE OF CONSENT

LINDSAY SMITH

The history of Lewis Carroll criticism is dominated by questions concerning the nature of his relationship with little girls. Regardless of whether it is his writing or his photographs that they are addressing, critics commonly identify the figure of the little girl as an index either of Carroll's potential sexual 'deviance' or of his irrefutable 'normality'.[1] Those critics who specifically consider Carroll's photographic practices, moreover, tend simply to collapse the author of the Alice books into the persona of Dodgson the photographer even though Carroll himself kept his literary persona distinct from his photographic one.[2] They fail to address, as a consequence, complex issues generated by the relationship of that photographic persona to the practice of photographing child subjects. From the 1850s onwards, the critical desire to read Carroll's interest in little girls as residing in the pleasure of their company, their language, the symbolism of their wit, has especially eclipsed the visual emphasis of that 'interest', the visualization of the little girl as spectacle which, nevertheless, is the strongest, most persistent interest that Carroll exhibits. As a result, the practices of his photographic sessions and his elaborate recordings of them in diaries and notebooks have been downplayed or gone virtually unnoticed, as have the ways in which they draw upon larger conceptions of childhood in the period. Not surprisingly, the particularities of this critical de-emphasis expose what is at stake in Carroll's photographic activities and their textual history, namely a production of the little girl that is inseparable from fantasies of childhood formulated in relation to Victorian concepts of majority and 'the age of consent'.

Marcuse Pfeifer for one exposes this relation. In a review of a collection of essays that seek to recuperate an unproblematic sexuality for Carroll, he writes the photographer into a somewhat inappropriate relationship with the Hollywood musical — albeit obliquely — by attributing to him the familiar line 'thank heaven for little girls' from *Gigi*.[3] In what might seem an initially fitting choice, Pfeifer takes Maurice Chevalier's song as the title of his essay. That title may seem apt, we might say, because the line that follows, 'without them what would little boys do', has assumed a refrain in Carroll criticism with such unmelodic phrases as 'if in fact Lewis Carroll has any claim to greatness in photography it is with his portraits of little girls.'[4] Yet, given the context of the rest of the song, this assumption about Carroll's dependency could not be further from the truth. For, as we shall see, if Carroll thanked 'heaven for little girls', he did so precisely because they need not 'get *bigger* every day' nor '*grow up* in a most delightful way'. He did so because 'little girls' could enter a substitutive economy, catalogued by their youthfulness and by the point at which it ran out. In this sense then, for Carroll, Chevalier would have had to have been singing the blues.

To remain, for a moment, with 1950s' musicals, but shifting from screen to stage, we might write Carroll more appropriately, and with different ramifications, into a relationship with Broadway. I am thinking in particular of a number by Vivian Blaine and the Hot Box girls from the musical *Guys and Dolls*, entitled 'Take back your Mink'. That song records the dressing up which goes too far because it ultimately signals undressing: 'what made you think that I was one of those girls?' This time, however, we could say that the shoe would be on the other foot, the singer no longer Carroll but the object of his affection. For Blaine's retort about her gift of a mink, 'go shorten the sleeves for somebody else', takes on particular dimensions beside Carroll's diary entry for 15 June 1880: 'Mrs Hatch brought Evelyn, of whom I took 2 photos in the spotted dress. In the afternoon I took the dress to the Hendersons, to have it reduced to fit Annie.'[5] Indeed, 'the spotted dress' first worn by Evelyn for a photograph, then efficiently re-tailored to fit Annie as next in line for the lens, is just one example of quasi-bespoke children's tailoring in Carroll. In *Guys and Dolls*, the point about sleeve-shortening establishes the status of the mink as fetishized commodity in consumer capitalism. Mink is the legendary token along with diamonds by which the woman is supposedly best ensnared. But implicit in the knowledge that 'those worn-out pelts' may be easily reduced in size for the next object of affection is the recognition that the act of couturial offering effectively amounts to no more than a *prêt à porter*. It is an offering designed by the giver, along with necklace, gloves, shoes and hat, primarily for his pleasure in their removal: 'last night in his apartment he tried to remove them all.' We find in this phrase, uttered by the recipient, an explicit link between commodity fetish and prostitution.

The couturial games of Carroll are, however, different from those enacted in *Guys and Dolls*. Whereas the latter involve a consenting adult who returns the mink to indicate her contempt for its potential transferability, the former require the dressing of a child to be photographed. The concept of consent thus emerges as a crucial point of differentiation. For Carroll's post-shrunk children's clothes (together with those borrowed from museums and theatres) circulate in an adult economy of exchange. Within that circulation they become, as a rule, garments which no little girl gets to keep, as Carroll maintains the wardrobe to which costumes are repeatedly 'take[n] back'. The little girl, thereby, merely enjoys the pretence of exchanging one exotic garment for another while Carroll stages, in miniature, what we might call a dress rehearsal for an exchange of commodity fetish, literally transporting theatrical spectacle into the context of the photographic studio by means of the wardrobe. In so constructing photographic masquerades, Carroll puts the little girl into a situation in which she can enact a return of the gift, become, so to speak, the consenting subject who, like our Broadway heroine, may return the 'mink' at will. He thereby appears to allow consent but his wardrobe door is, in fact, a revolving one, the clothes only on approval to begin with. Moreover, the child's apparent status of consenting subject is not what it seems, for it is linked by a common deception to the larger paradoxes of what is meant by the 'age of consent' in terms of power relations in concepts of majority and minority during the second half of the nineteenth century.

By means of such photographic practices, Carroll's formulation of desire assumes a visual enactment of cultural difference across the intricately clothed body of the little girl as object for the photographic lens. His dressing up or dressing down of the child for photography acts in accordance with an intricately formulated rhetoric of consent which, as we shall find, functions in one sense as a ruse. For, repeatedly, Carroll rehearses in his photographs fantasies of racial, cultural and sexual difference through the visual intricacies of costume dramas and child masquerade, intricacies that are in turn underwritten by contemporary issues of children's rights and age of consent legislation as negotiated in various cultural spaces. More specifically, Carroll deploys a personal logic of consent through legal and social definitions of the term 'consent' in costume fantasies that register, above all else, an insistence upon height as a barometer of childhood and infantile sexuality.

The medium for Carroll's personal logic is the letter, especially those letters to child friends and their parents in which he negotiates photographic sessions and costumes. Throughout his photographic career, Carroll situates his compulsion to photograph young girls according to contemporary laws of propriety. But he has to re-write continually the limits of those laws in order for them legitimately to accommodate that compulsion. Consent is crucial to this process, whether it be the consent of a child to walk out with him, to be photographed in his rooms at Christ Church or, as was common in later years, to stay with him at the seaside at Eastbourne. Defined as 'the age at which a person is legally competent' to assent to certain acts, 'especially marriage and sexual intercourse', 'consent' also marks the point at which a recently matured child subject may be legally 'taken'. Derived from '*consentir*', 'to be of the same mind: to agree: to give assent to: to yield: to comply', it suggests therefore not so much an equivalence, but rather an imbalance in power relations. For to agree, to give assent, to yield, all suggest capitulation to a more powerful agent, that the person consenting is not by definition occupying the role of initiator but that of yielder or complier.

The vexed issue of consent in Carroll's photographic practices, especially as inscribed in the use of little girls for photography, allows, I want to argue, his (linguistic) narratives of consent to remain detached from, whilst seeming to participate in, Victorian debates around age of consent legislation. Indeed, it is in this way that Carroll's concern with historical questions of consent operates, at one level, to deflect attention from the particularities of his psychic investment in the term as manifest in the small girl, the miniature. In such a scheme, the intersection of the psychic and social resonances of 'consent' means that 'size', a desire for the child precisely not to get bigger, produces for Carroll an urgent relation to historical and cultural determinants of the 'age of consent'. The problematical nature of a concept of adolescence is, as a result, displaced to height, and thereby linked to consent in such a way that height, rather than the more obvious signs of puberty, comes to stand in for markers of the psycho-sexual development of the subject.

One incident recorded in Carroll's letters concerning the visit of the young actress Polly Mallalieu to Eastbourne in the summer of 1892 stresses the importance of child-measuring to issues of consent. In a series of letters to Polly's parents, Carroll dwells upon the significance of a discrepancy between the child's professed height and her actual one. In short, when upon measuring Polly he finds that she is '4ft $10\frac{1}{2}$ ins. *without* her shoes', although she herself claims to be 'only 4ft 10 ins. *with* them', and explains that the discrepancy might be owing to her parents' desire 'to secure some engagement she was trying for', Carroll mounts an extended attack upon the motives of what he calls Mr Mallalieu's 'lie'[6] and causes a subsequent break in relations with the family. He reads in(to) the extra half-inch the implication that Polly's father is having her masquerade as more of a child than her height confirms her to be. For Carroll, pretending to be smaller is tantamount to possessing reduced authenticity. Height marks the physiological and psycho-sexual development of the child and occupies the place of visual differentiation that occurs with puberty, but which cannot be articulated as such. At the same time, as we shall find, the concept of consent operates for Carroll in a psychic economy reliant upon a reduction of the figure of woman to that of little girl.[7]

'RETURN TO SENDER'

Carroll corresponded with Lord Salisbury, during 1885, about the well-known exposé in the *Pall Mall Gazette* of organized child prostitution and vice by the editor Thomas Stead (1849–1912). His two letters to the Prime Minister on the subject of Stead's revelations to this magazine in the articles entitled 'The Maiden Tribute of Modern Babylon', position historically and culturally Carroll's photographs of children within the sphere of larger issues of children's rights during the period. These letters of 7 July 1885 and 31 August 1885 testify to the fact that it is not viable for critics to read Carroll's photographic activities as in some way divorced from the whole issue of the definition of childhood that was under debate and manifesting itself in various new legal and social structures. For, as I have said, Carroll's photographs of children inevitably engage questions of children's rights as they centre upon the huge and highly topical issue of consent and, moreover, Carroll regarded his literary and photographic practices within a context which included the various movements engaged in agitation for reform. But the question becomes one of precisely how to read this relationship of photographic practice to contemporary definitions of childhood.

The public outcry generated by Stead's articles of 6, 7, 8 and 10 July 1885 appears to have provoked Lord Salisbury's short-lived conservative government to address seriously in the House of Commons the Criminal Law Amendment Bill, and to restore to public attention the issue of child prostitution which had been obscured by agitation over the Contagious Diseases Acts. The Bill, known as 'Stead's Act' was passed in 1885 and raised the age of consent from thirteen to sixteen for girls. Prior to the Act of 1885, the Offences Against the Person Act of 1861 had deemed it a felony for a man to have sexual intercourse with a child under ten and a misdemeanour if the child were between ten and twelve years of age. The age of twelve in the 1861 Act went back to legislation of the thirteenth century.[8] During the 1870s, however, the Social Purity movement worked to legislate for a higher age, resulting in 1875 in its raising the age to thirteen. But the Act of 1885 did not represent a consensus; people campaigning for the protection of female children held divergent points of view about the age of consent. And as Deborah Gorham points out, 'Some people in the Social Purity Movement were pressing for an age as high as twenty-one, while many of their opponents still believed that the traditional age of twelve was more suitable.'[9]

Significantly, Carroll's two letters to Lord Salisbury do not directly address either questions of reform or state regulation of prostitution. Instead, Carroll directs his protest against the sensationalist rhetoric of Stead's articles; his concern is with legislating against the types of material which documented the exposure of prostitution. But he was not the only one to be so worried. As Gorham writes, 'By providing a set of vivid images that caught the public imagination, [Stead] generated a sense of outrage with which a wide spectrum of public opinion found itself in sympathy. In the summer of 1885, Anglican bishops and socialists found themselves working together to protest against the sexual abuse of children.'[10] At the forefront of Carroll's letters to the Prime Minister is his concern that 'the publication, in a daily paper sure to be seen by thousands of boys and young men, of the most loathsome details of prostitution' was likely to increase the problem by informing, and thus inciting to action, those who had previously been unaware of such 'vice'.[11] Carroll's position is clearly on the side of censoring the medium that had led to its exposure. In the second letter he writes: 'It was not the *Pall Mall* that I meant to suggest as a subject for prosecution: it is too late to think of that *now*: but surely the *other* similar publications, which are now flooding the streets, might be checked without any risk of increasing *their* popularity.'[12]

In writing this letter, Carroll implies an unquestioning belief in a direct causal relation between a written account of prostitution and its perpetuation, advocating a straightforward call for censorship as a primary form of protection. But protection for whom? For at the same time that he protests against Stead's exposé, Carroll chooses to situate himself, and by implication his child friendships, within this public debate. In one sense, then, his letters to Lord Salisbury simply confirm other instances in which Carroll shows a marked social awareness of the potential significations of his own interest in female minors. Indeed, Carroll frequently had recourse to the caricatured figure of 'Mrs Grundy', and that recourse suggests, as it off-sets, his repeated evaluation of 'laws' of public decency, together with the invention of new ways to transgress them, whilst never failing to communicate the fact that in his case there is no 'real' transgression as he regards the child's consent as paramount. In another sense, these letters clearly indicate an anxiety about the ways in which his relations with little girls might be construed at an historical moment when the realities of child abuse were being vividly exposed in the popular press. But this anxiety simultaneously works as a cover for his visual investment in little girls. Indeed, Carroll's interpretation of consent, in relation to the agency of the child, precisely involves the desired construction of the little girl as a diminished consenting subject, accompanied by a desire not to recognize the existence of consent in legal and social structures.

Carroll thus constructs an elaborate epistolary framework in which letters and diaries function in some ways as an exercise in the symbolic logic of consent, the meanings of which are changed when read in relation to the cultural debates around the Criminal Law Amendment Act of 1885.[13] As Carroll is regularly obliged to negotiate the parameters of his child friendships within the context of contemporary constructions of childhood, the letter (he wrote multiples of thousands of them) becomes the main medium by which he juggles the significance of his interest in little girls; friendship is the dominant trope of the narratives of his desire. In much of his correspondence with parents, Carroll is then in an impossible position of (innocent) transgressor (legally and culturally so to speak), and constantly faced with having to account for the peculiarity of that position. This fact explains, to some extent, the frequently authoritative rhetoric of Carroll's letters to parents asking to 'borrow' their children for photography. This is particularly so in the cases of nude studies, where the caution employed to ensure an absence of 'unhealthy' interest exacerbates the sense of a linguistic cover-up. Social and cultural constraints mean that he has to construct his child friendships as different from illegitimate relationships. But because there is no respectable historical precedent in Victorian culture for Carroll's interest in little girls, the question of how to represent the specificity of his desire and its manifestations becomes an insurmountable task that generates more and more purple-inked prose. In any case, he has to speak about the current state of child abuse against which to measure the respectability he posits for himself; to acknowledge child abuse as a real threat while simultaneously proving that his case requires no parental vigilance.

A transference of his sense of transgression of propriety to an unhealthy suspicion on the part of a child's parents typifies Carroll's epistolary use of consent. This process is evidently the cause of his breaking off relations with Mr and Mrs Anthony Lawson Mayhew in 1879 over the issue of consent to nude photographs.[14] In a first letter on this subject to Mrs Mayhew, 26 May 1879, Carroll goes to great lengths to detail desired photographic poses for her three daughters Ruth, Ethel and Janet, whose respective ages are thirteen, twelve and six: 'I should like to know *exactly* what is the minimum of dress I may take [Janet] in, and I will strictly observe the limits.'[15] In a second letter on the subject, written the next day to Mr Mayhew, Carroll writes:

> As to the photography, I am heartily obliged to Mrs Mayhew for her kind note. It gives more than I had ventured to hope for, and does not extinguish the hope that I may yet get *all* I asked [. . . .] If Ruth and Ethel bring Janet, there is really no need for [Mrs Mayhew] to come as well — that is, *if* you can trust me to keep my promise of abiding strictly by the limits laid down. If you *can't* trust my word, then please never bring or send any of the children again![16]

These preferences are followed by a highly detailed elaboration of prospective poses of the children (back and frontal views), and Carroll's subsequent letter to Mrs Mayhew, May 1879, which outlines his regret at the previous one, indicates the offence she had taken to it:

> After my last had gone, I wished to recall it, and take out the sentence in which I had quite gratuitously suggested the possibility that you *might* be

> unwilling to trust me to photograph the children by themselves in undress. And now I am more than ever sorry I wrote it, as it has accidentally led to your telling me what I would gladly have remained ignorant of [. . . .] I should have no pleasure in doing any such pictures, now that I know I am ~~not thought fit for~~ only permitted such a privilege ~~except~~ on condition of being under chaperonage.[17]

The question of chaperonage is, not surprisingly, a difficult one for Carroll to get around without in some way offending or distancing parents. For Mrs Mayhew to insist upon a chaperone is, Carroll writes, to mistrust his 'word' that he will abide by 'the limits [she] has laid down'. By these means, Carroll constructs the request for a chaperone as an unreasonable demand when in fact it is Mrs Mayhew who is merely abiding by convention and he the one asking for a concession to transgress an established social code. Carroll's response to her reply to his first letter on this issue, 'it gives more than I had ventured to hope for, and does not extinguish the hope that I may yet get all I asked', seems for a logician more than calculated illogic; the note gives 'more' than Carroll 'had ventured to hope for' but does not preclude the fact that he 'may yet get all he asked'. Thus, Carroll asks for more than he hopes for. Semantically, Carroll's use of the word 'hope', its shift from noun to verb, demonstrates the fact that in order to attempt to gain his desire, he has actively to situate the unnameable desire/hope into the commerce between himself and the parents; Carroll has to verbalize it (both speak it and make it into a verb), and 'more than I had ventured to hope for' becomes '*the hope* that I may yet get all I asked'.

The method of bargaining whereby Carroll plays the parents and successively plays the children against the parents shows to what extent he transgresses contemporary standards of decorum while transferring culpability to the parents. Carroll's strategy necessitates his placing the parents in a position of determining moral standards. He performs a subtle transference of transgression by which agency is delegated to the parents. The method of the letters, therefore, is to make the parents themselves initially define the quality of 'innocence' which, reciprocally, sets the limit of transgression; once the onus is on the parents it becomes difficult for them to raise subsequent qualms.

The crucial point, however, is that such a strategy requires Carroll to allude to sexual transgression through discourse in this way. Not in order 'to conceal sex: a screen discourse' as Foucault has written, but to expose it.[18] Carroll's masked allusions to sex are not attempts to gloss over the issue of sex but ruses to mask the fact that sex — at least as the parents might suspect it — is *not* the point. For Carroll's self-conscious references to the logistics of consent operate in one sense as a cover for his obsession with height; his compulsive interest in smallness as played out in costume fantasy works as a means of disavowing symbolic castration. But so great is the need for this disavowal that he is led to use a ruse of consent that is in some ways more transgressive than the act of photographing female minors that he hopes to perform by using it. However, aware of the risk he takes in constructing this discourse on transgressive sexuality to hide a different transgression, Carroll works continually to prevent the one from being extricable from the other.

'SARTOR RESARTUS'

Writing to one of his favourite 'child friends' Gertrude Chataway, 2 January 1876, Carroll explains: 'I want to do some better photographs of you. . . . And mind you don't grow a bit older, for I shall want to take you in the same dress again: if anything you'd better grow a *little* younger — go back to your last birthday but one.'[19] Here, a desire for 'the same dress' determines Carroll's characteristic request for a reversal of growth. In another letter of the same year (1 October 1876) written from his annual summer haunt of this period, the Isle of Wight, Carroll similarly requests Gertrude Chataway's help in dressmaking matters, this time pattern-cutting, for he wants to replicate the style of her bathing costume for other girls to wear:

> I have been buying, for photographing children at Oxford, two of those blue jerseys, like what you used to wear, the smallest two sizes, and I'm not sure if I shall want a larger size or not: so I want you to measure yours, and send me the length and width, both of the jersey and the bathing drawers, when they are simply spread out flat, without any stretching. I have lent my two to two little girls here, one 10 years old and one 6, and they look very nice in them.[20]

Such meticulous attention to details of costume is followed, in the same month, by an invitation to the child to go to Oxford to be photographed in the aforementioned garb: 'You had better bring the blue jersey and the bathing drawers with you. I shall want to take 8 pictures of you, so I send you 8 kisses.'[21]

The effect of these references to dress is in no way to exaggerate the way in which masquerade determines the nature of Carroll's photographic practices.[22] The catwalks of his photographic imagination display a spectacular ethnic sartorial mix: Chinese, Indian and Greek (costumes/models) rub shoulders with Turk, 'native' New Zealander and Dane, together with nationally displaced or indeterminate 'veils', 'rags' and 'primitive' costume. As Beatrice Hatch recalls: 'He kept various costumes and "properties" with which to dress us up . . . . What child would not thoroughly enjoy personating a Japanese or a beggar child, or a gypsy or an Indian.'[23]

In masquerading little girls before the camera, it is as if Carroll sees himself as offering to a child a place in a sartorial democracy, through a ritualized stripping away of contemporary fashion, a liberation that is equally achieved by encouraging — in the case of Gertrude Chataway, for example — her mother's sanctioning of the girl's wearing 'bathing pants and a fisherman's jersey' on the beach, 'a thing quite unheard of in those days'.[24] By 'freeing' little girls, in social situations, from strictures of propriety, he allows them to personate consenting adults. In the case of another 'child friend' Adelaide Paine, 'gloves' are recalled as the article of clothing about which Carroll offers advice to the parents. They are recommended 'not to make little girls wear gloves at the seaside; they took the advice, and I enjoyed the result.'[25] Such detail is further substantiated by Adelaide Paine's memory (documented originally by Collingwood) of the supply of safety pins that Carroll habitually carried at the seaside to prevent wading girls from spoiling their frocks.

According to the reminiscences of his 'child friends', Carroll apparently always made it plain that children should not be persuaded to do anything that they did not wish to do. Thus, by effectively granting consent to children of all ages (taking all children at their word, giving them the right to decide what they will assent to in terms of photographic poses and costumes), he paradoxically negates the legal status of the term. While such licence might be regarded as a radical liberation of the child subject, and clearly in one sense Carroll rationalized it in this way, it is difficult to separate his attribution of consent to a child of five from that which Carroll clearly wants to gain from it for himself. This is especially the case as he downplays the legal significance of consent, whilst, as we have seen, over-determining the relevance to the concept of the statistic of height.

At the same time, the links between Carroll's sartorial persona and issues of theatricality and role-playing have crucial connotations for his larger constructions of the realms of fantasy and reality in visual culture — that bipolarity upon which so much of his work hinges. Role-playing, it is important to note, is what Carroll seeks both in the fantasy 'set-ups' of his 'costume' photographs and in his interaction in contemporary social contexts as dramatized by his repeatedly voiced dislike of contemporary styles in children's clothing. Indeed, it has become something of a well-known maxim that Carroll could not 'bear' an unnatural child in real life. However, somewhat paradoxically, the elaborate cultural personae of his costume photographs are conceived by Carroll as proximate to the 'natural' child (as encoded in tousled hair and bare feet, for example), itself a fantasy of the child as exempt from the 'civilizing' and regular sartorial characteristics of Victorian culture. That is to say, fantasies of other nationalities share a territory of 'naturalness' with photographs of upper-class English girls barefoot in nightdresses. For Carroll forges an equivalence between the unadorned nude (or, as he so tellingly calls it by means of a transference of agency, the child's 'favourite state of nothing on'), or between the child in simple nightgown, and the elaborately clothed and posed subject who is always enacting a fantasy of cultural and/or 'racial' difference.

If we compare, for example, two photographic portraits of Gertrude Chataway and Irene MacDonald, we can see how Carroll formulates this equation. The portrait of 'Gertrude Chataway, age seven, Lying on a Sofa' (plate 1) from the 1870s combines the familiar makeshift qualities of Carroll's studio with a centrally placed couch. Taken from an elevated position, the photograph registers a distinctive literal point of view and is quite different, for example, from a photograph of 'child friend' Xie Kitchin reclining on a sofa, where the subject appears centred through cropping. The former represents a little girl reclining in a specific but incongruous context, the opulently embossed fabric of sofa and cushions contrasting dramatically with the tatty sections of carpet in the foreground. The figure of the child appears highly lit, deathly pale, eyes tightly closed, hands tensely clasped in front of her, long white feet stretched out, ankle and lower calf exposed. She wears a long-sleeved, high-necked nightgown of a netural tone rather than white. The figure is stiffly posed, feigning sleep in what seems a vast expanse of interior space. The surrounding blurs and faults give the impression that one is viewing it through an aperture or a partially opaque medium.

'Irene MacDonald, autographed', July 1863 (plate 2), fixes the child in recumbent pose among highly patterned shawls and variously textured animal skins.

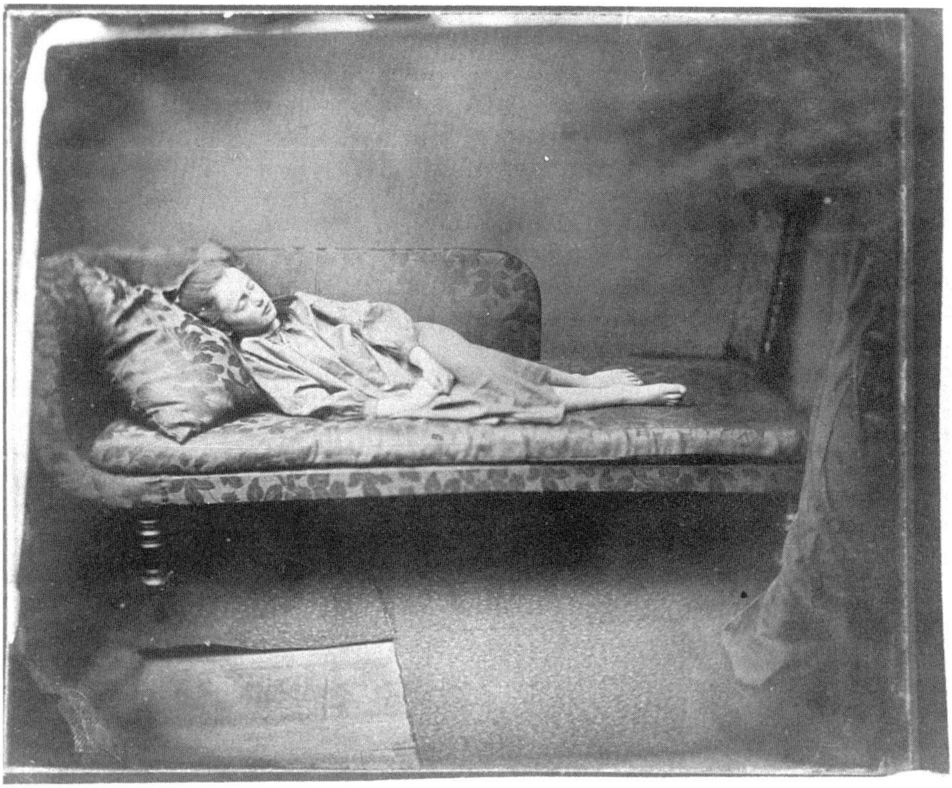

1 C.L. Dodgson, *Gertrude Chataway*, photograph, Gernsheim Collection, Harry Ransom Humanities Research Center, The University of Texas at Austin

The narrower depth of field in this photograph is exaggerated by the cropped oval format of the print and the overall effect of the drapery is one of exoticism. What looks to be a tiger or leopard skin lies in the foreground, while the girl's head rests on the base of a table covered by a fur. 'India shawls' are draped over the upper part of her body and, crucially, the composition articulates a contrast between the white skin of bare arms, shoulder and lower legs above the socks, together with brightly lit face, and the clothed areas in between: the nightdress hitched up to reveal crossed legs, ankle-strap shoes alongside oriental signifiers of adornment. The girl looks out, clasping a tuft of fur in the palm of her left hand. In one sense, she assumes the look of an English child who has nestled beneath unfamiliar Oriental drapery, but the image is highly staged, the figure personating a classic recumbent pose of the female nude. What we have is a fantasy of the English child as semi-Eastern, as taking on some but *not all* of the sartorial markers of that other culture. This point is crucial because, in this reduced format, the Oriental does not pose the type of threat that it would in its full form; there are sufficient markers of English childhood in this photograph for us never to lose sight of the fact that the figure is dressed for a staged spectacle, that a child masquerades as a reduced form of the Oriental.

Such reduced size is vital, then, to Carroll's formulation of a fantasy of

2 C.L. Dodgson, *Irene MacDonald, autographed*, July 1863, photograph, Gernsheim Collection, Harry Ransom Humanities Research Center, The University of Texas at Austin

childhood. Herman Rapaport, in 'The Disarticulated Image: Gazing in Wonderland', has identified in the Alice books and in Carroll's photographs of little girls a dependency upon miniaturization as representing 'inhibition' in a Freudian sense.[26] In 'Inhibitions, Symptoms and Anxiety' (1926), Freud explains the way in which an activity when it becomes too eroticized is 'subjected to neurotic inhibitions'. That is to say that 'the ego-function of an organ is impaired if its erotogeneity — its sexual significance is increased.'[27] Moreover, Freud defines 'inhibition' as 'the expression of a *restriction* of an *ego function*'.[28] A desire to miniaturize or to infantilize features in Freud in cases of failed repression in which the instinctual impulse has found a substitute. But it is 'a substitute which is very much reduced, displaced and inhibited and which is no longer recognizable as a satisfaction [. . . .] When the substitutive impulse is carried out there is no sensation of pleasure; its carrying out has, instead, the quality of a compulsion.'[29] With an inhibition describing a restriction or lowering of a function, Rapaport reads Carroll's photograph entitled 'The Elopement', which shows Alice Jane Donkin perched upon an upper window ledge, about to descend a ladder, as an affirmative statement of desire on the part of the photographer, such as 'I want to be with you', that is 'immediately refused or negated by the figure's size and age'. Furthermore, he contends that what occurs in this process is that the distance that articulates desire 'is repeated again by the "inhibition" of the "figure", the reduction of the woman into a little girl'.[30] The disarticulated image of Rapaport's title thus derives from the photographer's simultaneous assertion and denial of the distance between himself and his model.

Although Rapaport does not extend his analysis to Carroll's wider interest in reduced physical proportions, his approach provides a framework which we may apply to a reading of the intervolvement of the psychic and the social in Carroll's photographing of children. A psychic investment in the miniature or 'inhibited' figure of the little girl (as identified by Rapaport) finds its crucial decoy, as we have seen, in the anxieties Carroll expresses around the social determinates of 'the age of consent'. The tiny model ensures a negation of a real sexual union, whilst at the same time staging its possibility. Furthermore, the staged possibility is, we could say, repeatedly upstaged.

In the case of Gertrude Chataway, miniaturization is achieved by the physical dwarfing of the figure to the surroundings, as somehow incongruous, vulnerable, 'wedged' (to use Carroll's term) into the sofa.[31] In the case of Irene MacDonald, however, the child is transformed into an object of fantasy on the one hand — as viable object of sexual desire — while reciprocally this status is undermined by the signifiers of her size: shoes and socks which, like the bare feet of Gertrude Chataway, remind us that this is a reduced version of an authentic. The general subordination of the Oriental is exacerbated in the Other as female child, and correspondingly the Eastern girl can serve more satisfactorily the purposes of disavowal that he seeks. The miniaturization of the Oriental becomes for Carroll doubly representative of the impossibility of reciprocity with a minor, for the child in Oriental masquerade serves as one with whom it would be culturally impossible to have a sexual relationship.[32] In this sense, the dressing up of little girls to simulate cultural difference constitutes for Carroll the furthest removal from the possibility of reciprocity with a woman.

Carroll's obsession with the fact that little girls grow 'bigger' is not only signified in his photographic preoccupation with the miniature. It is recorded also in the fact that he charted their growth in mathematical calibrations on the door of his rooms at Christ Church, and in the fact that references to height occur repeatedly in letters to 'child friends' and to their parents. On 17 April 1868, for instance, he writes to Agnes Argles, 'Some children have a most disagreeable way of getting grown-up: I hope you won't do anything of that sort before we meet again.'[33] And in a letter to F. H. Atkinson, written twenty-two years later, 10 April 1890, Carroll remarks '*What* a tall daughter you've got! But I can see the child-face still, on the top of that mountainous maiden!'[34] Particularly noticeable here is the feeling of surprise, as if an increase in height swiftly undermines the matrices of his conception of childhood. At the same time, there is present a drive to find the child subject still, as identifiable in the 'child-face' of the 'maiden', to find her in spite of increased physical proportions. To preserve the little girl, as miniature, prior to puberty is to preserve her prior to the age of consent, as pre-sexual, and reciprocally as sexual. The photographic medium therefore operates to fix childhood in the manner of autographs and letters of child friends in which jokes about expanding maidens invoke variations upon the expanding/shrinking Alice of the books.[35]

'OFF WITH HER HEAD'

Carroll's desire to fix height by means of his impersonation of a sartor finds a further manifestation in his interest in tailors' mannequins as potential subjects for photography. Since not any old mannequins will do for his photographic purposes, a lack of available child-size ones — 'they are all adult proportions' — puts a stop to one of his schemes in 1872 to buy a mannequin 4ft 3in high with the measurements of the eight-year-old Julia Arnold so that he might dress it in 'a suit of [her] clothes', and then 'take a picture of it so dressed'.[36] In a letter to Mary Arnold, Julia's sister (later Mrs Humphrey Ward), Carroll, in explaining his plan to 'get an exact duplicate of Julia in papier-mâché', speculates upon the number of people that such a 'duplicate' would 'take in'.[37] His explanation makes it seem as if the photographic process suggests for Carroll new possibilities in deception, in duping the viewer, as defined by masquerade. For he envisages the photograph operating as a sort of theatrical trick, a classic trompe-l'oeil staging the credibility of which might be crafted by meticulous attention to details of pose and costume. 'Of course,' writes Carroll, 'the face must be turned away, and there would be a slight deficiency of hair! But nothing to signify.'[38] If averted face and a lack of hair do not signify in such an instance, then we are left with the question of what would be of consequence?

The mannequin idea would obviously liberate the photographer from the restrictions of photographing live child models, problems of movement during exposures. If, on the other hand, there would be nothing to distinguish a mannequin with averted face from an 'authentic' child, then it suggests that, in some ways, the face is not, for Carroll, the most engaging part of the child model. He desires instead to retain the clothed body in a static form of miniaturization. Thus, we are back to couture as suggested by the assimilation of tailor's dummy and live model: Julia Arnold and her clothes transformed into 'Miss Julia Arnold duplicate'.[39]

The implications of what became an abortive plan are significant, as they focus upon height, within the larger context of Carroll's elaborate schemes for posing and photographing little girls. Clearly, the plan somewhat dispels the predominant notion that a large part of Carroll's fascination with girls involved the befriending of the individual with the photographic session forming a mere adjunct to a friendship. For the mannequin preserves only the height, proportions and clothing of the original model; it salvages precisely those details with which we have been led to believe that Carroll was least concerned. We might then perhaps be surprised to find that where we expected individual character traits we are left instead with a set of 'vital' statistics.

Of those statistics preserved by the mannequin, 'height' is most pressing for Carroll: the one which, of course, the mannequin idea could uniquely solve because it could arrest a child subject at what he considered the optimum height for photography. Both photograph and mannequin therefore function as memorials to a past fantasy. They work as displacements to dupe Carroll himself, for the photographed mannequin (in the permanent and doubly fixed form of a photographed duplicate) offers a means of avowing and denying sexuality in the miniature. We can further understand the function of the little girl as miniature,

3 C.L. Dodgson to Xie Kitchen, 15 February 1880, pen and ink, Henry W. and Albert A. Berg Collection, The New York Public Library. Astor, Lenox and Tilden Foundations

however, if we consider yet another way in which height operates in Carroll's economy of vital statistics. A reference to proportion in a letter to Alexandra Kitchin brings together the psychic investment in height with particularities of the photographic medium itself and the capacity of photography to impress a unique sense of physical proportion. In this case, the 'off with her head'/castration theme from *Alice* is re-figured in relation to photography in a sketch by Carroll (plate 3). This sketch depicts Xie Kitchin as a half-decapitated subject of a *carte de visite* photograph, accompanied by the statement: '*Please* don't grow any taller, if you can help it, till I've had time to photograph you again. Cartes like this (it always happens if people get too tall) never look really nice as a general rule.'[40] On the one hand, Carroll here reiterates a common joke about how the photograph cuts off important bits of a person, but the idea that she will be too big for the frame, that her physical proportions will exceed the limits of the vertical format of the *carte*, resulting in partial decapitation, would seem to bear out the point that to photograph little girls is a primary method of disavowal. For Carroll's fantasy of the truncated image raises a crucial question of the significance of that which lies outside the frame in photography, and graphically situates the photograph as a means of disavowing castration.

Christian Metz has compared the off-frame in photography and in film and has concluded that it is much more subtle in the former than in the latter. This conclusion arises from the fact that in photography 'the spectator has no empirical knowledge of the contents of the off-frame, but at the same time cannot help imagining some off-frame.'[41] Moreover, he continues: 'The off-frame effect in photography results from a singular and definitive cutting off which figures castration and is figured by the "click" of the shutter.'[42] Metz, however, is theorizing that which lies completely outside the frame; Carroll is conversely drawing attention to the crude cropping potential of the photographic medium. But if, as Metz writes, 'the off-frame effect in photography results from a singular and definitive cutting off which figures castration', then Carroll's fantasy about a semi-decapitated Xie represents his anxiety about making the relationship of that which lies outside the frame of the photograph to castration all too evident. Carroll jokingly displaces his fear to a cartoon fantasy of a failed *carte de visite*, failed because half of the head is missing and the format is that of a portrait.

Another important component of the fantasy here is, however, that of size, that a person or thing can become *too* large to be accommodated within the border of the photograph. This is, of course, an impossibility, but it articulates a persistent anxiety that Carroll's photographs work to displace by way of their predominantly wide depth of field and clarity of focus. Thus, anxiety is clearly centred here upon the miniature again. For in projecting Xie's increased size in this way, Carroll forms an equivalence between the proportions of the little girl and the photographic medium. To be too old is to be too big. To be too big is not to be able to function as miniature or inhibition. It is to suggest that which lies outside the frame, thereby making the relationship of the off-frame to castration all too evident.

To be too big is also, however, to be too old, a fact borne out by incidents in Carroll's letters in which he radically underestimates a little girl's age, or literally refuses to believe her height until he *sees* it.[43] The equivalence forged here, in the Xie sketch, brings us back to the importance to Carroll of a simultaneous assertion and denial of reciprocity in his relation to child subjects, that which Rapaport identifies as 'the wish to be recognized by the child as a lover [while] at the same time the demand for such recognition must be dissimulated'.[44] This movement replicates the duality of the photograph's function in relation to the fetish, with its combination of fear and desire, its meaning both of 'loss (symbolic castration) and protection against loss'.[45] For the photograph of the little girl constitutes a double miniature in that it represents a reduced woman and may serve as a keepsake or fetish.

The staging of a desire for reciprocity with a girl below the age of consent therefore operates in Carroll's narratives as a cover for a different compulsion. Like a complex acrostic his voicing of concern over the issue of consent in photographic practices functions as a false allure to deflect attention from his visual compulsion. But because the cover he weaves around questions of consent is potentially so dangerous in itself, it has to produce, as a screen, its own narratives to counteract the problematics it generates. Thus, Carroll toys with a persona (the bachelor with an interest in little girls) the inappropriateness of which, under the circumstances, testifies to just what is at stake in the ruse. Carroll repeatedly voices the affronts he feels, proclaiming the suggestions by parents of 'child friends' tha he cannot be trusted. For this he complicates and abandons several friendships. But such affronts are his own necessary constructions, and they become determinates of his visual fantasies, transgressive covers, we might say, for the fact that he knows he *can* be trusted. For Carroll does not want — as so many critics have suggested — sexual reciprocity with the child. What he does want is the freedom to perform his visual compulsion, through a repeated photographic fixing of the minor; to perform it, that is, in the knowledge that the representation of his desire, in the little girl personating consenting subject (and its dependence upon the medium of photography), is rendered invisible, its visual register readily absorbed by the social and legal discourses on childhood of his day.

Lindsay Smith
University of Sussex

NOTES

1 Several critics re-iterate the claim that there has been excessive interest in Carroll's sexuality, when in fact there have been few attempts to discuss the politics of sexuality in relation to the politics of the medium of photography. Those critics who bemoan a surfeit of interest in sexuality in Carroll studies in order to exempt the author from any 'deviant' tendencies merely enter the fantasy of repetition which characterizes Carroll's photographs, letters and diary entries. We find a persistent construction of Carroll as unwilling bachelor. See, for example, Helmut Gernsheim's preface to the revised edition of *Lewis Carroll Photographer* (1967), and Morten N. Cohen (Edward Giuliano, *Lewis Carroll in a Changing World: An Interview with Morten N. Cohen*). Cohen attempts to preserve a normative heterosexuality for Carroll, by shifting his role from that of sexually problematic 'bachelor' to the more comfortable position of unrequited lover. Critics who refute so-called 'Freudian readings' of Carroll produce a psycho-biographical approach, paraded as other than such, in which the preservation of the myth of the transcendence of the nuclear family is inextricable from a notion of Carroll's transcendent appeal.

2 For photography he uses his 'real' name rather than his pseudonym. See, for example, letter to Mary E. Manners, 7 February 1895, *The Letters of Lewis Carroll*, Morten N. Cohen (ed.), 2 vols., II, London: Macmillan, 1979, p. 1051, and, letters to Catherine Laing, 30 November 1880, *Letters* I, p. 395, 14 June 1881, p. 433, and letter to Coventry Patmore, 6 March 1890, *Letters* II, p. 779. Hereafter cited as *Letters* followed by page reference.

3 Marcuse Pfeifer, 'Thank Heaven for Little Girls', *Book Forum*, 1979, pp. 504–8.

4 ibid, p. 507.

5 *The Diaries of Lewis Carroll*, Roger Lancelyn Green (ed.), 2 vols., vol. 2, New York: Oxford University Press, 1954, p. 387.

6 Letter dated 17 July 1892, *Letters* II, pp. 918–19.

7 On the issue of determining an 'ideal' age of consent in arguments around age of consent legislation during the 1880s see Deborah Gorham, 'The "Maiden Tribute of Modern Babylon" Re-Examined: Child Prostitution and the Idea of Childhood in Late Victorian England', *Victorian Studies*, 21 (Spring 1978), p. 369. See also Michael Pearson, *The Age of Consent*, London: David and Charles, 1972.

8 See also Deborah Gorham, *The Victorian Girl and the Feminine Ideal*, Bloomington: Indiana University Press, 1982; Charles Terrot, *The Maiden Tribute: A Study of the White Slave Traffic of the Nineteenth Century*, London: Frederick Muller, 1959.

9 Gorham, 'The "Maiden Tribute of Modern Babylon" Re-examined', op. cit., p. 364.

10 ibid, p. 354.

11 Letter to Lord Salisbury, 7 July 1885, *Letters* I, pp. 586–7.

12 ibid, 31 August 1885, *Letters* I, pp. 599–600.

13 We should, therefore, question how the status of Carroll's concern (with regard to nude portraits) about the age at which a child should no longer be asked to undress is re-defined after 1885 with the change in the age of consent. By definition, it is likely that Carroll was in favour of raising the age; to raise it would mean an increase in girls below the age, an increase in miniaturization so to speak.

14 Carroll's acquaintance with the Mayhews began in November 1878. The four daughters with whom he became increasingly friendly were: Mary Ruth (1866–1939), Ethel Innes (1867–1919), Janet, who died in 1891, and Margaret Dorothea (1883–1971).

15 *Letters* I, pp. 237–8.

16 ibid, pp. 339–40.

17 ibid, p. 341.

18 Michel Foucault, *The History of Sexuality Vol. 1: An Introduction*, Robert Hurley (trans.), New York: Vintage Books, 1978 (reprinted 1980), p. 53.
19 *Letters* I, p. 238.
20 ibid, p. 258.
21 ibid, p. 259.
22 Carroll criticism repeatedly side-steps the persistence of costume fantasies to the extent that influential photographic historians and collectors like Helmut Gernsheim distinguish Carroll's 'costume pieces' as 'banal' and separate from his more 'serious' and, we are urged to accept, more representative child portraits. (See my 'The Politics of Focus: Feminism and Photography Theory', *New Feminist Discourses*, Isobel Armstrong (ed.), London: Routledge, 1992, pp. 134–60.) Such a separation denies that odd continuum of visual cultural fantasies that hinge upon a particular paradigm of consent, represented especially for Carroll in the intersection of photography with the garb of child actors (especially from pantomime) as a legitimate context for exotic *tableaux vivants*.
23 Reminiscence of Beatrice Hatch from the *Strand Magazine*, London, April 1898, xv, pp. 212–23, quoted by Isa Bowman, *Lewis Carroll as I Knew Him*, New York: Dover, 1972, pp. 16–17.
24 Reminiscence of Gertrude Chataway, *Lewis Carroll, Interviews and Recollections*, Morten N. Cohen (ed.), Iowa City: University of Iowa Press, 1989, pp. 138–9.
25 Quoted by Stuart Dodgson Collingwood, *The Life and Letters of Lewis Carroll*, New York: The Century Co., 1898, p. 373.
26 Herman Rapaport, 'The Disarticulated Image: Gazing in Wonderland', *Enclitic*, vol. 6, no. 2 (Fall 1982), pp. 57–77.
27 Sigmund Freud, 'Inhibitions, Symptoms and Anxiety' in *Standard Edition*, vol. 20, London: Hogarth Press, 1974, p. 89.
28 ibid.
29 ibid, p. 95.
30 Rapaport, op. cit., pp. 66–7.
31 Letter to E. Gertrude Thomson, artist, 2 October 1893: 'P.S. You don't seem to know how to *fix* a restless child, for photography. I wedge her into the *corner* of a room, if standing; or into the angle of a sofa if lying down.' (*Letters* II, p. 982).
32 There is not space here to discuss in depth the staging of Orientalism in Carroll's photographs, but it is explored more fully in my forthcoming book.
33 *Letters* I, p. 117.
34 *Letters* II, p. 785.
35 See Nancy Armstrong, 'The Occidental Alice', *Differences: A Journal of Feminist Cultural Studies*, 2.2 (1990), pp. 3–40; in particular her discussion of appetite and consumption in the Alice books: 'For even though [Alice's] size increases at the story's end, she retains the prepubescent shape distinguishing her from the other women in that story.' (p. 18).
36 Letter to Mary Arnold, *Letters* I, p. 174.
37 ibid.
38 ibid.
39 ibid.
40 Letter to Alexandra Kitchin, 15 February 1880, *Letters* I, p. 370.
41 Christian Metz, 'Photography and Fetish', originally published in *October*, 34 (Fall 1985), reprinted in *The Critical Image*, Carol Squiers (ed.), Seattle: Bay Press, 1990, pp. 155–64, 161.
42 ibid.
43 See, for example, *Diaries*, II, p. 385: 'Brought in "Atty" Owen [. . .] to wait in my rooms until Owen was at leisure. She does not look fourteen yet, and when, having kissed her at parting, I learned (from Owen) that she is seventeen, I was astonished.'
44 Rapaport, op. cit., p. 66.
45 Metz, op. cit., p. 158.

Art History Vol. 16 No. 3 September 1993 0141—6790 pp. 386–407

IYOBA, THE QUEEN MOTHER OF BENIN: IMAGES AND AMBIGUITY IN GENDER AND SEX ROLES IN COURT ART

FLORA *EDOWAYE* S. KAPLAN

Given the pervasive imagery of nubile women and of women with children in African art, it is striking that no such images appear in the art of the royal court of Benin, Nigeria. Instead, the woman most often represented is the queen mother, whose title, *Iyoba*, may be literally translated as 'mother of the Oba'. Her status derives from female sex roles as wife and mother; as queen mother she is a widow of the former Oba — distinguished from his other queens by having borne his first son, the heir to the throne. She is past menopause and her sexuality is muted and rendered ambiguous in art. In sculptures and tableaux of cast bronze and in carved ivory, she is represented as a senior chief and equated with a male.[1] She is usually attended by prepubescent females, and on occasion either by two adult females or, more rarely, by two males. All have reference to her status and roles based on male gender (plate 4).

Among the Benins, the Edo-speaking peoples of southern Nigeria, the *Iyoba* manifests the intense mother-and-son dyad that underlies the ranked and hierarchical patrilineal society — suffused with a male ethos and organized around a divine kingship. The *Iyoba* embodies the possibilities for women to acquire wealth, prestige, influence, and even immortality. She marks the potential of women for achieved status and power in a system where royalty is ascribed. In a society where women's roles have little visible permanence and where only Obas' wives may be given chiefly titles, the queen mother is notable in being represented in court art. Our notions of her roles have been based mostly on analogy with other ethnic groups, and on indirect and brief contacts.[2] Despite the absence of prior and sustained ethnographic fieldwork on the subject of royal women and limited historic resources, political power has often been attributed to the role of queen mother of Benin. Female chieftaincies and titles among the Yoruba, who have an historic relationship with Benin, for example, have been the bases for assuming comparable female power among the Edos. Similar titles among the Sagi and Sonya of the Nupe, the royal princesses of the Kanuri of Bornu, in Nigeria, the Asante of Ghana, and the Mende of Sierra Leone have led to similar conclusions. In these places women called queen mothers and other royal women have played a role in the governments of various ethnic groups (see Awe 1977: 144).

4 Altarpiece, *Iyoba*, Queen Mother of Benin with attendants, Royal Court of Benin, Nigeria. Bronze, late 17th–early 18th century. Collection of the Staatliche Museen zu Berlin, Preußischer Kulturbesitz, Museum für Volkerkunde Germany

In researching women's power at the court of Benin with particular reference to their political and ritual roles, I have drawn on the extensive corpus of the art itself, on the history of people and events that oral tradition has preserved over the centuries, and on my own ethnographic fieldwork since 1982, during the lifetime of the current *Iyoba* (see Kaplan 1984; 1985; 1990).[3] Prior to the coronation of *Iyoba Aghahowa N'Errua*, crowned Queen Mother of Benin, 21 August 1981, the last woman to hold court was *Iyoba Iheya* or *Iha II*, mother of *Oba Ovonramwen*, who reigned from about 1890 to 1897.[4] In 1897 a British military expedition conquered Benin and sent the Oba into exile at Old Calabar, in eastern Nigeria. It is uncertain what happened to the queen mother, except that her palace, like that of her son, was burned at the time of the conquest. In interpreting the art I have relied on the way Benin people view their world, in juxtaposition to the art itself and oral tradition, to help illuminate the symbolism noted in the literature, and to help assess the degree of political power various queen mothers have had in Benin. My research shows that the relationship between court imagery and power, between sex and gender roles, and between men and women in Benin is more subtle and complex than has hitherto been suspected.

BENIN QUEENS AND QUEEN MOTHERS

In Benin, as in Africa generally, a woman's most important status derives from her role as mother. Motherhood is the focus of her economic activity and her life. It is as the bearer of children, especially males, that a woman defines her status in the polygynous family and forges lasting ties to her husband, home and kin. It is as a mother and through her children that a woman is assured of support in case of abandonment by her husband; in her old age; and 'in memoriam', when a proper burial is carried out by her son, or a daughter if she has no sons, and by other relatives. A woman begins her life cycle as a daughter and sister, continues as wife and mother and then concludes as a widow. And so it is with the queens — *iloi* — the wives of the Oba of Benin. In the case of the queen mother, it is her son, the Oba, who directs the burial rituals and memorializes her at his palace, and at Lower Uselu, now part of Benin City, where the *Iyoba* traditionally lives and where shrines perpetuate her memory.

First among all *Iyobas* and best known to this day is *Idia*, mother of *Oba Esigie*, who reigned from about 1504 to 1550. As any Benin can tell you, *Idia* is 'the only woman who went to war'. Oral tradition credits her with having raised an army and used her magical powers and knowledge of medicines to aid her son in overcoming his enemies. Her strong ties with her family and village, *Ugieghudu*, in addition to her outstanding personal abilities, probably gave her the base and the means to assist him. As Oba, *Esigie* created the title of *Iyoba*, making his mother the first Queen Mother of Benin. At the same time that he honoured his mother, he reified his claims to the succession: her presence asserted the union that marked him for kingship. He built a palace for her at *Eguae Iyoba*, Uselu, then outside the city, which every Oba since then has done.

The iconography of court art and works identified with *Idia* frequently invoke the Portuguese who, like *Idia*, contributed to the expansion of the kingdom under *Esigie* and to its wealth. With early contact at the end of the fifteenth century, the two kingdoms, Benin and Portugal, exchanged ambassadors and engaged in active trade. Portuguese fought as mercenaries in the Benin armies, providing manpower, instruction and weapons. As such, they are images of power associated with the first queen mother and *Esigie*'s reign. Portraits of Queen Mother *Idia* are delineated on ivory pendant belt plaques now in the British Museum, the Metropolitan Museum of Art, the Seattle Art Museum (plate 5) and elsewhere in Europe; and on bronze pendant belt plaques too, worn by important chiefs (and most often identified as male, as the ivory 'FESTAC Mask' has been; Kaplan 1990; 1991). Images of Portuguese or Europeans, royal motifs and water symbols are integral to the overall design of these and other art works associated with *Idia*. They include ancestral queen mother heads of bronze and leaded brass, plaques, ivory altar tusks, sculptures and other carved and cast works.[5] Europeans are characteristically

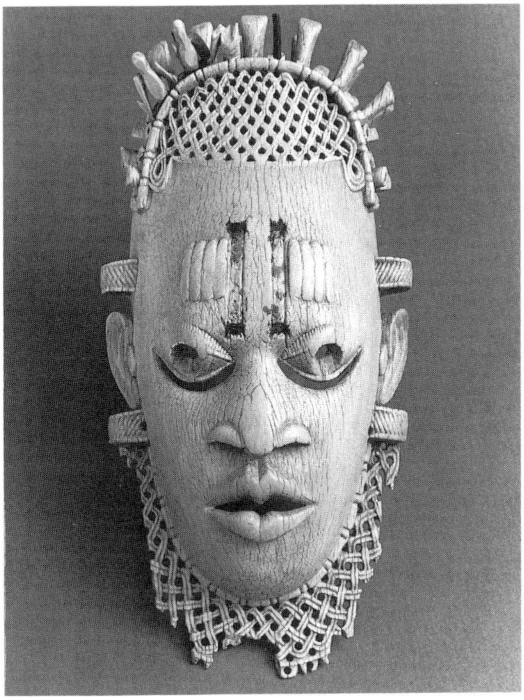

5 Pendant belt plaque, Queen Mother *Idia*, Royal Court of Benin, Nigeria. Ivory, 16th century. Collection of the Seattle Art Museum, Washington State, United States of America, Katherine White Collection. Photograph: courtesy of the Seattle Art Museum

bearded, with large noses, wearing foreign dress, and shown with and without the guns and weapons they used as the Oba's mercenaries.

From the 1500s on, virtually all court art created for royal women focuses on the *Iyoba* (sometimes in other guises: as a priestess, for example); others depicted are her attendants and retinue. These images are found on traditional objects and shrine furnishings in various media: bronze and leaded brass, ivory, works in wood, terracotta, iron; and coral beads, printed and woven cloth. Art associated with royal women comprises about 10 per cent of the known corpus of Benin art.

The *Iyoba* is quintessential woman in Benin, embodying the virtues and accomplishments desired among women, generally, in society. She, like other women, is part of a polygynous household in which relations between wives are competitive. It is not known who will bear the first son and future heir, although the first wife and the favourites are most likely to conceive. Nonetheless, Benins do not view this event as accidental. They believe an *Iyoba* is 'chosen', predestined for her role even before she is born, and that her success in bringing forth the next Oba is a result of both destiny and individual ability. Her special role is recognized through her son, and recorded for posterity in the court art of Benin.

This avenue for achievement is open to all young girls in Benin. The Oba may have as many wives as he chooses. Either he or his chiefs acting for him may take a wife from any segment of society. Girls may also be given to him as gifts, in fulfilment of parents' vows, and even as punishment for rebellious ones, effectively removing them from natal households and the larger society. The qualities admired in a queen are those sought in all Benin wives: she should be physically attractive, that is, well proportioned and slender, smooth-skinned, and of sound body and mind; she should be intelligent, and restrained in manner and bearing. A queen should be of good character and deeds; of agreeable disposition; faithful; and submissive to her husband's will. Undesirable wives are those who are troublesome, envious and quarrelsome, I was told by the head of the Oba's harem, *Chief Ine of Ibiwe* (personal communication, 6 March 1985). Such traits are recognized by men and women alike as the causes of problems, conflict and even divorce.

Iloi who met expectations, bore children, and gradually earned the confidence of the Oba might be rewarded with a title in their lifetime. These titles were like those of town chiefs, *Eghaevbho n'ore*, and palace chiefs, *Eghaevbho n'ogbe*: for example, *Obazuwa, Obazuaye, Eson* and others. Unlike their male counterparts, the queens have no functions to perform publicly. However, titled queens do perform secret functions inside the palace harem. Perhaps the most important titles reserved for queens are the seven body titles, *Egiegbe*, each of which refers to a part of the Oba himself, like his body, *Egbe*, his eyes, *Aro*, his forehead, *Ohan*, his spirit or soul, *Ehi*, and so on (see Kaplan 1984: 20). They were usually given to favourites and, in the past, the wives with body titles were buried with him.

Other wives who died 'unblemished' — without stain to their reputation, behaviour and good name — and who had exhibited the devotion and deeds expected of them, were buried in a special place, a village reserved for the Oba's wives. If a wife had been quarrelsome, or had been accused of witchcraft, envy, or selfishness, her family would have to bury her somewhere else, privately, and without ceremony. A queen who was banished or disgraced was unlikely to be buried at all, as anyone who aided the offender would also be declared 'an enemy of the Oba', and suffer for it along with his or her family. In the old days to be declared an enemy of the Oba and ostracized was tantamount to death and ruin for a family. A queen who ran away, therefore, would try to live discreetly and to die unnoticed, to avoid bringing harm to her family. A queen who was admired and respected for her good deeds and accomplishments might be long remembered in oral history and tradition, but not recorded in court art.

Royal wives still live with their children and attendants in seclusion, in the Oba's harem, *erie*. There are no concubines in the harem, only wives and intended wives. Until the end of the nineteenth century the harem was maintained by female slaves and male eunuchs, under the general supervision of the *Ine*, head of the *Ibiwe* palace society, and the *Oshodin*, responsible for the *erie*. The queens owned lands and property in the villages that were looked after by servants, slaves and relatives, both male and female, chiefs and emissaries from the Oba; and except for slaves, such people still serve the queens outside the palace. Only members of the Oba's family were permitted to enter the harem, and those female members of the queens' families who served them, but their mothers could not enter. Neither could fathers, brothers nor male relatives, nor could men generally come near them or touch them. These customs persist to this day. The taboos apply as well to the Queen Mother of Benin, at Uselu. She maintains herself as other queens do now, as in the past, through emissaries to her villages and properties. And like the others she maintains ties with her place of origin.

These local ties find expression in oral tradition, local cults and masquerades in which the deeds and fortunes or misfortunes of queens, the Oba's wives, and ordinary women are remembered. Unlike the *Iyoba*, such remembrances were not rendered in court art, but by natural phenomena, performance and rituals, music and song, masks and objects that are non-gender-specific. For example, women transformed into spirits and hero-deities, worshipped locally, have taken natural forms like a river (the Ovia and Ikpoba Rivers), a tree (*ikhimwini*) and even certain leaves (*ewere*). (For extended descriptions of these cults see Bradbury 1957: 54–7; 1973: 140–200; Lopasic 1989; 1992.) A queen, *Ovia*, became the focus of a local cult.

Remembrances of women and men who became part of the spirit world have other natural and vernacular art forms, produced in villages and towns: carved and painted wood masks, clay sculptures, shrines, chalks in various shapes, peeled sticks, and even single parrot feathers. Ritual offerings include cockerels, goats, cows, cowrie shells, chalks, snails, fish and other things. Pottery used in the worship of *Olokun*, the god of the sea, has special, although not exclusive meaning for women concerned with bearing children. Contemporary shrines to this deity are the most naturalistic with near life-sized figures, clearly identifiable as males and females, modelled in clay and painted. *Olokun* pots made in Benin City have small clay, nude figures modelled on the exterior body. On them, men may be shown playing a drum or side-blown horns; the women may be shown either pregnant or nursing infants. Traditional *Olokun* pots made in Use village, however, have only incised geometric designs, and sometimes cowrie shells modelled on the rim (plate 6). The Use pots are likely to be older designs than the modelled pots made at Igun Street, in Benin City (see Kaplan 1990: 325).

Village art is often neutral or ambiguous in representing, denoting, or referencing sexuality. However, some few objects are sexually explicit: pairs of somewhat crude, small, nude, half-figures of adult males and females are modelled in clay and chalk, and used as portents and offerings (children also may use these objects as toys). Knowledge of objects used by local cults, in ritual and masquerades, is shared among initiates and members of the local, and to a lesser extent, wider culture. They know the sex and gender roles of those whose stories are being enacted or who are being portrayed — which those outside the circle of knowledge cannot. Vernacular art objects, like court art, are often subtly differentiated, and sometimes not, like those contemporary modelled and painted clay shrines already mentioned. *Olokun* is the giver of children, which the Benins regard as another form of wealth. When depicted, he is shown as a king, an Oba, with his wives around him, some nursing children (plate 7). The general muting of overt sexuality, publicly, in village and court art is consistent with mores in the culture generally, and is encouraged by the omnipresent vows of secrecy in Benin. With regard to women, in particular, court art emphasizes images of power and roles socially defined by gender.

Court art is important because it is 'there' in the most tangible and unchanged way — as antiquities that have survived centuries of use, change and appropriation by foreigners. It provides insights into women's roles and the nature of polity in Benin. It is a statement, albeit 'official', in being made for court use and display, about who and what was important in society; and it enables us to seek and compare those subjects given artistic representation with extant historical accounts, oral

6 Potter, Mrs Edomwandiro Omoigui, making a ritual pot, Use village, Benin City vicinity. Photograph: Flora E. S. Kaplan, 1986

7 Queen's *Olokun* shrine (detail), Benin City, Edo State, Nigeria. Clay, painted (Location not disclosed). Photograph: Flora E. S. Kaplan, 1988

tradition and ethnographic findings. The art of the royal court attests to the contacts, trade and conflicts with neighbours and foreigners since the late fifteenth century; and it lends physical credence to the oral traditions and histories that recount expansion and contraction of the Benin empire, up to the end of the nineteenth century. The works embody ideas and values that still shape society ethnographically, and affect women's lives. The restricted use of rare materials like ivory and bronze and the specialized techniques associated with them bespeak the nature of rank and power in Benin. The import of their use by the queen mother needs more sufficient attention. Fortunately, because of the materials, most of the art is available as aesthetic and historic documents for future study. The art provides tangible and visible records of symbols of state and style, of deeds and events associated with the reigns of particular Obas and *Iyobas*.

The present Oba of Benin, *Omo N'Oba N'Edo Uku Akpolokpolo Erediauwa*, is thirty-eighth in direct line of succession from the Second Dynasty, begun in the twelfth century. The Oba's palace is in the centre of Benin City, the capital of modern Edo State. The palace site, occupied since the ninth century, remains the centre of the culture, and the place from which, since medieval times, the Benin kingdom has expanded to dominate most of what is today southern Nigeria. The palace itself was a city within a city, and the Oba the hub of all civic and religious life which was conjoined in his person. He endures as the literal embodiment of his people — his proclamations having the power to come to pass. When the Oba venerates his ancestors, he does so on behalf of all Benins, to assure their well-being and continuity (plate 8). The bronze heads of past Obas, displayed on palace

8 *Omo N'Oba N'Edo Uku Akpolokpolo Erediauwa*, the Oba of Benin, salutes his ancestors with his brass ceremonial sword, *Eben*, and ancestral rattlestaff, *Ukhurhe*, during annual *Igue* cycle of ceremonies, Benin City, Edo State, Nigeria. Photograph: Flora E. S. Kaplan, 1992

altars, affirm the dynastic line and illustrate the royal succession in history. It is to the palace, replete with symbols and shrines, that those who owe allegiance to the Oba come to salute him and to declare their fealty to him. In the past these included subjugated peoples as well as Benins. The Oba's palace and its shrines offer visible proof of the longevity, prescience and power of the divine kings of Benin.

The Queen Mother of Benin has her own altars and furnishings in her palace at Uselu. She, like her son and all other Benins, it should be noted, worship their 'head' at annual ceremonies and, more often in the past, used to worship their 'hand' as well. The head and right hand were important symbols in Benin art (plate 9). They impart two seemingly contradictory notions: one, predestiny, and two, that personal effort is needed to prosper in this world. Benins believe the head is the locus of reason and affects an individual's ability to realize his or her potential

9 Queen Mother Altar-of-the-Hand, Royal Court of Benin, Nigeria. Brass, 18th Century. Collection of the British Museum. Photograph: courtesy of the Trustees of the British Museum, London

in life; the hand is the means to wealth and prestige. To succeed everyone must strive, but predestiny also means no one completely controls the outcome — both important ideas and values in the culture. Art reflects the culture's ethos — its competitiveness, self-reliance and energy. The head is its leitmotif, made evident in annual ceremonies honouring the head of the living Oba, the polity of Benin, and the continuity of the Edo-speaking peoples, made manifest in the display of royal ancestral heads. Before the British conquest these ceremonies were performed with blood sacrifices of humans; nowadays, cows, goats, cockerels and other animals are used. At one time circular altars-of-the-hand, *ikegobo*, were offered prayers and sacrifices as well, in thanksgiving for good fortune.

The symbolism of rank in art extends to the materials and production by royal guilds, and to the use of important ritual objects, all of which are controlled by the Oba. Now as then, he alone can give permission for members of the court and village elders to use certain items of regalia, bronze ornaments and coral beads. Palace and town chiefs are allowed to use wood for their ancestral heads, staffs and altars-of-the-hand. The Oba permits the royal bronzecasters to use terracotta heads on their ancestral family shrines. But brass and bronze heads, ancestral rattlestaffs, *Ukhurhe*, and ceremonial swords used by the Oba, *Eben*, along with various bronze altarpieces and decorations for them, the ivories — tusks and certain ornaments, instruments, and furnishings — are solely the prerogatives of the Oba, and to a lesser extent, the *Iyoba*.

The materials of art have 'colour' and meaning. Three important and ritually significant materials — bronze, ivory and iron — are identified with the primary colours recognized in Benin — red (bronze), white (ivory) and black (iron). Bronze, *eronmwon equehun*, does not decay or rust. Like kingship, it endures forever. The impregnable surface and sheen of bronze deflects evil, and protects the Oba and *Iyoba*. The colour of bronze, red, is symbolic of both life and danger, the forces of creation and destruction. These forces are associated with the ancient god of iron, *Ogun*, and the Oba himself, who alone had ultimate power of life and death over his subjects. Red is also the colour of corals, and of life-giving blood, which is spilled on the ground in sacrifices and offered to 'feed' the gods, the ancestors and the Oba with its life force. In pre-colonial days, human blood was offered on important occasions, now animals are offered.

The god *Ogun* is associated with the metals that come from the earth, and with the red 'blood' of bronze that flows over and covers the clay core in 'lost-wax' casting. Iron is also linked to the power of the earth — the place struck to awaken the ancestors. Through the fire of the blacksmith's forge and the bronzecaster's molten crucible, new images are cast to become part of a chain that joins the living and the past. Red, the colour identified with *Ogun*, is worn by the Oba on occasions when there is danger, and when he is angry or threatening. He never, however, wears black — the colour linked to the earth in association with night, earth and evil. In the earth, the place where the deceased are buried, there is fire, pain, and forbidden and hidden things. Mourners daub themselves with black charcoal and wear black-patterned clothes. But the Oba must have no contact with or knowledge of death and disease. His state of mind, quite literally, reflects the state of the Benin people.

In contrast, the Oba most often wears white, the colour associated with purity, peace and happiness. It calls up the power of the elephant, from which precious ivory comes. It refers to the uniqueness of the elephant, its dominion over the bush, its strength and endurance, its capacity for swift response, as well as such human qualities as single births and 'hand-like' trunks. Elephant tusks had to be offered first to the Oba, to whom they belonged, before the hunters were allowed their share. Apart from royal use by the king and his mother, ivory was an important item of trade with the Europeans from the sixteenth century onwards. Chalk, like ivory, is white and is used in worship of the god of the sea or waters, *Olokun* (plate 10). People offer chalk at shrines, they drink it in water and eat it; they mark their bodies with it, their faces and arms, to show their happiness on having a baby, on being given a title, when worshipping their heads or giving thanks, and on any joyous occasion. The Oba will wear white as he does red, with meaning for the occasion — dressed in red, he is a manifestation of *Ogun* on earth, and in white, he is the counterpart of *Olokun* on land.

The Queen Mother, *Iyoba*, also wears clothing imbued with meaning — red on some occasions and white on others — but she is not identified as the female counterpart of either the associated deities or her son. In a formal photographic portrait of her, taken during the 1981 ceremonies for her title-taking, she appears as a senior chief, identified with the highest level of town chiefs, *Eghaevbo N'Ore*, displaying the privileges given her by the Oba (plate 11). She wears coral insignia of the highest rank: the headband, *Udahae*, the high coral collar, *Odigba*, coral anklets,

10 Queen Mother *Aghahowa*, with chalk mark of happiness, at her personal shrine for *Olòkun, Iyoba's* Palace, Uselu, Nigeria. Photograph: Flora E. S. Kaplan, 1990

Ivie Owe, and the coral bandelier. She wears the special red flannel cloth, *Ododo*, with wrapper in the formal shape, *Eyoen*. Her wrapper is filled out and billowing, rather than tied in the more casual ram's-head style, *Uhunmwun-Ogho* (see Aisien 1986: 57). She holds the chiefly sword, *Eben*, used to pay homage to the Oba, in front of her, touching the ground. *Iyoba Aghahowa N'Errua* sits on a rectangular, carved, wooden throne, *Agba*, firmly planted on the ground, in regal fashion. Despite the modernity of the media, many of the most important coral insignia of rank in the photograph are also retained in printing her image on commemorative cloth, designed in honour of her final title-taking, on 21 August 1981.

Images of the *Iyoba* on antiquities often show her wearing a coral shirt, and privileged coral insignia, like those above, denoting a high-ranking male chief. Her uniqueness is closest to the war chief, the *Ezomo*, who is the only other chief who enjoys comparable status and a number of privileges approaching those of the Oba. For example, aside from the *Iyoba*, no person other than the *Ezomo* may wear a similar coral shirt. Although these similarities and gender roles may cause confusion at times, the queen mother may be identified by a number of distinctive features, apart from the coral shirt. Her wrapper differs from that of males in antiquities, being straight and decorated with three horizontal, decorative bands. The *Iyoba*'s special conical, curving headdress is more easily and generally recognized. Sometimes, however, in smaller and less well-cast or carved pieces, its resemblance to the conical, but upright headdresses of other senior chiefs is

11 Formal portrait of Queen Mother *Aghahowa Ovbi N'Errua*, at Uselu, Benin City. Photograph: S. O. Alonge, 1981, Collection of Flora E. S. Kaplan

mistaken. The unique hairstyle of the queen mother that forms the basis of her headdress covered with netted corals was invented by *Idia*, and is compared with a parrot's beak.

Other distinctive features of the queen mother and her attendants are the number and position of female body tattoos, *iwu*. These were reserved for women, and were given to young girls who entered palace service. They consist of five pairs of long black blades on the upper body, and five radiating blades below the navel. The latter are of the utmost reliability in identifying women versus men. Non-royal women who became wives had an additional short blade just below the right breast, *ovbiwu*, as a sign of origin (see Aisien 1986: 11, 24-6, 34). Tattoos are generally faithfully rendered in virtually all media. Secondary sex characteristics have been used as indicators of biological sex. In court art, however, breasts are not reliable indicators of the sex of the person represented. They may be prominent or rendered as simple, incised, pendant triangles (on both bronze and ivory works). Bare-chested chiefs, who are often, literally, the 'big men' at the Oba's palace today, frequently are heavy-set, thickly muscled, with well-developed pectorals. As the physical features of these men — their size, weight and powerful builds — denote wealth and health in Benin, gender is rendered in art as in life. But sex differences are ambiguous and have confused scholars from time to time. This is likely to occur where size of image, quality of casting, and crude rendering of details have blurred less well-understood, distinctive features (see Kecskesi 1987: 164); and lends support to my thesis that images, and women's images in particular in court art, are ambiguous and gender-based.

On antiquities, it is best to look to the sex of the young attendants, who are always shown naked and whose private parts are plainly visible. Young girls usually accompany the Queen Mother of Benin. On bronze altarpieces and carved ivory sculptures used to decorate her ancestral altars, they are 'clothed' only with ornaments — having many strands of beads, *ika*, possibly corals, around their necks, ankles and wrists. Their high, crescent-shaped hairdo, *Eme*, is also special, and is tied with a particular intertwining thread. These young girls may be daughters of chiefs or from wealthy families, or intended wives of the Oba, sent to the queen mother to serve her and to learn palace ways, until they reach puberty. The band of beads worn about the hips symbolizes their unmarried state. These and similar details appear on numerous altarpieces and art works (see Kaplan 1981: plates 23, 24, 33, 36, 40); *Oba Erediauwa* suggests these females were accompanying the queen mother to *Ugie* (personal communication, 6 January 1991). The present *Queen Mother Aghahowa* is attended by her grandchildren, great-grandchildren, distant relations and members of important families in Benin. As she is quite an elderly lady, new and intended wives are trained by the Oba's senior wives in the palace.

Young boys who attended the Oba, pages and swordbearers, were naked as well. They used to wear only brass anklets. Nudity for both sexes was formerly a sign of immaturity, purity and lack of sexuality. In the palaces it was also a protection for the Oba and *Iyoba*, because those close to them could not conceal anything harmful on their persons, including magical substances. With few exceptions (two out of nearly one thousand plaques known, and some late examples), traditional court art rarely shows females in the presence of the Oba. (Some pieces, as I noted earlier, do show adult males in attendance on the *Iyoba*: see Kaplan 1991: 122.) Indeed, there are only two ceremonial occasions at which young girls have specific functions to perform for the Oba, because of their symbolic and actual purity: *Esukporu*, a young virgin, plays a role once, during the Oba's coronation ceremonies; another prepares the medicines applied to his head and body during the annual *Igue* festival. But they do not otherwise attend him.

Ambiguity and even neutrality of sex in gender roles characterized prepubescent girls and boys in court art, and were part of custom before and even after the British conquest in 1897. In these works as in life, young people at the palace were assigned tasks based on biological sex; girls attended the queens and queen mother, and boys attended chiefs and the Oba. As royal attendants their gender roles were neutral. They had to be celibate and sexually inactive. But their nakedness and visible lower body parts, tattoos and ornaments, left no doubt as to their sex, albeit immature in their sexuality. Some palace attendants might be kept past puberty, and served at the discretion of the Oba until he released them — often with a wife and land with which to start life, as rewards for their loyal service. Until they married, however, neither boys nor girls were clothed in Benin, in the old days. Their representation on bronze plaques, altarpieces, sculptures and other works makes their status and roles clear. Although royal attendants are clothed today, young boys and males are still celibate and cannot be touched by women until they are released from palace service by the Oba. Young female attendants, too, are still prepubescent and sexually neutral. They must remain celibate until released from palace service, ready to marry and have children. Today an intervening period of further education may come before marriage.

As late as the first two decades of the twentieth century, attendants and young people generally went about unclothed. In the early years of his long, forty-five year reign, *Oba Akenzua II* (1933–78) became aware of British sensibilities about nudity; he instituted various items of dress for attendants and chiefs at court, and he abolished tattooing among Benins of both sexes. Tattoos are seen only among very old people now. The tattoos used to be made by traditional surgeons, *Osiwu*, in distinctive patterns and sets for males and females; they marked all free Benins (see Aisien 1986: 22-7), and were recorded on antiquities.

The role of ethnographic data and oral tradition is important in reassessing court art with regard to royal women, images of power, sex roles and gender. In particular, they informed my interpretation of the famed ivory pendant plaques and the ancestral bronze heads, as well as other works (rectangular altarpieces, altars-of-the-hand, and ivory tusks and sculptures). The art and practice of tattooing which still is known and can be seen among old people today provide important data for distinguishing not only sex but differences in ethnicity, as *Iwu* identified Benins in battle and in history.

The importance of facial tattoos (as well as body tattoos) in identifying royal women (who began life as non-royal women, being the ones chosen for marriage with an Oba) is best illustrated with an oral tradition told to me by His Highness, *Omo N'Oba N'Edo Uku Akpolokpolo Erediauwa*. It illuminates *Idia*'s distinctive facial marks, and enhances recognition and interpretation of the art generally (personal communication, 26 September 1989). Most scholars have noted the inset strips of iron between her brows on her forehead. They mark a place of important expression, a place from which spirit, power and thought emanate (see Nevadomsky 1986: 42). But of equal importance these marks, where strips of iron are usually inset, relate to the story about how she came to be a queen in the first place. It is also consistent with current ideas and values in Benin culture. *Idia*'s parents did not want her to become the Oba's wife, and so they consulted an oracle. He advised them to make her ugly in the Oba's sight; and to accomplish this the native doctor made two incisions between her eyes, and put medicines (magical substances) in them to repel the king. The Oba, sensing something was wrong, ordered his doctors to treat her before she came into his presence. This was done. She became an *oloi*, and the mother of *Oba Esigie*. The two marks on her forehead, however, are not cicatrices nor tattoos; such women's marks consist of either single or triple marks on the forehead, not two.

The sixteenth-century ivory pendant plaques, and some possibly carved later, all portray *Iyoba Idia*, the first queen mother. They are replete with symbols of

12 Pendant belt plaque, Queen Mother *Idia*, Royal Court of Benin, Nigeria. Ivory, 16th century. Collection of Linden-Museum Stuttgart, Staatliche Museum für Volkerkunde, Stuttgart, Germany. Photograph: courtesy of the Linden-Museum Stuttgart

water and wealth, with fish, bearded Europeans, and royal entwined motifs that form the ruff around her chin and surmount her headdress. The decorative ruff of this kind of plaque is a flattened perspective of the rows of coral beads that encircle the queen's neck. An ivory pendant in the Linden Museum Stuttgart, Germany, is atypical, with a headband of coral beads, *Udahae*, threaded through it; *Oba Erediauwa* and his chiefs consider it something possibly added later as an embellishment (plate 12). Some pendant plaques are also a kind of charm. They have special features: the plaques in the collections of the Metropolitan Museum and Seattle Art Museum, for example, have secret compartments where medicines were hidden to protect the Oba during the annual *Igue* and *Emobo* ceremonies (see Kaplan 1991: 134, 136, 137, 139, 141). As part of his regalia on such occasions, the Oba wears two strings of carved ivories around his waist, but only one pendant with the face of the *Iyoba*. The main string consists of pairs of ivories, found in various museum collections: heads of Obas, crocodiles, elephants and leopards — symbols of royal power. The present *Oba Erediauwa* wears a total of seventeen such pendants, eight pairs and the lone *Idia*, and a second string that consists of thirty-nine thin, pencil-like ivories, carved with decorative motifs. The number worn depends on the waist-size of the king (Oba of Benin, personal communication, 6 June 1988).

Perhaps the largest corpus of ivories is the altar tusks, now being dated to the eighteenth and nineteenth centuries (see Bassani and Fagg 1988; Blackmun 1991). Nearly two-thirds of the known tusks studied include at least some females in conjunction with a queen mother. The suggestion has been made that the mothers of *Oba Osemwede* and *Oba Obanosa* are represented on some of them (see Blackmun 1984: 204, 232, 303; and 255, 268, 270, 273, 275-276, 281, 286, 289). This coincides with other ideas put forward about the identity of some bronze queen mother ancestor heads (see Kaplan 1984: 21); *Oba Osemwede*'s mother *Omozogie* is a likely candidate for representation on the tusks and in court art because of the high regard in which she was held and because of her wealth. But it is questionable whether or not *Ose* was intended, as she is considered notorious for joining the enemies of her son *Oba Obanosa*.

Single ivory sculptures of standing female figures used to decorate the shrines of queen mothers at the Oba's palace and at Uselu (see Kaplan 1981: 36). Similar figures, in three pairs, appear at each side of the queen mother on rectangular bronze altarpieces, *Urhoto*. On these tableaux two adult figures, usually males, hold shields above the queen's head to ward off evil — or they may be shown supporting her arms in full-festival position, just as chiefs and the Oba are supported. The young females, like the ones on the circular altar-of-the-hand, *Ikegobo* (plate 9), hold a variety of objects, very often a circular fan, *Ezuzu* (held discretely over their private parts), used to 'cool' the queen mother, and a netted calabash, *Ukuse* (a musical instrument which women use to accompany themselves when singing, along with drums and other instruments).

Ancestor heads were the most important bronzes cast for the *Iyoba, Uhunmwun Elao*, lasting proof of her place in Benin history. Grouped and arranged chronologically on the basis of style, into 'early' and 'late', these heads are neither idealized nor generalized royal representations as scholars have suggested. Rather, they are portraits, from the Benin's point of view, and were meant to represent the particular *Iyobas* for whom they were cast. Like the Oba's own, they were cast after they 'passed', and were placed on altars, decorated with other ritually prescribed bronze, ivory and wood shrine furnishings produced by royal guilds.

The 'early' Queen Mother *Idia* heads are thin castings, delicately modelled with great naturalism, and nearly life-size (plate 13). All five early heads show *Idia*'s distinctive curving headdress with its latticework of coral beads: the *Ukpe-Okhue*, or 'parrot's beak'. It is pointed and curving, and is worn by subsequent queen mothers (despite some confusion with male chiefs' headdresses, mentioned earlier). Again, only the *Ezomo*, like the *Iyoba*, was permitted to use a coral cap, but I stress it is not considered a 'crown', but a rare privilege granted to them by the Oba. The leader of the town chiefs, the *Iyase*, wears a tall, conical cap, but it is made of leopard skin and red flannel cloth, *Ododo*. Other senior chiefs may wear a type of conical headgear of cut *Ododo*, or 'pangolin' cloth. The Oba, of course, wears the most elaborate and distinctive headdress of all, his royal crowns.

It is, however, by no means certain that the stylistic classification is entirely correct. Accumulating hard evidence, and thermoluminescence tests on some bronzes, so far, indicate dating of Benin pieces is more complicated than the accepted chronology suggests (see Craddock and Picton 1986). Furthermore, the virtual absence of ongoing and intensive archaeology in Benin provides scant context for chronology. Suitable samples from existing pieces are also scarce because, early

13 Ancestral head of Queen Mother *Idia*, Royal Court of Benin, Nigeria. Brass, 16th century (Early period). Collection of the British Museum. Photograph: courtesy of the Trustees of the British Museum, London

14 Ancestral head of Queen Mother, Royal Court of Benin, Nigeria. Bronze, 18th century (Late period). Collection of the National Museum, Lagos, Nigeria

15 Ancestral head of Queen Mother, Royal Court of Benin, Nigeria. Bronze, late 18th–early 19th century (Late period). Collection of Linden-Museum Stuttgart, Staatliche Museum für Volkerkunde, Stuttgart, Germany. Photograph: courtesy of the Linden-Museum Stuttgart.

on, European conservators cleaned, repaired and resurfaced many Benin bronzes. Also, the practice I observed in the field — of recycling scrap and raw materials for castings — yields contaminated samples and inconclusive results (see Kaplan 1990). Such practices seem to have been followed for a long time, creating confusion where trace elements might have yielded valuable comparative data, and shed light on sources of raw materials. Nonetheless, a few 'late' heads, for example, are yielding earlier dates than might be expected, and a few 'early' heads, later dates (see Craddock and Picton 1986; Dark 1975; Fagg 1963; Kecskesi 1988; Tunis 1981, 1983).

Queen mother heads have multi-layered symbolism. The head itself has many meanings for Benins: the serenity of the features, the facial marks, the headdress and its many related motifs all implode on ancient history. Ornaments and insignia of rank — indeed the materials themselves — draw added meaning from being identified with 'maleness', and are bestowed on the basis of gender roles and rank. The same motifs used on ivory pendant plaques are found on bronze heads. Two 'early' bronze heads of queen mothers are raised on truncated pyramid bases (National Museum, Lagos, and Berlin Museum, Germany). Both are decorated with a fine tracery of guilloche or 'royal rope' designs: one (Berlin Museum) has fish cast in high relief within its design borders. These fish are neither mudfish nor any other small riverine species, but great and 'mighty fish', say Benins, that symbolize the fertility and power of *Idia*. They connote the riches that came from the sea after contact and trade with the Portuguese, and the power of *Idia* who helped in the expansion of the kingdom.

The 'early' queen mother heads were not necessarily cast at the same time. Fieldwork in Benin suggests all ancestor heads, early and late, as presently categorized, were probably recast from time to time for different shrines in the palace and at Uselu. Of these five early heads, two (National Museum, Lagos, and British Museum, London) were apparently made by the same hand, at about the same period. A third head in the Berlin Museum is evidently the work of another artist, made about the same time; it belongs stylistically to the sixteenth century. Another early queen mother head, somewhat thicker and heavier, but finely modelled (Liverpool) may have been cast later than the other three. Finally, a rather coarse head in the University Museum, Philadelphia, is problematic and was probably not made before the nineteenth century.

Of the 'late' bronze queen mother heads, some forty-five castings are known. Like the Oba's heads, they are arranged chronologically on stylistic grounds (see Dark 1975: 31, 46–53; Fagg 1963), becoming larger, heavier and thicker castings from the seventeenth century onwards. From the mid-eighteenth to nineteenth centuries, especially, necklaces of coral beads encircling the neck, gradually became high, cylindrical bases for heads that rested on a flanged base. The smaller, more finely detailed heads rest on flattened bases with royal rope designs, and probably date from the eighteenth century (plate 14).

Heads of this tentative period can probably be subdivided further, on the basis of an interesting detail that has not been remarked on: some heads have five fine lines incised on each cheek. Benins did not scar their faces with incisions or true 'cicatrices' — despite the latter being widely described in the literature, as such, and as 'tribal marks' when they appear above the eyes. These marks have even been regarded as characteristic of male and female heads (see Ben-Amos 1980: 81) — which they were not (see Aisien 1986: 27, 34, 42). Neither were they significant chronologically (see Williams 1974: 141–2); nor were they 'cicatrices' which are true scars. But they appear to be, I agree, likely stylistic features (see Blackmun 1984: 17; Kaplan 1985; Nevadomsky 1986: 41). Queen mother heads with incised cheek lines may have reference to her ethnic identity or an event in which she figures prominently. Kecskesi also points to the possibility that some heads were cast for particular queen mothers, e.g. *Ede* and *Ohogha II*, mothers of *Oba Erosoyen* and *Oba Akengbuda* respectively, because an eighteenth-century date has been obtained in some tests (personal communication, October 1988). Other heads, as noted, lack this feature (see Kecskesi 1987: plate 162; Celenko 1986: 110; Powell 1985: 25). Nineteenth-century queen mother heads display a profusion of symbols as does Oba's head, on the flat, flange bases — frogs, celts, snails, etc. — modelled in high relief on top of the flat flange.

Late heads are generally less subtly modelled than the early ones. The facial planes are less rounded, the eyes wide open and staring, and the expression rather fixed and frozen; the head itself is of larger-than-life proportions. The face, once near life-size, is reduced between the wider, elaborated headdress above, and the heavily ringed, tall neck base below. While late heads look less like 'portraits' to the Westerner's eye than the naturalistic early heads, it is best to look again, closely. Fieldwork suggests that what appear to be minor variations in details have greater meaning for Benins. Those minor differences may prove useful in identifying different queen mothers. More detailed knowledge of deeds and oral tradition will, I believe, connect 'minor' variations to major innovations of particular queens, meant to be remembered. This connection will transform later ancestor heads into portraits, from the culture bearer's point of view, with increased historical and stylistic import for chronology.

It appears a generally 'fuzzy' category of 'late' heads can be divided, even now, into at least two main types, with a third possible; and the 'early' heads prove to be of different dates, though not necessarily of a different subject. To separate the two types, the presence or absence of the following distinctive features can be used: a coral headband, *Udahae*, is worn with long strings of coral beads hanging down at the left side; one or more large, tubular agate or coral bead(s) is placed at the front of the headband or headdress; and a single or two pair(s) of large coral bead rosettes, called *Ititiako*, is added at either side of the headdress (plate 15).

The apparent hiatus between the early and late ancestor heads of queen mothers may be connected with the reported destruction of the royal Oba's palace by *Ogbebo, Oba Osemwede*'s brother. This usurper is said to have seized the throne in 1816 and waged considerable warfare. Then, after destroying its treasures, he is said to have set fire to the palace and hanged himself. He had reigned only eight months (see Egharevba 1968: 43). Mid- to late eighteenth-century heads may be associated with *Ede*, mother of *Oba Eresoyen* (*c.* 1739), and with *Ohogha II*, mother of *Oba Akengbuda* (*c.* 1752). Both Obas actively expanded the Benin kingdom and amassed great wealth. *Oba Eresoyen*'s reign brought a florescence of the arts. The ornate nineteenth-century bronze queen mother heads may represent *Iyoba Omozogie*, mother of *Oba Osemwede* (*c.* 1816). She is reputed to have been very wealthy and, like *Idia*, she is credited with assisting her son's important conquests, at *Akure*, for example (see Egharevba 1968: 75). Nineteenth-century visitors to Benin during *Osemwede*'s reign lend credence to accounts in oral tradition; they also remarked on the splendour of the queen mother's court (see Egharevba 1968: 44-6).

SUMMARY

In Benin the art reveals the ethos of the culture with its desires for individual achievement, wealth, recognition and popularity, all of which are valued and sought by men and women. They not only assure success in this world, but good name and remembrance afterwards, and constitute an important part of a person's legacy. Proper burial and ritual observances are overwhelming concerns of each Benin man and woman. Children, especially males, are crucial for their parents' passage to the next world, and are greatly desired. Family name and continuity are still expressed throughout Benin with the setting up and maintenance of an ancestral shrine in the family house, other religious denominational affiliations notwithstanding. In the case of the Oba, the family shrines are the state's and stand for all the Edo-speaking peoples. The court art displayed on shrines at the palace extols and asserts the power of divine kingship, the ruling dynasty, and the belief system of the Benins.

Court art displayed for the *Iyoba* privately, in the palace, and publicly at the shrines at Uselu after her death, acknowledges the power of all women in ensuring the continuity of the family; and, in the case of the *Iyoba*, in ensuring the continuity of the state and the Edos. In fulfilling her roles as wife and mother, the queen mother attains visibility and a kind of immortality. As mother of the Oba, she is portrayed and her memory and deeds preserved in the ritual furnishings of ancestral altars and shrines, on chiefly ornaments, in masquerades and cults, and in oral tradition. The proposal here, that individual queens are portrayed in court art, enhances a chronology based on style (see Kaplan 1984; 1991). Ancestor heads are cast in remembrance of departed rulers and to mark succession, and include queen mother heads.

Paradoxically, the Oba's mother attains her status through female sex roles, but achieves the highest rank in society as a widow, past menopause, in a role based on male gender, as a senior chief. Thereafter, as the *Iyoba*, she is consulted and remains vigilant on her son's behalf, although the two never meet face to face again. She takes up residence in a new palace built for her by her son, at Uselu. She plays an active role in settling disputes and furthering prosperity and peace in his reign. The present *Iyoba Aghahowa Ovbi N'Errua* holds court at Uselu and deliberates cases together with her male chiefs and retinue, as did her predecessors. In a society suffused with a strong male ethos and organized around a divine kingship, she fulfils her destiny as a female and is honoured as a male, senior chief.

The *Iyoba* illuminates both the complementarity and ambiguity of sex and gender roles in Benin, as they were determined from the culture bearer's point of view. As a wife, the queen mother was seldom visible, being secluded in the palace harem, *Erie*. As a widow, in the guise of a senior chief of highest rank, she emerges and becomes visible in a male gender role with special privileges, regalia and a distinctive lifestyle. Her 'femaleness' and sexuality are muted, and only the vestiges remain discernible in her body tattoos. She achieves recognition, expresses her individuality and identity, and attains immortality in art and memory within the confines of a traditional society — at the crossroads between sex and gender roles.

Flora *Ẹdowaye* S. Kaplan
New York University

NOTES

1 Ethnographic fieldwork in Benin commenced at the royal court in 1982, and was continued from late 1983–85, as a Fulbright professor, Department of Sociology and Anthropology, University of Benin, and at CenSCER (Centre for Social, Cultural and Environmental Research). Additional periods of research in Benin, from 1986 to 1992, followed. The fieldwork on which this study is based included research, observations, and interviews in the palace harem, as well as more than fifty in-depth interviews with members of the royal family, chiefs, and other individuals of varied backgrounds.

I am deeply grateful to His Highness, *Omo N'Oba N'Edo Uku Akpolokpolo Erediauwa*, the Oba of Benin, for his permission to conduct my research; and for his critical reading, comments, and discussion of earlier drafts of this and other articles. The *Iyoba Aghahowa N'Errua* offered her enduring friendship, knowledge and experiences at court. Members of the CenSCER faculty seminar provided thoughtful questions and comments that stimulated eventual interpretations. I acknowledge in particular the contributions of professors Fred Omu, Pauline Makinwa-Adebusoye and Philip Igbafe; and the participation of Joseph Nevadomsky and Arlene Enabolele.

2 Historic and ethnographic references to the *Iyoba*, her court and royal women have generally been limited in scope. King (1823), Bacon (1897) and Ling-Roth (1902) are among the visitors, traders, administrators and missionaries to Benin who remarked on the queen mother. Contemporary references usually are limited, and based on indirect or brief contacts (Awe 1977; Blackmun 1984).

3 An ethnography of Benin royal women, based on intensive fieldwork among them, is the subject of a work in progress, *In Splendour and Seclusion*. Theoretical issues and studies of elite women in Africa, focusing on their political and ritual roles, including Benin, are discussed in an edited volume of papers entitled, *Queens, Concubines, and Consorts: Case Studies in African Gender*, forthcoming.

4 In a series of interviews at Uselu, in the palace and her private quarters, *Iyoba Aghahowa Ovbi N'Errua* graciously discussed some sixty years of her life at court.

5 An abundance of Benin carved ivory altar tusks has been available for study (some 130 have been reported); and the *Iyoba* appears on nearly two-thirds of the 90 examined (Blackmun 1984: 298–9; 301–302). Representations on the tusks currently viewed as priestesses are likely to be the *Iyoba* herself, in other guises and roles. Several past queens as well as the present queen mother, are considered powerful priestesses.

REFERENCES CITED

Adams, Capt. J., *Remarks on the Country Extending from Cape Palmas to the River Congo*, London, 1823.

Aisien, Ekhaguosa, *Iwu: The Body Markings of the Edo People*, Benin City: Aisien Publishers, 1986.

Awe, Bolanle, 'The *Iyalode* in the Traditional Yoruba Political System', in *Sexual Stratification: A cross-cultural view*, Alice Schlegel (ed.), New York: Columbia University Press, 1977, pp. 140–60.

Bacon, Sir R. H. S., *Benin, City of Blood*, London: Arnold, 1897.

Bassani, Ezio and William Fagg, *Africa In the Renaissance*, New York: Center for African Art, 1988.

Ben-Amos, Paula, *The Art of Benin*, London: Thames and Hudson, 1980.

Blackmun, Barbara, The Iconography of Carved Altar Tusks from Benin, Nigeria. Unpublished Ph.D. dissertation, University of Califormia, Los Angeles, 1984.

Blackmun, Barbara, 'From Trader to Priest in 200 Years: The transformation of a foreign figure on Benin ivories', in *Art Journal*, vol. 47, no. 2, 1988, pp. 128–38.

Blackmun, Barbara, 'Who Commissioned the

Queen Mother Tusks? A Problem in the Chronology of Benin Ivories', in *African Arts*, 24(2), 1991, pp. 54–65, 90.
Bradbury, Robert E., *Benin Studies*, London: Oxford University Press, 1973.
Bradbury, Robert E., *The Benin Kingdom and the Edo-speaking Peoples of South-Western Nigeria*, London: International African Institute, 1957.
Celenko, T., *A Treasury of African Art from the Harrison Eiteljorg Collection*, Bloomington: Indiana University Press, 1982.
Craddock, P. T. and John Picton, 'Medieval Copper Alloy Production and West African Bronze Analyses, Part III', in *Archaeometry*, 28, 1986, 1: 3–32.
Dark, P. J. C., *An Introduction to Benin Art and Technology*, Oxford: Clarendon Press, 1973.
Dark, P. J. C., 'Benin Bronze Heads: Styles and chronology', in *African Images: Essays in African Iconology*, D. F. McAll and Edna G. Bay (eds.), New York and London, 1975.
Egharevba, Jacob, *A Short History of Benin*, Ibadan: Ibadan University Press, 1934 (1968).
Fagg, William, *Nigerian Images*, London: Lund Humphries, 1963.
Fagg, William, *Divine Kingship in Africa*, London: British Museum, 1970.
Kaplan, Flora S. (ed.), *Images of Power: Art of the Royal Court of Benin, Nigeria*, New York: New York University, 1981. Introduction, and Of Symbols and Civilization.
Kaplan, Flora S., 'Doing anthropological fieldwork at the royal court of Benin', Paper presented, Faculty Seminar, CenSCER, University of Benin, 18 December, 1984.
Kaplan, Flora S., 'Royal Women at the Court of Benin', The University Lecture, University of Benin, 1 March 1985.
Kaplan, Flora S., 'Some Uses of Photographs in Recovering Cultural History at the Royal Court of Benin, Nigeria', in *Visual Anthropology*, vol. 3, nos. 2–3, 1990, pp. 317–41.
Kaplan, Flora S., 'Benin Art Revisited: Photographs and museum collections', in *Visual Anthropology*, vol. 4, no. 2, 1991, pp. 117–45.
Kaplan, Flora S. (ed. and contributor), *Queens, Concubines, and Consorts: Case studies in African gender*, Carbondale, Illinois: University of Southern Illinois Press (forthcoming).
Kaplan, Flora S. *In Splendour and Seclusion: Royal women at the Court of Benin, Nigeria* (forthcoming).
Karpinski, Peter, 'A Benin Bronze Horseman at the Merseyside County Museum', in *African Arts*, vol. 17, no. 4, 1984, pp. 54–62, 88–9.
Kecskesi, Maria, *African Masterpieces and Selected Works from Munich: The Staatliches Museum für Volkerkunde*, New York: Center for African Art, 1987.
Kecskesi, Maria, Personal communication, 28 June 1988, Munich.
King, Lieut. J., in *Journal des Voyages*, vol. 13, Paris, 1823.
Ling Roth, H., *Great Benin, Its Customs, Art and Horrors*, Halifax: F. King & Sons, 1902.
Lopasic, Alexander von Vortrag, 'Provinzkulte and Kunst in Benin', in *Mitteilungen der Berliner Gesellschaft Für Anthropologie, Ethnologie und Urgeschichte*, vol. 10, 1989, pp. 23–30.
Lapasic, Alexander von Vortrage, 'Gender and Traditional Village Art in the Benin Province, Nigeria', in *Queens, Concubines, and Consorts: Case studies in African gender*, Flora S. Kaplan (ed.), Carbondale, Illinois: University of Southern Illinois Press (forthcoming).
Nevadomsky, Joseph, 'The Benin Bronze Horseman as the Ata of Idah', in *African Arts*, vol. 19, no. 4, 1986, pp. 40–7.
Nevadomsky, Joseph, 'Brass Cocks and Wooden Hens in Benin Art', in *Baessler-Archiv, Neue Folger*, vol. 25 (1987), Berlin, pp. 221–47.
Powell, Richard J., 'African Art at the Field Museum', in *African Arts*, vol. 18, no. 2, 1985, pp. 24–36.
Tunis, Irwin, 'The Benin Chronologies' in *African Arts*, vol. 24, no. 2, 1981, pp. 86–7.
Tunis, Irwin, 'A Note on Benin Plaque Termination Dates', in *Tribus: Veröffentlichungen des Linden-Museums*, no. 32, December 1983, pp. 45–53.

Art History Vol. 16 No. 3 September 1993 0141—6790 pp. 408–423

PICTURING A PERSONAL HISTORY: THE CASE OF EDWARD ONSLOW

KAREN STANWORTH

Hanging on the walls of a stately country home, images of a boy's childhood, youth and maturity seemingly reproduce fleeting moments in the private life of an English gentleman. At Clandon Park, the Surrey home of George, Lord Onslow, pictures of his second son Edward (who left the family home in 1781), depict with chronological regularity the child alongside his elder brother and the youth playing chess with his peers (plate 16).[1] These are followed eventually by pendant portraits of Edward and his wife (plates 17 and 18), and of his wife and son. These images provided a testimony to the ordered life of a favoured son. There is no hint of anything other than the normative vision presented in these portraits — portraits whose presumption of being 'true-to-life' functions to smooth the historical gaps between the images. At the same time, the spatial interstices between the points of display establish a physical distance which affirms the apparently uneventful passage of time. Nothing beyond the isolated moments of portrayal is allowed to intrude upon the life story constructed around and through the chosen moments of representation. This conspicuously neutral interweaving of time and space frames the story of Edward Onslow. It is my intention to unpick the threads of his story (history) in an effort to explore the complexity of familial representation within a wider context of social relations. I shall suggest that the very unremarkableness which characterizes both family and portrait representation is intrinsic to a sequence of normalizing strategies which, when identified, indicate how apparently conventional, small portraits may signify in relation to gender, sexuality and social class in diverse, powerful ways.

As the household inventory of 1778 confirms, there was an extensive range of family portraits distributed throughout Clandon Park.[2] In addition to paintings of family ancestors, there were portraits of living family members including 'Lady Onslow and three other Family Portraits in oval Frames'. Possibly these include the picture of 'Hon. Thomas Onslow and Hon. Edward Onslow, sons of George, 1st Earl of Onslow' listed in the inventory of 1911 (whereabouts unknown).[3] This portrait of Edward as a young man may be one of the three 'family portraits' hanging in Lord Onslow's bedchamber or among the other twenty-eight portraits in the principal rooms which are not individually identified in the inventory of

16 Daniel Gardner, *Edward Onslow, Lord Fitzwilliam and Lord Herbert Playing Chess*, *c.* 1780, Clandon House. Photo: Mellon Centre

17 Anon., *The Hon. Edward Onslow*, Clandon Park, Surrey. Photo: The National Trust

18 Anon., *Marie de Bourdeilles, Mrs Onslow*, Clandon Park, Surrey. Photo: The National Trust

1778. In the small drawing room is located 'a gilt frame chimney glass in five compartments with oval crayon drawing glazed with portraits of Lords Onslow, Pembroke and Fitzwilliam by D. Gardiner [*sic*]' (*c.* 1777–8, plate 16).[4] A portrait of Mrs Edward Onslow with her son (1790, whereabouts unknown) is described as an oil painting in a gilt frame. A pair of portraits of the Hon. Edward Onslow and his wife (*c.* 1800) and 'a plaster relief in a velvet frame of Georges Onslow, son of Hon. Edward Onslow' (also missing) are also listed. Over half a dozen, perhaps more, portraits of Edward and his immediate family members, were hung at Clandon Park in the last quarter of the eighteenth century. While six portraits done across a lifetime are not exceptional by contemporary standards, certainly the second son of Lord Onslow was pictured with regularity. The images date from before and after his departure from the family home in 1781. Furthermore, it is apparent that significant stages of his life are being visually remarked (those of childhood, age of majority, marriage, fatherhood, maturity). Of the images in this life series, the group portrait of the three peers at a chess game (plate 16), becomes charged with greater significance when viewed in the light of lived experience; this image marks the point after which the sustaining visual narrative begins to unravel. In part, this is due to a combination of details of date, subject, framing and sitters which, in conjunction with knowledge of contemporary events, invites interpretations of the image beyond those available to an 'innocent reading' of the chess game.

Various details of the image and of its installation suggest that the pastel was likely to have been commissioned *c.* 1780. The figures referred to in the 1911 account are Lords Pembroke, Fitzwilliam and Onslow. Specifically, the image is believed to represent George Augustus Herbert, future eleventh Earl of Pembroke, standing with his arm resting on the shoulder of Edward Onslow. Edward is playing chess with either John or Thomas, future Viscounts Fitzwilliam. The black servant portrayed, but not described, has an apocryphal role in the traditional family story about the picture. It is said that his future services were the stake in the chess game. While this story has been dismissed, there was a reason for diverting viewers of the image from a discussion of the known sitters to a story revolving around the unknown servant.

The male society represented in the chess game was an unusual subject for Daniel Gardner, whose pictures almost universally portray softly rendered women and/or children, often in small groups, frequently in oval frames.[5] Also out of the ordinary is the manner in which the chess players are depicted. Contemporary literature often portrayed the game of chess as a battle of individual will, employing militaristic metaphors in the poems and strategy books which were popular at the time. Here, however, the languid movement of Fitzwilliam's fingers trailing across the incorrectly set chess board does not elicit impressions of confrontation. Only the dog and the servant pay attention to the game. Edward, seated opposite, focuses on his distant cousin's eyes. Herbert's oblique glance penetrates the space beyond the picture frame; his arm rests awkwardly upon Edward's shoulders. The three main protagonists of the picture are plainly not paying much attention to the game. Any element of risk-taking which may be present in the chess game is quelled by the richness of handling of both the paint and the objects represented. The brilliant scarlet of Herbert's military coat, Fitzwilliam's deep blue coat with red trim, and the blue-green worn by Edward are equalled by the extravagance of the servant's costume and the ornamental superfluity of drapery, column and garden urn.

The picture surmounts a multi-compartmental mirror which, in turn, forms the overmantle of a classicized Adam-style fireplace surround which was 'modernized' by Edward's father as part of a programme of renovations commenced soon after his accession to the title in 1776. Both the mirror and the glossy surface of the picture reflect the light of the contemporary French chandelier hanging a few feet away. Thus, the group portrait in the mirror is subjected to the larger framing devices of both the gilt frame and the small room. The gilt frame of the mirror cornice extends the theme of comfortable decadence into the small drawing room which houses the overmantle. Drawn into the decorative scheme of the room, the interpretative possibilities expand to encompass a further set of linkages. Located at a distance from the formal spaces of the house, associated with hunting and sport and used for gaming (a Pembroke table was listed as in this room in the 1776 inventory), the small room comfortably established a homosocial space.[6] In its amenable environment, the retreat of the men from the public spaces of the saloon or the Palladio room can easily be envisaged (see plate 18). However, when Edward, one of the sitters, is accused of desiring sexual intimacy with his male peers, the portrayal of the languid hand, the casually draped arm and the directed gaze threatens to suggest other, less comfortable stories.

THE SCANDAL

Within days of the incident which unalterably changed Edward Onslow's life, the tenth Earl of Pembroke wrote to his son (one of the sitters in the painting of the chess game):

> In the name of wonder, My dear George, what is this Mindening [*sic*] story of our cousin Ned Onslow, & Phelim Macarty [*sic*] Esq . . . I should hope that no kinsman of ours *donne dans le sexe masculin* . . .[7]

Despite being Edward's third cousin, twice removed, Lord Pembroke immediately understood the implications of any event which cast aspersions upon the sexual proclivity of a member of his extended family.

Lord Pembroke was responding to public accusations that, on 2 May 1781, while in attendance at the Royal Academy Exhibition, Edward (popularly known as Ned) had attempted 'an infamous familiarity with a Gentleman'.[8] Although no account of the event specifies exactly what passed between Edward and Felix McCarthy, James Stephen's *Memoirs* provides a long and personally motivated, yet generally accepted recitation of the whole affair.[9] Stephen and the newspapers, in varying degrees of detail, report that Edward was challenged and struck by McCarthy for having made repeated sexual advances towards him while he was viewing the exhibition. It was particularly noted that Edward fled from the scene, refusing McCarthy's challenge.[10] In an attempt to contain the social implications of the incident, a meeting was held within a few hours at the nearby Salopian Coffee House with friends of both parties in attendance. While they were in the midst of negotiating a solution, Lord George Onslow arrived with a magistrate ready to charge McCarthy and his friends with conspiracy to libel.

McCarthy was charged with accusing Edward of making 'infamous advances to the perpetration or excitement of the crime he meditated'.[11] The crime being 'meditated' was that of sodomy, an act which had been a capital offence since Henry VIII had enshrined it in law in 1533.[12] Meditation of the offence, proven by the witnessing of a 'sodomitical advance', was punishable by confinement to the public stocks; in 1763 two men were stoned to death whilst serving their time in the pillory.[13]

The initial public response of Edward's social peers to the charges was one of incredulity and support. James Stephen specifically recalled the rapport demonstrated between the accused and his male peers/Peers:

> It soon became unequivocal not only that the criminal was determined to stand his ground, but that he had persuaded his Friends in the upper circles to believe and treat him as innocent. I saw him the next day, to my terror, come into the House of Commons and be received there with marked and solicitous attention and respect. He took his seat on the Treasury Bench; and Lord North immediately placed himself beside him, shook him cordially by the hand, put his arm even round his waist, and continued long in close conference with him, doubtless on the subject of 'the foul conspiracy by which he had been beset'. Many respectable men also of both Parties came up to him and shook him cordially by the hand.[14]

The Prime Minister, Lord North, had been highly visible in Parliament for the previous few days in the discussions regarding America, and his physically expressed reassurance to the young Edward would not have gone unnoticed in the House.

That Stephen particularly remarks the actions of the other Members of Parliament in taking Edward's hand is confirmation of Lord North's physical vote of confidence.

The assumption of Edward's innocence (or perhaps the unlikelihood of the accusation withstanding the counter-pressure of his peers/Peers) is evident in a letter sent by George Selwyn MP to Lord Carlisle on Friday night, 4 May, in which he insists that 'all the part of the world in which I live seem to acquit absolutely the young man, and the circumstances make the story highly improbable . . .'.[15] Although the story is 'abominable', the circumstances cause Selwyn to view the incident as a youthful escapade — the sort of thing that one outgrows.

Before examining the nature of these 'circumstances', it is worth considering how behaviour which could result in execution could still fall under the rubric of a 'scrape'. There is, perhaps, an answer to this paradox which exists in the contemporary type known as a 'libertine' or 'rake', that is, someone who lives his (*sic*) life as a 'freeman' — free of moral and physical restraints (the type celebrated in many of the male-authored novels of the eighteenth century, such as those by Richardson and Smollet).[16] Certainly, Edward had a reputation, at least within his family, of being sexually indolent. A ribald poem, penned by his brother Thomas for his father, satirizes Edward's escapades. Joking about Edward's lack of social finesse, apparent in his inability to keep his sleeves out of his dish or a tea table upright, Thomas teasingly calls Edward, 'great Garbage my Brother'. The poem, written in the form of a letter, recounts,

> Miss Loveit . . . cou'd not resist him;
> When he sat in her lap the poor creature xxx him [word scratched out]
> Great Garbage wan't cruel; Gave ear to her sigh,
> And for dancing this Jig, she'll lie-in in July,[17]

Edward's actions were, it seems, regarded with little concern by his family. Similarly, describing a sodomitical advance as a 'prank' may perhaps be understood as signalling contemporary acceptance of a notion of male behaviour which was condoned by other males if it occurred in a homosocial setting (club, coffee house, university and race meeting).[18] The intra-male social world of Edward and his peers seems to have permitted or at least overlooked excessive behaviour when it was restricted to the acceptable place, time, or social grouping. The idea that the bounds of social behaviour shift according to circumstances is reiterated in Selwyn's later comment that discretion on the part of the offender would have lessened the likelihood of offending individual sensibilities.[19]

What then were the circumstances which apparently served to preclude the probability of the act in the minds of Edward's acquaintances? The various descriptions call particular attention to the site, the time and the witnesses of the incident. The 'attack' was described as occurring in 'the public rooms of the exhibition of paintings in Somerset House, at mid-day and in a crowded company of both sexes'. Both Stephen and the papers considered it newsworthy that Edward had been 'talking with two or three beautiful young women, the honourable Miss Keppels' before he turned from them 'to the object of his unnatural passion'.[20] Here beauty is opposed to unnaturalness, a juxtaposition which is supported by the association of beauty with nature. This traditional conflation of beauty and nature in art is historically specified within the Royal Academy through the relationship of the Misses Keppel and Reynolds, their primary portraitist, who codified the notion in the many likenesses of the women which he produced at this time.

The time of the 'attack' at midday added insult to injury. The apparent disregard for the respectability of the largely upper-bourgeois crowd and for the sensibilities of the female portion of the audience was magnified by the full light of 'mid-day'. Added to this lack of regard for the witnesses was the circumspect aura of the Academy rooms themselves. These rooms of 'grace and simplicity'[21] had been the subject of much debate in recent years as the Academy sought ways to limit admittance to the exhibition to a more desirable audience.[22] They had 'not been able to suggest any other means than that of receiving money for admittance to prevent the rooms being filled by *improper* persons' (my emphasis).[23] The efforts to forestall the entry of an inappropriate public through the imposition of monetary obligations obviously served to eliminate the classes of people who could not afford to purchase art, but could not guarantee that the favoured would behave once granted admittance.

It would appear that, for George Selwyn and his peers, the circumstances which mitigated against Edward's guilt were a combination of place, time and mixed company — for who could believe that such an attempt would be made in a space as public as the Royal Academy Exhibition rooms at midday in front of a mixed audience? Another MP, Anthony Storer, was also confounded by the attendant facts, 'considering the place, the person, and all the circumstances, it must have been no less than frenzy by which [Edward] was actuated, otherwise it would have been impossible to have believed either the charge or his confession.'[24]

The impossibility of imagining Edward's guilt, *given the circumstances*, virtually guaranteed his innocence in the minds of his peers; this judgement was underwritten by McCarthy's relatively lower social status (he was merely styled as a gentlemen, with no claim to title, land, or public position). James Stephen indicated that he saw little likelihood of McCarthy escaping from the charges of conspiracy to libel, that is, until he received the promise of moral assistance from a Colonel Michael Cox of the Guards, the 'son of an Irish Archbishop and highly esteemed in the fashionable circles'.[25] Cox's public avowal of his belief in the innocence of McCarthy at Brooks's, the club to which he belonged, resulted in a rising social pressure which Edward's bravura could not withstand.[26] Edward's 'confession' to his father quickly became public knowledge. Anthony Storer, another intimate of Brooks's Club, reported to Lord Carlisle, 'as for poor Onslow, it is all over with him, and he had better be dead. He has made his confession to his father, and is gone off . . . !'[27] Edward's flight to France not only 'sealed his doom' but also condemned his father to public disgrace.

GEORGE ONSLOW: THE SOCIAL EMASCULATION OF THE FATHER

At the very moment when Storer was expressing his pity, George Onslow was basking in perhaps his greatest public tribute to date; he had been included in

Copley's *The Death of the Earl of Chatham*, then on display in the Great Room in Spring Gardens. One of the great group portraits of the period, the painting had received wide public attention which focused on the names of the Peers of the House of Lords who pressed around Chatham when he had his eventually fatal stroke after expressing his outrage at the government's handling of the affairs in America. Listed fourteenth in the published list of Chatham's attendants, Lord Onslow was portrayed firmly ensconced amongst his peers as a public figure.[28]

The threat to that public standing posed by Edward's predicament probably accounts for the rapidity with which George Onslow publicly countercharged Felix McCarthy's accusations by having a number of newspapers print a rebuttal to the stories.[29] The same motivation was presumably behind Lord Onslow's attempt to enforce a charge of libel against the accuser as a means of regaining control of public opinion.[30]

Edward's confession of his guilt in the affair, which several contemporaries noted was made before his father, served to nullify his father's efforts. Thus the question might be raised as to why George Onslow imagined that it was possible to repair his son's reputation as the confession was generally known and Edward's self-exile was understood as proof positive. It may be that it was the nature of the crime itself which motivated the father. A hint of the way in which the sins of the son are visited upon the father is suggested in the only rebuke which was publicly administered to Edward. In the absence of the guilty party, criminal proceedings could not proceed. The only action which could be taken was his expulsion from the fashionable clubs to which he belonged, the grounds being 'that he had received a blow from a gentleman in a public room without resenting it'. Being expelled from the club spelled the literal rejection of the individual from male society. Felix McCarthy had administered a similar social justice, when he refused to accept Edward's demand for the satisfaction of a duel (which Edward's friends had suggested as an honourable way of resolving the situation). James Stephen claims that he would not suffer McCarthy 'to degrade himself by meeting on equal terms one who had forfeited his title, not only to the gentleman, but the *man*' (my emphasis).[31]

Recent theoretical approaches to gender definition in eighteenth-century England have often been complicated by anachronistic interpretations of homoerotic behaviour as 'homosexual'. Furthermore, the ambiguity of the term 'man' has to some extent been acknowledged in the recognition that gender, as a social construction, is constituted through shifting signifiers which only appear stable when confined to an historically specific moment. Randolph Trumbach has argued that a shift in the processes by which gender identity is organized results in a growing fear of sodomists as effeminate in eighteenth-century London. Thus the emasculation of the son through the loss of his social status as gentleman, and of his gendered identity as a man, would inevitably draw into question the social definition of the father whose procreation is deemed unsuccessful by his peers, a point which Storer and Onslow himself quickly appreciated. It is however necessary to complicate this idea of effeminacy somewhat, as we must acknowledge that Trumbach has also suggested that males seduced by sodomites often did not conceive of themselves as sodomites.[32] In other words, there was room within their sexual identity for behaviour which did not fit the publicly declared norms. Moreover, it has been suggested that at least in one county of England, the reputation of a man so accused (whether proven or not) was ruined only when the limits of sexual tolerance were breached, that is, 'where enclaves exist in which sexual norms differ, definitions of reputation are adjusted to accommodate them.'[33] Thus, it is argued, deviant sexual practices were tolerated in Somerset within certain social groups and 'popular definitions of buggery differed sufficiently from the official, legal ones to permit considerable latitude in sexual practice.'[34]

The possibility that homoerotic behaviour was both more acceptable in some places than in others and that participants in such activity saw themselves as normal suggests that the variation in punishment was not arbitrary but, rather, that it conformed to these perceptions. In particular, the place of enactment seems significant. This assumption is reinforced by the outcome of an incident which took place within weeks of the Onslow–McCarthy affair. At the end of May, the nephew of Lord Chedworth (John Howe), the heir of his title and estate, 'got into the same scrape at Epsom as Onslow did at the Exhibition'.[35] If their actions were the 'same', one has to wonder why Howe escaped the same fate as Edward? Perhaps the location of Howe's infamy at Epsom races, a male-oriented event, served to moderate the public condemnation by his peers, i.e., the 'circumstances' were different.[36] As in the reports of the Onslow case, an emphasis on the rejection of the 'natural' sexuality of men is constantly present in the trial for libel pressed by Howe. In prosecuting the action for defamation of character against Mr Dive, who stood accused of calling Howe a 'b-gg-r-r', Mr Peckman, council for Howe, emphasized the damage that the mere accusation of sodomy had caused:

> the charge being once made was equally fatal to Mr. Howe . . . [he] must look forward, not with pleasure to a good old-age, not with hope to the honours he is to receive, but with detestation, horror, and dismay to the life which God may be pleased to curse him with . . . How will he bear the opprobrium of being a disgrace to manhood, and the outcast of society![37]

Similarly, the defence advocate argued that his client, Dive, was perfectly justified in using language which expressed his horror at the unnatural actions of Howe. Dramatically interrupting himself in the midst of this defence, he exclaims:

> Good God! I am reasoning upon this subject! Nature has not left to reason the vindication of her rights. She has implanted an instinctive horror of the crime which acts independently of thought — which reason was not intended to controul [*sic*].[38]

The crime is perceived as defying God, nature and society. It is a sin, an aberration, and a social infamy. According to the prosecution, the charge alone is enough to ruin a man's life.

The events of this case further resembled the Onslow affair in that Howe reputedly made an advance in a public place (Epsom races) which Dive rejected violently. Howe also fled from the scene without defending himself (therefore also refusing, like Edward, to respond to the attack of a 'gentleman'). However, it seems that some of the circumstances differed significantly. This time the approach took place in the crowded stands of a racecourse where the 'victim' was surrounded by men, not women, as in Edward's case. The collision of art and nature, unremittingly visible in the Academy's exhibition rooms, was palpably present in the public judgement of Edward's crime. Furthermore, Edward's confession resulted in his consolidation in the social imagination as being guilty as charged. Ironically, Dive's exclamation at the races ratified the public indictment of Edward, as Dive's libel charge arose from his having called after Howe, 'Do you take me for an Onslow!'[39]

Edward's departure from England deprived him of the social and aesthetic pleasures of the Royal Academy and the leisure activities found at Bath and Epsom. Lord Onslow, his father, for his part, was doubly deprived. He lost his son both physically and figuratively, as the departure signalled Edward's full culpability. The evidence of the language used to describe the sodomist strips him of his membership in male society. 'A disgrace to manhood and the Outcast of society!', Edward had 'forfeited his title, not only to the gentleman, but the man'.[40] Thus, Lord Onslow was the father of a son who was not considered to be a man. If Edward was not a man, how could he be Lord Onslow's male progeny? With fatherhood erased by social castigation, patriarchal stability and, therefore, family continuity were threatened. Perhaps this portent of structural damage to the family was at the root of the horror expressed in Lord Pembroke's letter to his son Lord Herbert — that a kinsman of his *donne dans le sexe masculin*.[41]

As a result of Edward's confession, which ruptured the rapidly constructed, yet tenuous, legal and social safety net drawn over Edward in the first few days after the incident, the rehabilitation of both the father and the son took another form. A number of actions taken by George Onslow over the next twenty years can be seen as contributing to the re-creation of his son's sexual and social status, and, in consequence, of his own status as a father. He must have aided Edward's escape from England. He certainly visited the refugee in France, and assisted him in the purchase of an estate in order to ensure that a proper marriage could follow; Edward's marriage in 1783 to Marie de Bourdeilles, the daughter of a French chevalier, was predicated upon Edward obtaining French citizenship and purchasing a landed property. The money for this could have come only from his father, who was himself already in financial difficulty.[42] However, the debt must have been justified to Lord Onslow as a means of restoring Edward's social and gender identity. The quick arrival of Edward's first son Georges in 1784 and the inheritance of an income-generating estate in the same year confirmed this restoration. Thus, George Onslow's fatherhood could be understood as also having been regenerated through his grandson, his male namesake. Furthermore — and it is here that material culture can be seen to function in the unfolding of family history — Lord Onslow appears to have attempted to create a visual narrative at Clandon Park which was intended to erase any suggestion of deviancy and to confirm the normative passage of time.

THE VISUAL NARRATIVE

To recall the numerous images of Edward which hung at Clandon Park is to review a series of portraits commissioned across a lifetime; there is archival evidence in the inventories of a range of portraits commissioned during his childhood, youth and maturity. Despite the impossibility of knowing exactly where each picture hung, they were clearly present in Clandon Park, his father's home. To describe these works as functioning within a totalizing narrative, that is, the story of his life from birth to maturity, is not to suggest that each represents a discrete event which is placed chronologically into a story.[43] Rather, the narrative may be better understood as a social construction, one of an unlimited number of other narratives that can be constructed in response to the represented events or perceived as related to them.[44] It is always bound within an allegorical framework which limits the possible figurative and metaphorical interpretations available to any particular reader. In other words, all the readers who confront a set of narrative possibilities at any given point in time will share some epistemological constraints. Given this rather wide parameter, there remains an immense range of narratives concerning Edward Onslow which could be constructed by the individuals who lived in and who visited Clandon Park. Despite the theoretically expansive choice of narratives, real limits are imposed through Lord Onslow's attempted closure of the implied plot and through the physical fabric of the house itself.

It has been suggested that history requires closure and that that closure is inherently moralizing, i.e., history can be understood as a totalizing narrative shaped through the moral rhetoric of the storyteller.[45] Such moral closure may be perceived in Lord Onslow's attempt to construct a visual family history which works against Edward's personal history and attempts to subdue or overwrite prior knowledge of the incident on the part of a visitor to the family home. The separate, lived events of childhood, youth and maturity present a coherent and ordered view of a life; an all-embracing impression is received which fills the gaps between the represented moments. A visual insistence upon the normative fulfilment of a son's potential may be realized through the representation of a sequence of images which seem to spotlight important moments in a seamless lifetime (see plates 16, 17 and 18). In essence, an imaginary whole or fiction is established as real history.

Patricia Spacks has convincingly argued that fiction creates and conveys its truths through the mechanism of plot.[46] In her analysis of eighteenth-century fiction, she proposes that fictions actively moderate the meanings of society's myths, i.e., they move beyond reflection to modification by expressing the author's desires and by satisfying those of the readers.[47] By functioning as social transactions, fictions cause truth and desire to coincide in eighteenth-century fiction. Thus, I would argue that in the fictionalization of Edward's life, Lord Onslow organizes the possible narratives by establishing a plot which imposes a morally and socially correct closure upon his contemporary readers. The story is about a young man who achieves all the success a father could desire. The markers of attainment are re-presented to an admiring public: the aristocratic wife, the male grandchild who, in turn, is successful.[48] The chess game becomes a crucial image in the sequence because it portrays Edward shortly prior to his disgrace. The physical closeness of Edward and George Augustus Herbert provides a point of speculation if the subsequent event can be read anachronistically into the scene. Similarly, the intense look directed at Fitzwilliam by Edward shifts from a sign of interest to, potentially, an indication of intimacy, regardless of whether the unspoken desire was shared or unfulfilled. Furthermore, John Fitzwilliam, like Edward, went into self-exile in France. Apparently in disgrace, he was denied all but the minimum legal inheritance from his uncle, the seventh Earl Fitzwilliam.[49] Thus the relations between the sitters become suspect; open to speculation, the constructed visual narrative is threatened by the spectre of scandal. However, the impeccable public reputation of the future Lord Pembroke must have assisted the narrator in his counter tale, forcing the story back into a respectable mould.

The picture, being incorporated into a mirrored overmantle, is likely to have remained in place in the years immediately following the affair. It is easy to imagine that the pendant portraits of Edward and his wife (see plates 17 and 18) would have hung, as presently, in the saloon, the room immediately adjacent to the small drawing room where the chess game was displayed, thus framing the chess game between other portraits in the life story. If the portraits — linked conceptually and by common subject and genre — fictionalize a life, the way those portraits are hung also produces and endorses fictitious narratives.

We cannot be certain about the hanging positions of the pictures or of the sequence of their reception during Lord Onslow's tenure at Clandon Park, but there are inventories for the years 1892 and 1899 which suggest a pattern of room usage and some likely locations for the images which in turn suggest a controlled sequence of viewing. Moreover, it can be said with some certainty that all these portraits were retained and hung at Clandon Park, located over twenty miles from the city, the site of the family's disgrace.

Giacomo Leoni's adaptation of a Palladian cube plan establishes discrete patterns of movement through the southern half of the house which direct the visitor through an *enfilade* — a sequence of rooms opening one on to the other (plate 19). The movement through space which is suggested in the ground plan is literally in place in the inventory of 1778.[50] Here the contents of the house are carefully listed room by room. The furnishings and the ornaments of the ante room (now the 'Morning Room') are listed before those in the 'Palladio Room' (still so-called). The inventory then describes the contents of the 'small Drawing Room' (the present 'Hunting Room'), followed by those in the 'Green Drawing Room' (as named presently).[51] Thus, Leoni's Palladianism was to affect the structure of any storytelling which the family portraits may have prompted. Whether author of the guidebook, personal guide, or contemporary visitor, the viewer encounters the images in a specific, spatially organized manner.

Regardless of the particular order of viewing, there is inevitably a succession of family-related images whose varying time-frames provide visual evidence for the separate elements or events which constitute a family history. When the power of authorship in that history is threatened by a loss of control caused by the disruptive forces of scandal, as when a favoured son admits culpability of a capital crime and flees the country, the attempt to heal the breach may be, at least in part, attained through subsequent representational strategy. Thus my interest resides not only in how the chess-playing image of Onslow, Pembroke and Fitzwilliam may have been understood by contemporary viewers, but also in how that image becomes

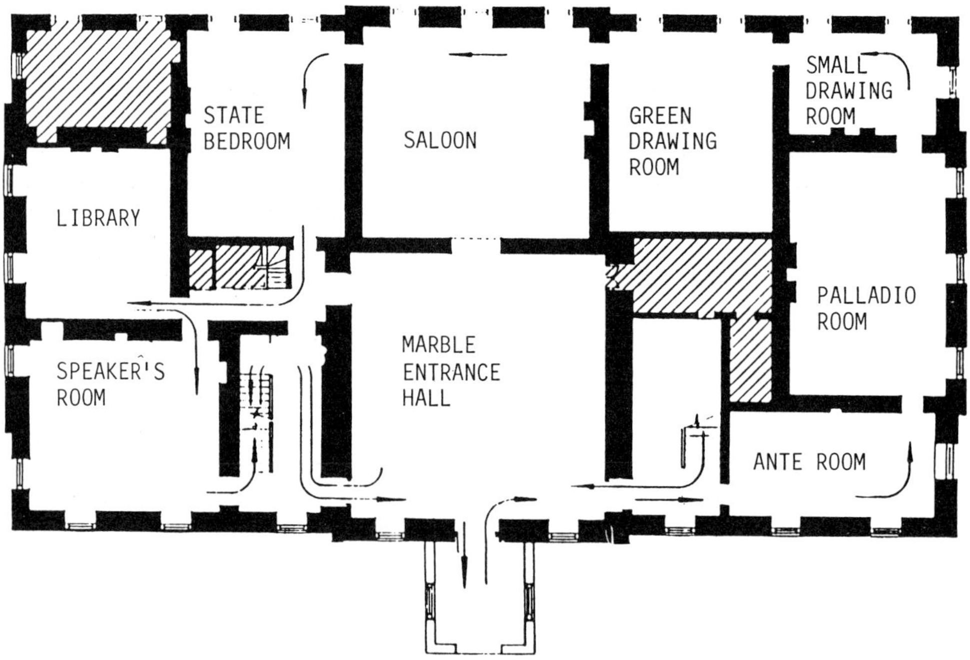

19 Floor Plan of Clandon Park, Surrey, adapted from the National Trust Clandon Park Guide Book. Photo: K. Stanworth

an event in an ongoing visualization of family history.

If we add to the immensely seductive (reflective) image of the chess game the series of subsequent portraits of Edward, his wife and son, the collective visual portrayal of Edward creates the impression of a younger son, complacent sibling, chess partner to his cousin, mate to a beautiful wife, and eventually father of another Onslow son. The life progression from being a son to having a male child follows the standard family narrative. Each image constitutes an element of the story of Edward's life. Storytelling is extended by the Gardner image of the chess game which employs a self-conscious representational strategy insisting upon readings which operate outside the frame. The group portrait functions to implicate in the social transaction of narration both the other images within the house and the known histories of those portrayed. The series of images of Edward and his family ageing gracefully along with the visual presences of Fitzwilliam and Herbert, cousins and peers/Peers, in the represented plot serve to mitigate the rupture threatened by the intrusion of real events into the fictionalized history of the family. The house, itself signifying the tradition of family through the generations, provides the frame within which the reading of Edward's story is ratified. The repeated patterns of father/son, father/son, perpetuate the dynastic ambitions of the aristocratic genealogy. Although Edward is the second son who does not legally inherit the title, in a family where two sons have already predeceased their father, the other son always holds the potential to replace the heir. While the birth of Thomas's son, Arthur George, in 1777 confirmed the passage of title and position through the elder son, the events of 1781 which implicated Edward in a scandal were perhaps more decisive in prohibiting his ever being the father of the next Onslow Baronet.

*

Although the normal events of a lifetime were visually encoded within Clandon Park, they were not remarked in the customary public way. The marriages, births, promotions and deaths of London 'Society' so assiduously followed in the *Gentlemen's Magazine* were markers of social advancement and fulfilment. Edward's name did not appear in that exhaustively inclusive journal even when he died, although Howe, absolved of the crime of meditation of sodomy, did receive an extended, if apologetic, eulogy.[52] An indication of the ultimate success of Lord Onslow's representational strategies is, however, evident at Clandon today. The attendant supervising the Hunting Room at Clandon Park on my initial visit to the house explained that the son of George Onslow pictured in the chess game had gone to France under the cloud of 'some family scandal' but that he had eventually 'made good'. She pointed out the portraits of Edward and his wife in the next room as evidence of his success in establishing the French branch of 'les Onslows'. So two hundred years later, George Onslow can be said to have won at least a reprieve for Edward from those now paid to guard his visual legacy.

Karen Stanworth
Toronto

NOTES

I wish to acknowledge the support of the Social Sciences and Humanities Research Council of Canada (SSHRC's Doctoral Fellowship) and of the Committee of Vice-Chancellors and Principals of the United Kingdom (CVCP's or ORS Award).

1 George Onslow was created Baron Cranley of Imbercourt, 20 May 1776; Baron Onslow of Onslow and of Clandon on 8 October 1776; Viscount Cranley of Cranley and Earl of Onslow on 19 June 1801.

2 Clandon MSS, National Trust Southern Region, at Polesden Lacey (NTSR). The original is missing. Another photocopy exists in the Clandon Park file, Victoria & Albert Museum. In addition to this inventory, there is a list of paintings in Clandon House in May 1778, Onslow MSS, Surrey Muniment Room [SMR] 173.3.20. Other inventories include a hand-written list of December 1899, Onslow MSS [SMR] 97.21.4 (1) & (2), and a typed 'Inventory of Clandon Park bequeathed by Will of William Hillier, Earl of Onslow', Onslow MSS [SMR] 173.53.1.

3 Listed in Hillier Inventory, 1911, Onslow MSS [SMR] 173.53.1, 50.

4 Onslow MSS [SMR] 97.21.4 (1), 44. The inventory of 1899 describes what is presumably the same overmantle in the following way: 'A chimney glass in several compartments in ornamental gilt frame (5′9″ × 4′)'.

5 See Daniel Gardner file in Witt Library, Courtauld Institute for examples.

6 See note 18 for definition of 'homosocial'.

7 Sunday, 6 May 1781, *Pembroke Papers*, (London: 1950), 123. 'Donner dans' has been generously translated for me by Professor Geoffrey Bennington 'as any one of: "to go in for", "to give oneself over to", "to indulge in", "to have a penchant for", with indeed a sense of some degree of transgression, but without any notion of aggression or of any particular sexual practice. There is nothing vulgar or crude about the expression itself.' (Personal communication, 8 May 1992). Alistair Laing, Picture Director of the National Trust, has suggested that 'Mindening' may be a contemporary expression for 'shaming', referring to the shame which accrued to Lord George Sackville from his part in the Battle of Minden.

8 *The Morning Herald, and Daily Advertiser*, 3 May 1781 [BM 708.b.Burney].

9 Bevington, Merle (ed.), *The Memoirs of James Stephen: Written by himself for the use of his children*, (London, 1954), pp. 343–360. Stephen says that he knew Felix McCarthy and that McCarthy regarded him as 'his surest friend and councellor', p. 345. Thus it must be assumed

that Stephen would represent Edward Onslow in the least favourable light. However, Stephen's account seems to be confirmed by the accounts of the incident found in extant reports.

10 *Whitehall Evening Post*, 3–5 May 1781, 2.

11 Stephen, *Memoirs*, op. cit., p. 343.

12 Sodomy was listed as a 'Capital Offence against the Person' — 'By 25 Hen. 8, c.6 (1533), 2 & 3 Edw. 6, c. 29 (1548), revived & confirmed by 5 Eliz. c. 17 (1562), capital punishment (deprived of clery and death) was appointed for sodomy and the crime against nature'. L. Radzinowicz, *A History of English Criminal Law and its Administration from 1750*, London, 1948), p. 632.

13 M. Hyde, *The Other Love*, London, Heinemann, 1970, p. 69.

14 Stephen, *Memoirs*, op. cit., p. 351. The parliamentary report in the *Whitehall Evening Post*, op. cit., also noted that Lord North and several friends had welcomed Edward to that day's session.

15 *Manuscripts of The Earl of Carlisle*, London, 1897, p. 478.

16 For a recent discussion of libertinism, see S. West, 'Libertinism and the ideology of male friendship in the portraits of the Society of Dilettanti', *Eighteenth Century Life*, vol. 16, 2 May 1992, pp. 76–104.

17 Thomas Onslow, *Family Poems*, Clandon Park Library.

18 G.S. Rousseau defines the terms used for the description of male sexual behaviour in 'In the house of Madame Vander Tasse, on the Long Bridge: A homosocial university club in early modern Europe', in G. Kent and G. Hekma (eds.), *The Pursuit of Sodomy: Male homosexuality in renaissance and enlightenment Europe*, New York & London, 1989, p. 341. Homosocial behaviour is defined as, 'referring to relations which are less than homoerotic friendship' [the latter referring to male-oriented friendship not necessarily oral or genital]. Homosocial behaviour is defined as more pronounced male-oriented relations than the 'homoerotic' which is male-oriented, male-centred and male-dominated.

19 31 May 1781 *Carlisle MSS*, 490. Comments made in respect to John Howe, also accused as Edward.

20 ibid., 342 and 344; also cited in the *Morning Herald*, 3 May, and in the *Whitehall Evening Post*, 3–4 May, 2.

21 Letter from 'Candid' on the Royal Academy in *Morning Chronicle*, 1 May 1781, expressing disapproval of young artists being exposed to 'a love of glare & bustle in a room of grace and simplicity'.

22 The problem of limiting admittance to a 'respectable' audience has been discussed in respect to the exhibition policies of the Society for the Encouragement of Arts, Manufactures and Commerce in 1761/62 by Iain Pears, *The Discovery of Painting*, New Haven, 1988, p. 127.

23 This apologia was printed in the Academy handlist for this and the preceding year.

24 7 May 1781, *The Earl of Carlisle MSS*, 480.

25 Stephen, *Memoirs*, op. cit., p. 355.

26 Storer also belonged to Brooks's Club, where he was said to have gambled for high stakes (*History of Parliament*, 486).

27 *Carlisle MSS*, 480.

28 Descriptions of the painting and lists of the represented Peers appeared in the *Morning Chronicle*, the *London Chronicle*, the *Morning Herald, and Daily Advertiser*, 3 May 1781, and the *Whitehall Evening-Post*, 1–3 May 1781.

29 The *Morning Herald, and Daily Advertiser*, 3 May 1781 and the *Whitehall Evening-Post*, 3–5 May 1781, printed the accusations against Edward. The *London Chronicle*, 3–5 May, the *London Courant, & Westminster Chronicle*, 4 May, and the *Whitehall Evening Post*, 3–5 May, printed the Onslow rebuttal.

30 The manner in which the magistrate, Sir Samuel Wright, took the information from the two parties, and his over-enthusiastic investigation, demonstrated such partiality towards the Onslows that he was subsequently charged for corruption. A rule for an information against the magistrate for 'a corrupt breach of duty in his Office was moved for in the Court of King's Bench' soon after Edward's departure for France.

31 Stephen, *Memoirs*, op. cit., p. 347.

32 R. Trumbach, 'Sodomitical assaults, gender role, and sexual development in eighteenth-century London' in *The Pursuit of Sodomy*, op. cit., p. 409.

33 Polly Morris, 'Sodomy and Male Honour: The case of Somerset, 1740–1850' in *The Pursuit of Sodomy*, op. cit., p. 386. While this study deals only with one area of England and focuses primarily on the holiday resort of Bath, its findings direct our attention to shifting definitions with regard to sexual practice in this period.

34 ibid., p. 387.

35 30 May 1781, *Carlisle MSS*, p. 490.

36 The obituary for John Howe in the *Gentleman's Magazine*, vol. 74, 1804, pp. 1242–43, is lengthy and complimentary, although it does refer to the Epsom races incident. The author explains that Howe appealed to law, won the case, and had the transcript of the trial published. The paper suggests that Howe's 'peculiarity of appearance and manner' caused a gentleman to receive an 'unfavourable impression', and so to assault him. The proceedings of the trial were published as 'Two Actions between John Howe, Esq. and George Lewis Dive, Esq. Tried by a special Jury before Lord Mansfield', 15 August 1781, 2nd ed., 1781, [B.L. 1417.k.22].

37 'Two Actions . . . Howe and Dive', pp. 11–12.

38 ibid., p. 21.

39 ibid., p. 22.
40 See above, note 31 re: Stephen on not letting McCarthy take part in a duel, and note 37 (Howe case).
41 See note 7.
42 The copy of Edward Onslow's Will [SMR] 173.3.32, makes mention of the sum of fifteen thousand pounds settled on him by his mother and father.
43 I do not accept Wendy Steiner's structuralist approach to narrative in *Pictures of Romance. Form against context in painting and literature*, Chicago, 1988. Her specification of the conditions of narrativity in painting confines narrative within the frame and insists upon the presentation of more than one temporal moment, repetition of the subject, and a minimally realistic setting, *passim*.
44 B. Herrnstein Smith, 'Narrative Versions, Narrative Theories' in W.J.T. Mitchell, *On Narrative*, Chicago, 1981, pp. 209–32. Smith seems to have conceived a theory of narrativity which permits me to propose that the rhetorical specificity of a particular time and place do limit the possible narratives. However, she does not discuss the idea of epistemological limits.
45 Hayden White, 'The Value of Narrativity in the Representation of Reality', *Critical Inquiry*, no. 7, 1980, p. 26.
46 P. Spacks, *Desire and Truth*, Chicago, 1990, p. 2.
47 ibid., p. 6.
48 Edward's son, Georges, became known as the 'French Beethoven'.
49 Although it is not clear which brother is the Fitzwilliam portrayed, John, the younger, was the same age as Edward. I found no evidence in the supporting literature to explain John's self-exile.
50 1778 Inventory of Clandon House, [SMR] 173.3.20.
51 The same order of progression is present in the inventory of December 1899, National Trust, Clandon Park MSS, 97.21.4. (1) & (2).
52 See note 36.

Art History Vol. 16 No. 3 September 1993 0141—6790 pp. 424–446

A CANON OF DEFORMITY: *LES DEMOISELLES D'AVIGNON* AND PHYSICAL ANTHROPOLOGY

DAVID LOMAS

'Studies of human morphology which each day assume greater importance draw art and science together on a terrain which is rich in lessons. Anthropologists, doctors, artists, archaeologists, etc. can only stand to gain from it.'[1]

I

Les Demoiselles d'Avignon (plate 20) has a mythic stature as the source from which cubism was engendered, along with the rest of modern art. The poet André Salmon helped to crystallize this myth about the *Demoiselles* when in 1921 he proclaimed it 'the ever-glowing crater from which the fire of contemporary art erupted', adding that 'Picasso has invented it all.'[2] At that moment, the tide of opinion in France had turned against what was regarded as the convulsive disorder of the pre-war avant garde in favour of a more ordered classicism. Salmon was a staunch defender of modern art against this hostile reaction and his exaggerated claim that the vital strands of modern art all originated from Picasso must be understood in this light. Yet the potent appeal of the myth — that *Les Demoiselles d'Avignon* erupted *sui generis* and the rest of modern art flowed from it — is such that it has proven remarkably tenacious, even in art history where it is often maintained that the picture marks an absolute breach with the artistic and cultural past.

Those few visitors who saw *Les Demoiselles d'Avignon* in the studio, mainly fellow artists and poets, were shocked by its gross distortions of the human form. Five brazen whores stare down a venerated classical past. This, above all, must have struck Salmon (an eyewitness to the creation of the picture) as absolutely new and unheralded, a volcanic fissure in the cultural landscape of his time. However, in this essay I will demonstrate that Picasso had recourse to an iconography of the prostitute already formulated by physical anthropologists in the late nineteenth century. *Les Demoiselles d'Avignon* was thus firmly embedded in a cultural terrain that provided the visual terms with which it could be read.

An overriding concern with the formally innovative character of the *Demoiselles*

20 Pablo Picasso, *Les Demoiselles d'Avignon*, June–July 1907, oil on canvas, 243.9 × 233.7 cm. The Museum of Modern Art, New York

has led to it becoming detached from the social and cultural context of its production, neglect of which weakens existing art-historical interpretations. Leo Steinberg, for example, has argued that Picasso conflates the prostitute with the primitive in order 'to personify sheer sexual energy as the image of a life force', creating out of this hybrid a vision of the 'nature beings who dwell behind all civilization'.[3] While prostitution was much discussed during the period, it was never in such glowing terms but rather in connection with the syphilis scourge, as a symptom of the dire malaise of French society. Michael Leja has convincingly shown that Picasso registers the prevailing attitudes toward prostitution in the numerous images dealing with the theme painted after his arrival in Paris in 1901.[4] For such reasons it is unlikely that he would have chosen the prostitute to symbolize either a Nietzschean vital life force (syphilis was on the contrary life-threatening), or nature beings outside civilization (the very fact of bringing Cézanne's bathers indoors, which Steinberg remarks upon, seems to foreclose this reading).[5]

Alternatively, *Les Demoiselles d'Avignon* has been viewed as a *mise en scène* of the artist's psyche with Eros and Thanatos, the warring parties, battling for control. William Rubin remarks that 'We sense the thanatophobia in the primordial horror evoked by the monstrously distorted heads of the two whores on the right of the picture, so opposite to those of the comparatively gracious Iberian courtesans in the centre.'[6] Rubin suggests that the primitivism of the *Demoiselles* has to do with its capacity to communicate the primal terror felt by primitive minds. Yet to connect the prostitute with primal emotions may once again be anachronistic when contemporaries viewed prostitution and venereal disease rather as evidence of an effete and degenerate France. It is relevant to note here that Freud, from whom the notion of conflicting life and death instincts derives, writing just two years before Picasso painted the *Demoiselles*, was himself still prepared to accept degeneracy as a causal factor in sexual disorders.[7] One must attend to this pervasive cultural discourse in order to explain in historically specific terms the pictorial amalgam of prostitute and primitive in *Les Demoiselles d'Avignon*. That conjuncture was forged primarily in the culture Picasso inherited, not in the depth of his own psyche.

It is not my intention to claim that Picasso consciously made use of the findings of physical anthropologists, though this cannot be ruled out. Instead I wish to draw attention to a shared mentality common to both Picasso's art and physical anthropology. Peter Burke has written that a history of mentalities is concerned primarily with 'collective attitudes rather than individual ones'. It takes into account, according to Burke, 'unspoken or unconscious assumptions [. . .] as well as conscious thoughts or elaborated theories' and explores 'the structure of beliefs as well as their content, [. . .] how people think as well as what they think'.[8] A complex set of unconscious assumptions, beliefs and values lie behind the breach of classical proportion in *Les Demoiselles d'Avignon*. The primary aim of juxtaposing the picture with a discourse of physical anthropology is to bring these collectively held attitudes to light, rather than to add yet another item to the burgeoning list of artistic and other sources that have been related to it.

Aesthetic concepts of symmetry and proportion were central to the discourse of physical anthropology, thus ensuring a convenient bridgehead between this notionally scientific discipline and the sphere of art. The idealized classical body acted within anthropology as a signifier for Western man whose superiority it underwrote in the colonial encounter with other races. In France, a classical heritage was also invested with connotations of a specifically French national identity. On the far right of the political spectrum, the leader of the Royalist *Action française*, Charles Maurras, promulgated a return to classicism as the cultural counterpart to his organic conception of nationhood rooted in racial and geographic belonging — an ideology of *le sang et la terre*.[9]

The classical body could thus mediate a sense of national identity as well as being a focus for its anxieties and discontents. Because of these powerful cultural resonances, any perceived deviation from a classical norm emphatically signalled inferiority — whether racial, moral, or intellectual — and when applied to a reviled subgroup worked as a virulent mode of exclusion from the social body. The normative and prescriptive power of the classical ideal served to organize and secure a group identity in the face of a multitude of threatening others, both outside France and within (notably criminals and prostitutes), whose contours it delineated and over whom it facilitated a regime of surveillance and control. The classical body and its deviant other constitutes a crucial binary opposition within anthropological discourse, linking up with a whole series of related binary terms. Of these, the most important from the viewpoint of this paper were the conceptual pair *dégénérescence* and *regénérescence*, which not only dominated *fin-de-siècle* medical and anthropological thought but also left their stamp on the literary and artistic culture of the period.[10]

Similarly, it is possible to consider the work of Picasso as structured around an opposition of classical and anti-classical stylistic idioms. This is especially so of the surrealist period where the classical body is often alluded to, or invoked in some way, but only to be aggressively dismembered. In a pithy statement in 1935, which could almost have been uttered by the surrealist writer Georges Bataille,[11] Picasso spells out his transgressive stance toward the classical ideal:

> Academic training in beauty is a sham. The beauties of the Parthenon, Venuses, Nymphs, Narcissuses, are so many lies. Art is not the application of a canon of beauty but what the instinct and the brain can conceive beyond any canon. When we love a woman we don't start measuring her limbs.[12]

An etching of 4 May 1933 from the *Vollard Suite*, known as *Model and Surrealist Sculpture*, which juxtaposes an impeccably classical nude and a whimsical surrealist assemblage, is a distilled visual formulation of these remarks.[13] The surrealist sculpture, a close relative of the *Une Anatomie* contraptions, is a riotous jumble of furniture, body parts and primitive mask in which the order and hierarchy of the classical body is anarchically overturned. In accord with surrealist principles, desire is the agent of an artistic transgression in which the propriety of the model, who adopts a chaste *Venus pudica* pose and turns away from the viewer, is cast off by the assemblage which provocatively flaunts its sexuality. That the artistic identity of Picasso is affirmed in the tension between the classical law and its transgressive other was astutely discerned by the German critic Carl Einstein who wrote in 1926 that Picasso 'lives in the tension between opposites and finds his own vital individuality and identity in the drama of antitheses'.[14]

Les Demoiselles d'Avignon inaugurates this artistic practice of transgression (and as a result enabled Picasso to enhance his avant-garde image enormously). While it is not as obviously pitted against a classical ideal as the surrealist sculpture in *Model and Surrealist Sculpture*, this is nonetheless implied as the law which is transgressed; indeed the Rose period images of classical youths from the summer of 1906 which narrowly precede work on the *Demoiselles* act as a foil to its anarchic force. On a superficial reading, then, Picasso appears as diametrically opposed to the physical anthropologists: where the latter affirm the classical ideal and identify themselves with it, the artistic posture of Picasso is predicated on a radical transgression of classical order. What I seek to elicit, however, is a more fundamental level of ideological agreement between them, such that the audacious departure from a classical canon of the body in *Les Demoiselles d'Avignon* relies on and brings into play what were, in effect, highly denigratory stereotypes of cultural otherness.[15]

II

Anthropology emerged as an organized discipline in France with the founding of the Société D'Anthropologie by the eminent neurologist Dr Paul Broca in 1859.[16] Its membership was drawn principally from medically trained professionals with a positivist scientific outlook and avowedly Republican politics — Broca himself became a senator under Léon Gambetta. From these few facts much of the programme of the Société followed. The medically trained pioneers in the field favoured an anatomical and strictly empirical approach. Craniology, a comparative study of skulls, the passion for which originated early in the century with the phrenology of Gall, came to epitomize the new science. Joy Harvey in her doctoral thesis on the Société observes that, boosted by new forms of instrumentation, craniology became 'a worldwide enterprise, with the collection of skulls carried on with the enthusiasm of shell collection, being shipped from all areas of the world to the Société d'Anthropologie, until it could boast many thousands of specimens'.[17] Correlations were thought to exist between skull and brain size, and thence with intellectual and cultural development. Proponents of craniometry claimed that raging controversies over the role and status of women and the potential for development of native populations might be settled by this ostensibly neutral, empirical technique.

The new science of anthropology was thus devoted above all to measurement, or anthropometry. Its data was expressed in ratios derived from artistic canons of proportion, as one of the advocates of the technique confessed: 'the first attempt at anthropometry for the purpose of determining the proportions of the human body, and craniometry, for analysing the physiognomy, are due to artists.'[18] This is confirmed by glancing at the earliest book on anthropometry by the Belgian statistician Quetelet in which, for instance, a diagram of the *homme moyen* plainly mimics Leonardo's famous drawing of a Vitruvian man.[19] Where academic treatises on ideal beauty once advised painters to generalize from the model in nature, eliminating accidental deformities to extract 'an abstract idea of their forms more perfect than any one original', anthropologists employed statistical averaging of data to put this procedure on a newly scientific footing.[20] Topinard predicted that art would, in turn, prosper by obeying the limits anthropology set: 'Art, then, ought to rest upon anthropology, in that its whims are tolerated, though under the express condition that they do not go beyond the individual variations which anthropology reveals to it.'[21]

Quetelet and Topinard encapsulate two antithetical stances regarding the use of proportional systems. Guided by a religious belief in the unity of the species, Quetelet affirmed one type of beauty in both men and women. His priority was to define this *type général* and only then to characterize the secondary traits of particular groups. 'Our species admits one type or module of which one can easily determine the different proportions,' Quetelet insisted.[22] From a study of Belgian subjects Quetelet concluded that this *type général* conformed almost exactly to the *beau idéal* of classical antiquity: 'Everything tends to establish that the human type, in our climate, is identical with that which is deduced from observation of the most regular ancient statues.'[23] The universal truth of the Greek ideal was thenceforth verified by science!

Topinard, on the other hand, hotly disputed this stance, arguing that 'It had not occurred to the ancients that there are differences in the proportions of the various races of mankind [. . .] It is now generally admitted, and we look for the negro ideal, or the Mongol ideal, as well as for the white ideal.'[24] Physicians at the Société like Topinard were secular materialists whose polygenic theory of the separate origin and parallel development of human races was a challenge to the biblical doctrine of the single origin of mankind. (Other factors also contributed to the imperative need to differentiate races and sexes on the basis of immutable physical characteristics, as we shall see.) Hostility to the religious attitude lay behind Topinard's efforts to rid anthropology of any metaphysical taint: 'Art by its nature is idealist, unitary,' he wrote, 'it admits but one canon and one human type and around it simple variations, whereas anthropology, necessarily realist, accepts multiple types and canons.'[25]

Despite theoretical arguments undermining the sovereignty of the classical ideal, in practice the white classically proportioned male was not so readily toppled from his pedestal. This is patently obvious from the frontispiece of Topinard's *L'Homme dans la nature* which depicts a 'Canon of the Adult European Male' directly facing the title page bearing the name of the author, implying an elision between the anthropologist himself and the old *beau idéal*. The ideological significance of this is clear: Harvey notes that doctors at the Société clung tenaciously to pejorative beliefs 'about other human societies as well as the innate superiority of civilized European man'.[26] Polygenism, with its emphasis on human diversity, dovetailed with a ranking of race and culture that placed the scientific Western male subject at the apex of an evolutionary pyramid.

While my primary objective is to define a common mentality rather than specify causal connections, one might reasonably ask whether channels existed whereby an artist could have had access to a specialized discourse conducted within the institutional bounds of anthropology. From at least the middle of the nineteenth century the potential value of anthropometry to artists had been extolled.[27] In 1878 Topinard wrote:

> We are not now living in the time of Albert Dürer and of Rubens when artists were satisfied with delineating the forms and features of those around them to represent those of foreign nations. Our annual exhibitions testify the progress which has been made in this direction [. . .] and at the Ecole des Beaux-Arts, the professor of anatomy knows that he must teach the different forms of the beautiful, as seen in every country and under every climate, and, therefore, must be an anthropologist.[28]

As a site where the interests of medical men and artists overlap and reciprocally inflect each other, the Ecole des Beaux-Arts was central to the dissemination of medical knowledge about the body of particular interest to visual artists. Dr Paul Richer, who as an assistant to Jean-Marie Charcot had contributed to the *Iconographie de la Salpêtrière*, was from 1903 Professor of Anatomy at the Ecole des Beaux-Arts and was the author of several books promoting and diffusing physical anthropology for the guidance of artists.[29] Texts by Richer incorporated advice on proportion and translated the raw figures of anthropology into a more palatable form by

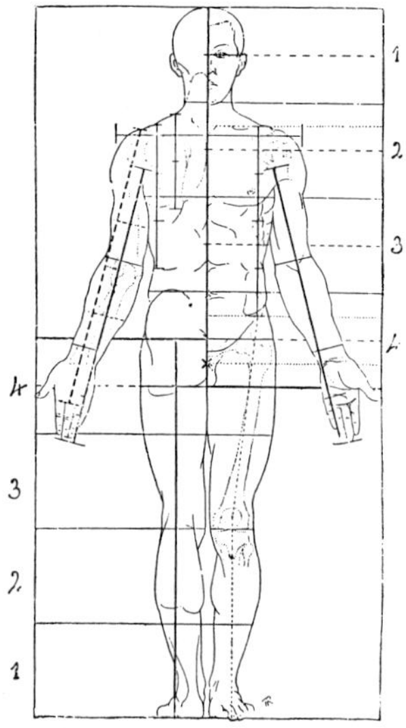

Fig. 46. — CANON DE L'HOMME MOYEN.

21 Canon of an Average Male. From Paul Richer, *Anatomie artistique*, Paris, 1980, p. 173

constructing diagrams artists could follow (plate 21). There is little doubt that a plate from Richer's *Artistic Physiology* provided a starting point for Marcel Duchamp's *Nude Descending a Staircase* of 1912.[30] Whether or not Picasso, who had a thorough academic training, was acquainted with texts such as those is not germane to my argument. However, a cluster of proportional studies in which he attempts to formulate a distinct canon of the primitive body must count as the first belated response by an artist to the calls of anthropologists since the middle of the previous century.

III

The proportion sketches of a figure with clasped hands, some drawn onto blank pages of a Daumier catalogue, were a startling revelation of the exhibition of *Les Demoiselles d'Avignon* held in 1988 at the Musée Picasso (plate 22).[31] The exercise was quite informal but a system of numbering suggests that some calculations which are now indecipherable must have taken place. Coinciding with final preparatory studies for the *Demoiselles*, they have been seen as a nostalgic backward glance to a mode of figuration Picasso was about to jettison; Yve-Alain Bois claims that 'the purging of such almost academic procedures was a necessary step toward achieving the disruptive character of the *Demoiselles*.'[32] While they recall classic studies of proportion, however, the studies do not conform to any standard source Picasso might have consulted. Dürer, for example, composed discrete canons for men and women of different heights and builds where Picasso employs a single module whose progeny, oddly enough, are of both sexes. Furthermore, a meticulous analysis by Pierre Daix shows beyond doubt that the studies are of a piece with the primitivizing

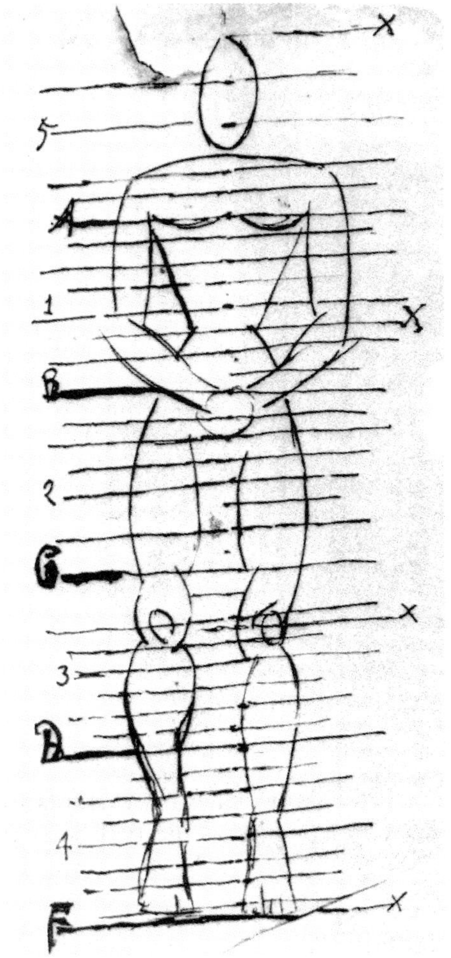

22 Pablo Picasso, *Study of Proportion*, April–May 1907, ink on tracing paper, 31 × 12.6 cm. Musée Picasso, Paris

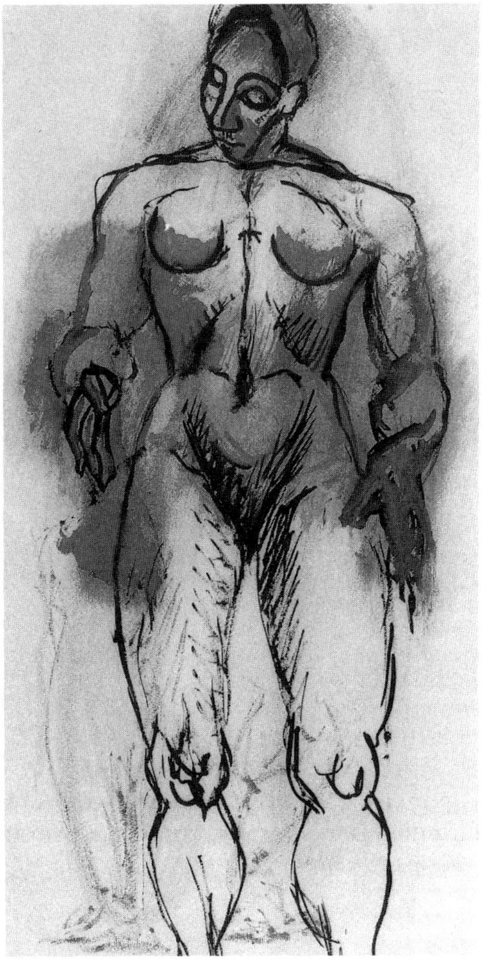

23 Pablo Picasso, Study for *Les Demoiselles d'Avignon*, Winter 1906–07, ink and gouache on paper, 61.5 × 42.2 cm. Formerly the collection of Douglas Cooper

trend that predominated at this moment. They spawn a cluster of primitivist works in which the frontal pose and clasped hands of the studies is preserved.[33] Sketches for a demoiselle later eliminated from the composition (plate 23), display the same compact torso, lengthy thighs and knobbly knees found in the proportional studies themselves. And the bizarre overlapping diamond lozenges of one drawing, for which no precedent exists in academic systems of proportion, feed into the triangular shapes of the *Demoiselles* and prefigure the more emphatic faceting of the following year.

The proportional drawings attest to the search for an alternative to the classical canon governing representation of the body in the West, and that prompted Picasso to turn to various non-Western sources.[34] But they are not the culminating point of his researches: in *Les Demoiselles d'Avignon* he opts for the even more radical and aberrant solution of a canon of deformity. In this, Picasso may have been influenced by a revival of symbolist aesthetics which posited a deforming tendency as the very essence of artistic creation. In his immediate circle, Mécislas Golberg wrote about the satiric drawings of André Rouveyre: 'that which is vulgarly called deformation is the very principle of human creation, our *anima Dei*!'[35] That caricature and primitivism are linked by their tendency to deform was recognized in a highly prescient essay on Picasso by the critic Max Raphael in 1933. Raphael argued that the existence of a caricatural impulse in non-Academic art from Daumier onwards was necessary before Picasso could respond to primitive art: 'Without the introduction of caricature, which has broken up the European tradition, Picasso could never have arrived at his affinity for Negro art.' This is because caricature abandons a conception of the body as an ordered and harmonious whole: 'The whole no longer determines the parts [. . .] the harmony of the whole has ceased to exist.' Caricature deforms the classical body, breaks up the European tradition, just as the incorporation of Negro art by Picasso 'deprives the antique of its character as absolute norm'.[36]

In broad terms, Picasso traces a similar path to that followed by Topinard, whose own study of the primitive races prompted him to reject a universal *type général* in favour of a multiplicity of types. Moreover, the specific issues of race, gender and deviancy that crop up repeatedly in debates at the Société are precisely the same constellation of themes as preoccupied Picasso at the time of painting *Les Demoiselles d'Avignon*. The following section will map this common ground in more detail.

Anthropologists legitimized the position of the colonizing west by the proofs of moral and physical superiority they purported to uncover.[37] The classical ideal, identified with the *race blanche* and placed at the summit of human evolution, gave a measure against which other groups subjected to anthropological scrutiny were invariably found to be deficient.[38] Dr René Verneau's 'Physical Characteristics of Women in Different Races', the first part of a four-volume compendium on *Woman* published from 1908, took the Venus of Medici as the exemplar of an ideal female physique.[39] By contrast Verneau offers caricatural descriptions of 'savages' which are openly derogatory. He ranks the different races according to their greater or lesser degree of physical charm, venturing the opinion that 'each of the types encountered in ethnic groups corresponds to a stage of human evolution.'[40] It is noteworthy that Polynesian races whose bodily proportions were said to rival even those of classical antiquity fared better than *peuples barbares* under the aesthetic hierarchies that such authors fabricated. A similar perception may govern Picasso's turning away from Gauguinesque imagery, Polynesian in inspiration, to barbaric Negro sources as he seeks to convey a more extreme departure from the classical canon.

Anthropometric techniques were applied with equal relish to deviant subgroups in the metropolitan French population. Robert Nye has argued that, in the wake of her ignominious defeat in the Franco-Prussian War, there emerged in France 'a medical model of cultural crisis'.[41] Signs of pathology were detected everywhere in the social body. The notion of *dégénérescence*, understood as evolution in reverse, came to encapsulate the widespread sense of decadence and decline. Sheer vagueness of definition enhanced its utility, to the extent that any and every ill besetting the French populace could be gathered under the rubric of degeneration. The term had wide currency in French psychiatry, being often invoked as an etiological factor in mental disorders following the publication in 1856 of Auguste Morel's *Traité des dégénérescence*. It has been plausibly suggested that French psychiatrists, faced with evidence of an increase in mental illness, lacked any effective response to the situation, and for this reason were particularly receptive to the idea of an irremediable inherited predisposition to madness.[42]

Anthropologists also joined the search for evidence of degeneration, male criminals and their female counterparts, prostitutes, being the main target of research by anthropologists who zealously looked for physical clues of atavistic regression. The fallen woman had, so to speak, toppled down the evolutionary ladder, and the stigmata of degeneration were read from her face, which took on the contours of a grotesquely deformed mask. Aesthetic criteria of beauty and proportion versus asymmetry and deformity figured prominently in the evaluation of the female subjects. An authoritative and much cited anthropometric study of Russian prostitutes was published in Paris in 1889 by Dr Pauline Tarnowsky who found that degenerative 'anomalies of the face present frequently as asymmetry, prognathism [a jutting mandible], or a perceptible disproportion of the diverse parts of the face.'[43] Meanwhile, doctors at the Société were engaged in developing a method for identifying criminals that was, according to Nye, 'largely a revamping of phrenological systems'.[44] Most notably, the criminologist Alphonse Bertillon set about compiling tables of photographs exhaustively recording the protean variations of the human ear (plate 24).[45]

Additional manifestations of *dégénérescence* in female prostitutes were imbecility and moral deficiency, the alleged causes of an innate attraction to vice. Tarnowsky reported in her sample 'a dimunition of the principal diameters of the cranium by several millimetres', this being 'entirely to the detriment of the intellectual and moral development of prostitutes'.[46] By adducing empirical evidence of this sort, anthropometry merely conferred a scientific aura on prevalent stereotypes through which Belle Epoque society channelled its fears and anxieties, principally about syphilis, into a scapegoating of the presumed source: the prostitute.[47]

Turning now to the grotesque masks of *Les Demoiselles d'Avignon*, Kahnweiler wrote that as Picasso worked on the *Demoiselles* he became interested in African masks, more so than in statuary. Even so, attempts to relate individual African masks to the picture are fraught, as an exhaustive study by Rubin has concluded that Picasso would not have seen most of the masks traditionally compared with the *Demoiselles*, nor did he slavishly follow those he did see.[48] In addition, the radical asymmetry of his solution to the problem of representing the primitive is at odds with the almost exclusive bilateral symmetry of archaic art. Rubin admits it is highly improbable that Picasso could have known a rare type of asymmetric *masque de maladie* which he relates to the *Demoiselles*.[49] Nor is his otherwise plausible suggestion that the picture reflects fears about syphilitic contagion advanced by a comparison of its distorted physiognomies with photographs of women horribly disfigured by disease. None of these images in fact show the ravages of syphilis, as Rubin erroneously claims.[50]

On the other hand, there are striking parallels between the way Picasso registers a deviation from classical ideals in the primitive masks of the *Demoiselles* and the stigmata of degeneracy as recorded by anthropologists. Daix characterizes the former

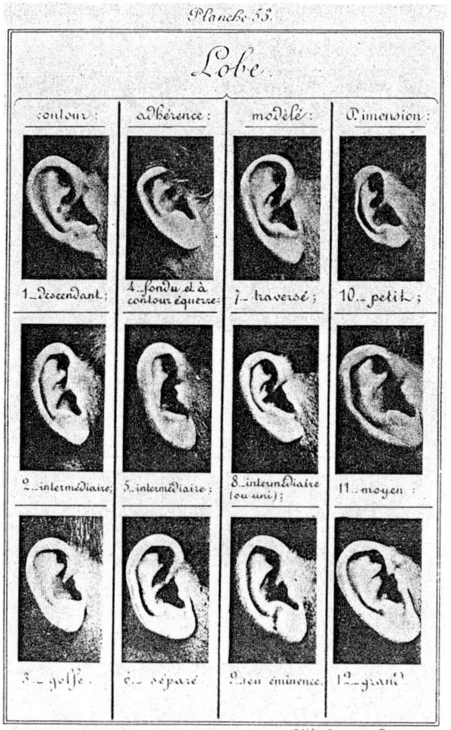

24 Classification of Ear Lobes. From Alphonse Bertillon, *Identification anthropométrique. Instructions signalétiques*, Paris, 1893, plate 53

in terms of a 'disequilibrated deformity of the face', 'uneven levels of the eyes' and 'a jutting jaw'[51] — a description that applies not only to the grossly distorted right-hand figures, but also to the Iberian demoiselles in the centre, whose uneven eyes (a distance cue) are no less disconcerting. Tarnowsky, meanwhile, includes photographs (plate 25) to illustrate the salient features of *dégénérescence* in prostitutes. These are enumerated in the captions and among them are asymmetry, prognathism or disproportion of the lower third of the face, misshapen ears and, curiously, 'deviation of the nose, [or] a deep depression of the root of the nose' (a perception that may have arisen from analogy with the saddle-nose deformity of congenital syphilis, even though the author separates the signs of venereal disease from degeneration).[52] One irresistibly recalls the bizarre scroll-like ear in studies for the *Demoiselles* (plate 26), for which the specific artistic source was an Iberian head, and the renowned nose *en quart de Brie*. For both artist and anthropologist the telltale sign of atavism is, above all, physiognomic asymmetry. The degree of overlap is so striking that one is tempted to speculate that Picasso, who visisted the Hôpital St Lazare in order to observe prostitutes incarcerated there, might have consulted Tarnoswky's book in the course of his researches, or at least garnered some knowledge of it from the medical doctors he encountered.

If medical and anthropological studies could confer a legible stamp upon the

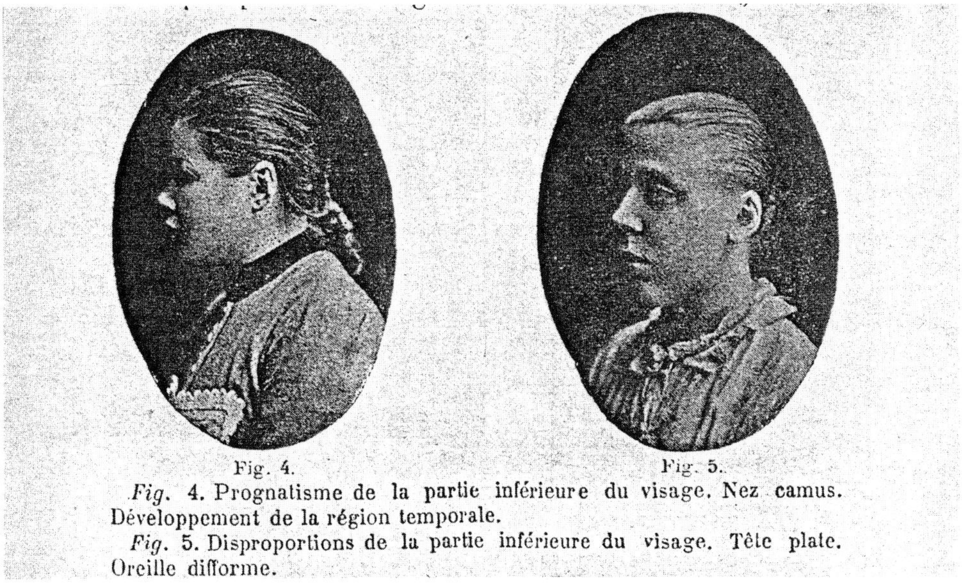
Fig. 4.
Fig. 5.
Fig. 4. Prognatisme de la partie inférieure du visage. Nez camus. Développement de la région temporale.
Fig. 5. Disproportions de la partie inférieure du visage. Tête plate. Oreille difforme.

25 Photographs of Facial Anomalies in Prostitutes. From Dr Pauline Tarnowsky, *Etude anthropométrique sur les prostituées et les voleuses*, Paris, 1889, p. 37, figs. 4 and 5

26 Pablo Picasso, Study for *Les Demoiselles d'Avignon*, June 1907, gouache and watercolour on paper, 60.3 × 47 cm. The Museum of Modern Art, New York

face of prostitutes then troubling uncertainties of identification in the urban crowd would be resolved. At just that moment, regulationists were clamouring for more policing and harsher controls of prostitution. The matter of visibility was a leitmotif of Cesare Lombroso's controversial, and hence much talked about, *La Femme criminelle et prostituée.*[53] Lombroso alleges that prostitute women, because of a natural selection imposed by their vocation, 'show fewer of the anomalies which produce ugliness, but are marked by more of the signs of degeneration'. They manage to conceal such blemishes by dint of a certain facility in the art of making up, but Lombroso warns sternly:

> When youth vanishes, the jaws, the cheek-bones, hidden by adipose tissue, emerge, salient angles stand out, and the face grows virile, uglier than a man's; wrinkles deepen into the likeness of scars, and the countenance, once attractive, exhibits the full degenerate type which early grace had concealed.[54]

In the moralizing contrast sketched in by the sanctimonious Lombroso, it is perhaps not too far-fetched to see an analogy with the polarity that Rubin detects in *Les Demoiselles d'Avignon* between the gracious Iberian courtesans in the centre and the scarified masks of the whores on the right, though by a Picassean twist of an otherwise hackneyed plot it is the masks which render visible the truth which early grace and art had concealed.

As for the body of the prostitute, anthropometry pronounced it devoid of female charm, coarsened by a *métier infâme*, coupled with the ugly taint of degeneration. Lombroso recorded in female prostitutes a virile appearance due to excessive body hair and a high incidence of male voices owing to enlargement of the vocal cords. This he cites as evidence of a 'tendency to atavistic return to the period of hermaphrodism'.[55] Lumping the prostitute with the primitive on the grounds of a masculine body habitus could be justified by recourse to a theory which linked sexual differentiation with the progress of civilization. In the *Bulletins de la société d'anthropologie*, for example, it was asserted that:

> There exists among different races a sort of seriation which corresponds roughly to how ancient their civilization is. The race which presents the greatest difference between men and women is the yellow race, the first to be civilized: then comes the European race, then the Americans. The negroes and arabs, who present the least advanced degree of civilization, where women work with men at the same hard labour, present the smallest sexual difference.[56]

Accordingly, femininity was only fully expressed in modern civilized societies where women were 'spared' the same hard labour as men. Lombroso found in the prostitute, a working woman *par excellence*, supposedly incontrovertible proof of the view. One suspects that this scientific argument was fuelled by the same sentiment as a popular stereotype which portrayed the modern, emancipated woman as a mannish virago, a kind of *hommesse* in the words of one commentator.[57]

Ambiguous gendering of body types from the period of Picasso's work coinciding

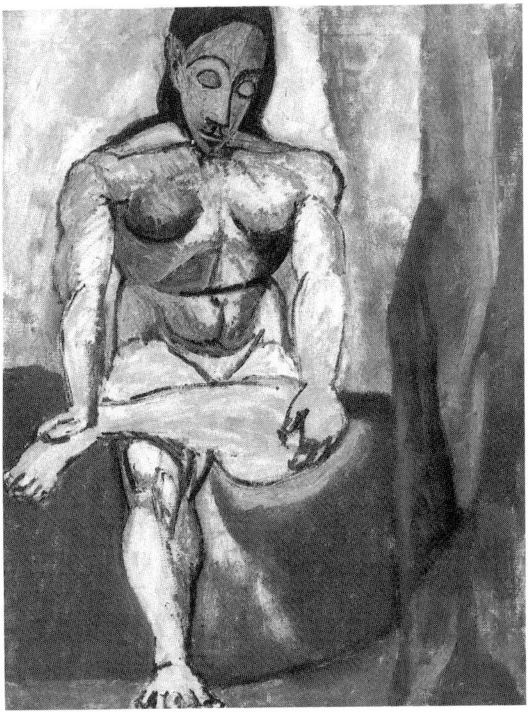

27 Pablo Picasso, Study for *Les Demoiselles d'Avignon*, Winter 1906–07, oil on canvas, 121 × 93.5 cm. Musée Picasso, Paris

with the *Demoiselles* is often noted, but its significance rarely explained. Though masculine traits are muted in the final picture by comparison with individual studies, the 'mannish' character of its women is not infrequently remarked upon. The marked ambiguity of the sketches led Zervos mistakenly to identify a drawing for the seated demoiselle (plate 27), later eliminated from the composition, as male. Moreover, it was noted that the proportion sketches which punctuated work on the *Demoiselles* are of a single androgynous prototype that spawns both male and female progeny. It seems unlikely that Picasso is reverting here to the unisex *type général* advocated by Quetelet among others. The more probable explanation is that he is registering the view popularized by Lombroso that female prostitutes display features of atavistic return to a more masculine type. Why Picasso should look to the androgynous dying slaves of Michelangelo as a source for one of the demoiselles, initially baffling given his rebellion against Renaissance conventions of figuration, can be understood in the light of this anthropometric discourse on the prostitute: Michelangelo was, after all, renowned for the masculine body cast of his women.

Studies for individual figures in the *Demoiselles* portray the body as an amalgam of distinct male and female parts, in the same way that medical authorities were busy espousing a detailed morphology of gender. Alexandra Parigoris has demonstrated that the seated demoiselle, for example, is derived from male antique statuary, adopting the pose of the *Spinario* and pastiching the *Belevedere Torso* which has been adorned with female breasts.[58] In another sketch of the arm, powerful deltoid and pectoral muscles are those of a male whereas the pelvis belongs to a female body.[59] At this very moment anthropometry was similarly engaged in producing an exact typology of gender applicable to every part of the body and every organ.[60] These attempts to ground gender difference in anatomy tended to naturalize the unequal social opportunities of men and women, and may have been a reaction to growing demands by women for emancipation (heated debate centred around the issue of relative brain size). A wry comment by Thomas Laqueur on an analogous situation in eighteenth-century France that 'wherever boundaries were threatened arguments for fundamental sexual differences were shoved into the breach' was no less applicable to the urgent task of anthropologists a century later.[61] The desire to demarcate the sexes on the basis of anatomy was accompanied by inordinate anxiety about borderline cases such as effeminate males, bearded women and hermaphrodites — numerous attempts being made to classify the assorted types of this latter anomaly. Dr Henry Meige in an article published in *L'Anthropologie* of 1895 looked closely at antique sculptures of hermaphrodites, as Picasso may have done, claiming that their composite nature should not be dismissed as mere artistic licence, because 'there exist in nature corporeal anomalies of which they are the exact reproduction.'[62]

IV

Alongside the pessimistic doctrine of *dégénérescence* various prescriptions to ameliorate the ailing social body were forthcoming from the medical profession. Dr Francis Heckel in 1908 accused experts obsessed by ideas of 'hereditary and ineluctable physical degeneration' of ignoring 'the degree of which the *matière* is malleable and keen to regenerate'.[63] This author claimed that vast individual and social benefits would accrue from exercise:

> If the State promotes equally physical and intellectual education, it increases individual gain and economic gain; it augments the national wealth [. . .] it also increases the possibility of expansion beyond the metropole, and it remedies depopulation in giving to each man confidence in himself and in his descendence.[64]

Repudiating 'the man hypertrophied in his muscular apparatus', Heckel turned to antiquity for a model of physical health based on balance and equilibrium. In a paraphrase of classical beauty he describes the desirable outcome of his *méthode myothérapique* as a 'harmoniously balanced appearance of all the segments of the body', a point comically underlined by a plate showing the unlikely transformation of a flabby present-day Frenchman into a simulacrum of an antique statue. Robert Nye remarks that amidst 'the extraordinary explosion of sport and physical culture in the *fin de siècle* [. . .] the body became an ideological variable in the first burst of modern sportive nationalism.'[65] And, as the case of Dr Heckel shows, 'medical terminology was deeply embedded both in the discourse of sport and fitness and in the pronouncements of the purity crusaders who wholehearedly believed in the healing properties of exercise.'[66]

The fad for physical culture may be implicated in the resurgence of classicism in the work of Picasso *c.* 1905–06, which was accompanied by a spate of images of gymnasts, an archetypal embodiment of balance, and circus strong men. Coinciding with the appearance of these subjects, from 1905 the fitness magazine *La Culture physique* ran a series of articles on circus acrobats with the aim of documenting this colourful, but fast disappearing, part of French life. Two articles written by Apollinaire appeared subsequently in *La Culture physique* in February and March 1907, closely echoing the pronouncements of medical men by advocating sport as a panacea for the twin risks of depopulation and degeneration.[67] The first of the articles, on dance as a sport, insists without evident irony that: 'Alcoholism and depopulation, these scourges of France, would find a sure remedy in the proliferation of balls and dances.'[68] The second on 'Guy de Maupassant athlète' is less adamant in tone. The subject of the study who, 'by certain sides of his talent is attached to the most French if not the most classical' tradition, in spite of devoting 'an important part of his existence to physical development', had the misfortune to end his days in an *accès au folie*, dying with 'his reason obscured'[69] — *une saine vie* clearly did nothing to preserve de Maupassant's sanity.

In a preface to the farcical drama *Les Mamelles de Tirésias*, outwardly concerned with the issue of repopulation, Apollinaire confesses to being unable to decide whether he ought to be taken seriously or not. Ironic equivocation also informs the attitude of Picasso to physical culture, as a caricature of Apollinaire from 1905, where the poet is portrayed as a strong man clutching a copy of *La Culture physique* in reference to his current enthusiasm, reveals (plate 28). Proponents of physical culture strenuously objected to excessive and unbalanced development of muscles yet this is precisely what Picasso depicts in a deforming style which may be derived from the caricatures of Rouveyre, so warmly praised by Mécislas Golberg. Although irony distances Picasso from the overtly nationalistic and classicizing rhetoric that surrounded physical culture, his image and the related articles by Apollinaire indicate their acute awareness of what was merely the obverse side of a discourse of *dégénérescence*.

Returning to *Les Demoiselles d'Avignon*, I wish briefly to consider a case of contested identity which copious expert testimony has failed to resolve. An early state of the composition discloses a male figure on the left who clutches, rather enigmatically, a human skull or a book — plate 29 is one of several drawings for this figure.[70] As the composition evolves he undergoes a sudden transformation into a partly clad female whereupon the puzzling attributes disappear. Lingering on the threshold of a brothel scene this character lacks a wholly satisfactory alibi. Picasso testified at many years remove that he was a medical student, but this leaves the reason for his presence unexplained. A consensus view held that he was a *memento mori* symbolizing the wages of sin, but this does not tally with Picasso's supposed bohemian disregard for conventional morality. Various alternative readings have been proposed: that he symbolizes distanced knowledge as opposed to action in the realm occupied by his counterpart, the sailor; that the medical student is a partial self-portrait and refers to Picasso's alleged syphilophobia; a reference to Max Jacob has also been mooted.[71]

The meaning of this protagonist continues to perplex. Indeed it is likely that a penchant for symbolist ambiguity guided Picasso's choice of such a resonant motif.

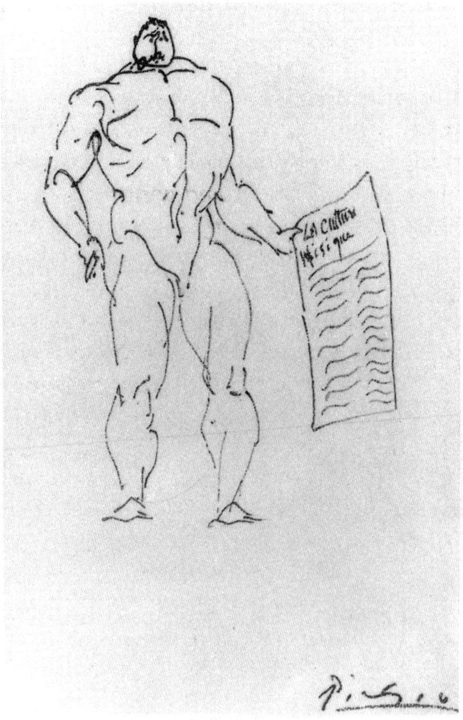

28 Pablo Picasso, *Caricatural Portrait of Apollinaire*, 1905, ink on paper, 31 × 23.5 cm. Location not known

29 Pablo Picasso, Study for *Les Demoiselles d'Avignon*, 1907, crayon on paper, 24.5 × 19.5 cm. Musée Picasso, Paris

However, one further association of a medical man clutching a skull may now be added: physical anthropology, which was closely allied with medicine and to the layman was virtually synonymous with measuring skulls. Drawing aside a curtain to render its company of prostitutes visible to our gaze, he enacts the cardinal function of physical anthropology in its relentless dedication to measuring limbs. Though this figure drops out of *Les Demoiselles d'Avignon*, its ultimate form owes much to the *fin-de-siècle* science he may represent.

V

Having noted that an artistic rivalry with Matisse for leadership of the Parisian avant garde loomed large as Picasso undertook to paint *Les Demoiselles d'Avignon*, John Golding then asks: 'But why should he have returned to the subject [of the prostitute] at this particular moment in his life, and why should he have chosen it to effect a major stylistic revolution?'[72] We have already gone part of the way to answering this question. Physical anthropology, as was seen, discovered in the body of the prostitute the very antithesis of classical beauty, and Picasso was able to exploit this signification in order to effect a stylistic revolution which sought to overturn a classical order of representation. But in order to understand how his decision to depict a brothel scene might relate to the contest with Matisse requires a further detour through anthropology.

Katherine Arnold, a social anthropologist, has made a study of the interaction of prostitutes and their clients in a Latin American society.[73] In the absence of more local data her findings can be extrapolated to other Latin cultures where gender relations are governed by the ethos of *machismo*.[74] Arnold describes the brothel as a site where masculinity could be proven but also threatened and contested. The prostitute flouts the female stereotype of these patriarchal societies by her active sexuality and economic independence; because of her challenge to the self-image of the *macho* she is feared and reviled, and the brothel is consigned to the very outskirts of town. But at the same time the brothel is where males display their prowess in rivalry with each other: 'It is a *parranda machista*, an orgy of masculinity,' Arnold writes.[75] This tensely ambivalent scenario is precisely what Picasso stages in *Les Demoiselles d'Avignon*, a picture whose daring breach of convention constituted his bid for supremacy within the coterie of mainly male artists that comprised the Parisian avant garde (the fact that the picture was not exhibited publicly until 1916, and was initially shown only to fellow artists and friends, supports this view of its original purpose). The ambiguity and disruption of gender distinctions that was noted in studies for the *Demoiselles* is equivalent to the flouting of traditional sex roles by prostitutes that Arnold describes. One might speculate that this crossing of gender boundaries enables an identification by the artist with his female subjects; their flagrant violation of gender norms can then signify metaphorically *his* transgression of artistic norms.

It is now apparent why Picasso should create an image of castrating *femmes fatales* that apparently threaten his masculine narcissism. As Freud writes in the essay on the *Medusa's Head*: 'What arouses horror in oneself will produce the same effect upon the enemy against whom one is seeking to defend oneself.'[76] Picasso exploits this paradoxical strategy with resounding success: *Les Demoiselles d'Avignon* was greeted with reactions of horror and incomprehension by its first audience, but at the same time it consolidated his reputation as the most heroic of modern artists.

It was suggested at the outset of this essay that a vanguard artistic practice transpires in the reciprocal interplay between the law and its transgression. A remark ascribed to Picasso acknowledges the fundamental ambiguity of avant-garde transgressions, their complicity, with the interdiction: 'Rules are necessary even if they are bad, because the power of art [and artist] is affirmed in the rupture of taboos.'[77] What perhaps Picasso could not have realized was the extent to which, even within the revolutionary format of *Les Demoiselles d'Avignon*, he was in fact playing by dominant cultural rules.

David Lomas
Courtauld Institute of Art

NOTES

An earlier version of this paper was presented as a seminar at the Courtauld Institute in 1989 and subsequently at Essex University and the Ruskin School of Art, Oxford. I am especially grateful to Christopher Green for his advice and encouragement, and to Ludmilla Jordanova and Marcia Pointon for their helpful comments. My research on this topic was facilitated by a grant from the University of London Central Research Fund.

1 'Les études de morphologie humaine qui prennent chaque jour plus d'importance, contribuent à rapprocher la science et l'art sur un même terrain fertile en enseignements. Anthropologistes, médecines, artistes, archéologues, etc., ne peuvent qu'en bénéficier.' H. Meige, 'L'Infantilisme, le féminisme et les hermaphrodites antique', *L'Anthropologie*, 6, 1895. Henri Meige was a physician who published numerous articles on art and medicine and subsequently became Professor of Anatomy at the Ecole des Beaux Arts in Paris.

2 A. Salmon, 'Picasso', *L'Esprit Nouveau*, no. 1, May 1920, pp. 61–80. Quoted from M. McCully (ed.), *A Picasso Anthology*, London, 1981, pp. 138–44.

3 L. Steinberg, 'The Philosophical Brothel', *October* 44, Spring 1988, pp. 53–4. This essay, extremely important in moving discussion of the picture beyond purely formalist parameters, first appeared in *Art News*, vol. 71, Sept–Oct 1972.

4 M. Leja, '"Le Vieux Marcheur" and "Les deux Risque": Picasso, Prostitution, Venereal Disease, and Maternity, 1899–1907', *Art History*, vol. 8, no. 1, March 1985, pp. 66–81.

5 A comparable instance may be *Die Brücke* painting where the combination of stylistic primitivism and figures in decadent urban settings conveys a very different mood from the same primitivized figures in pastoral scenes.

6 W. Rubin, 'Picasso', in *'Primitivism' in 20th Century Art*, vol. 1, exh. cat., Museum of Modern Art, New York, 1984, p. 254.

7 S. Freud, 'Three Essays on the Theory of Sexuality', *The Pelican Freud Library*, vol. 7, London, 1987, pp. 160–1. Referring to inherited factors disturbing normal sexual development which 'might be described as "degenerative" and be regarded as an expression of inherited degeneracy', Freud relates the 'remarkable fact' that in over half of cases of severe neurosis treated by him there was a history of syphilitic disease in the father. As none of the patients bore physical stigmata of hereditary syphilis 'it was their abnormal sexual constitution that was to be regarded as the last echo of their syphilitic heritage.'

8 P. Burke, 'Strengths and Weaknesses of the History of Mentalities', *History of European Ideas*, vol. 7, no. 5, 1986, p. 439.

9 Though it concerns a slightly later period than that being considered here, a detailed study of the implicit link between classicism and nationalism in French cultural ideology is K. Silver, *Esprit de Corps*, London, 1989.

10 Degeneration and regeneration are discussed in detail in sections III and IV below.

11 In 1930 Bataille praises Picasso for his trenchant assault on classical form, writing in a *Documents* special issue about the artist that 'academic painting more or less corresponded to an elevation — without excess — of the spirit. In contemporary painting, however, the search for that which most ruptures the highest elevation, and for a blinding brilliance, has a share in the elaboration or decomposition of forms, though strictly speaking this is only noticeable in the paintings of Picasso.' G. Bataille, *Visions of Excess. Selected Writings, 1927–1939*, translated by A. Stoekl, Minneapolis, 1986, p. 58. The close involvement of Picasso with the *Documents* circle, which also included disaffected surrealists such as Michel Leiris and André Masson, doubtless encouraged this disfigurative impulse evident in his work in the early thirties.

On transgression as an avant-garde textual practice in the work of Bataille see S. Suleiman 'Pornography, Transgression, and the Avant-Garde: Bataille's *Story of the Eye*', in N. Miller (ed.), *The Poetics of Gender*, New York, 1986.

12 'Statement by Picasso: 1935', A.H. Barr, *Picasso. Fifty years of his Art*, New York, 1966, p. 273.

13 Reproduced in H. Bolliger, *Picasso's Vollard Suite*, London, 1987, plate 74.

14 C. Einstein, 'Picasso: the last decade', in M. McCully (ed.), op. cit., p. 168.

15 For a contrasting, rosier picture of Picasso's primitivism *c.* 1907, see P. Leighton, 'The White Peril and *L'Art nègre*: Picasso, Primitivism, and Anticolonialism', *The Art Bulletin* (December 1990), 72, n. 4, pp. 609–30.

16 See J. Harvey, 'Races specified, evolution transformed: The social context of scientific debates originating in the Société d'anthropologie de Paris 1859–1902', Ph.D., Harvard, 1983. For a general historical overview of French anthropology see D. Bender, 'The Development of French Anthropology', *Journal of the History of the Behavioural Sciences*, vol. 1, 1965.

17 ibid., p. 127.

18 P. Topinard, *Anthropology*, London, 1878, Introduction.

19 A. Quetelet, *Anthropométrie. ou Mesure des différentes facultés de l'homme*, Brussels 1870,

p. 243. It depicts a standing figure with outstretched hands touching two corners of a square whose diagonals also form the circumference of a circle.

20 The quotation is taken from Sir Joshua Reynolds's *Discourses on Art*, R. Wark (ed.), 2nd edition, New Haven and London, 1975, p. 44. Ideal Beauty for Reynolds consists in a general form divested of any particularity: it is 'a rule, obtained out of general nature, to contradict which is to fall into deformity' (p. 46). The shortest road to this perfect form is through a study of classical sculpture. An analogous principle lay behind the use of composite photographs by anthropologists 'to establish a visual representation of an ethnic "type" by combining the physical features of a number of individuals'. See M. Banta and C.M. Hinsley, *From Site to Sight. Anthropology, Photography, and the Power of Imagery*, Cambridge Mass., 1986, p. 102.

21 Topinard, op. cit., p. 316. See also articles by Dr Patin, 'Projet de canon scientifique à l'usage des artistes', *L'Anthropologie* T.9, 1989 and 'Application des données anthropologiques au contrôle des canons de proportions artistiques', *L'anthropologie* T.10, 1899. Numerous articles in *L'Anthropologie* reiterate the optimistic predictions of these authors about the benefits accruing to both sides from the rapprochement of art and anthropology (see note 1 above).

22 Quetelet, op. cit., p. 13. 'Un grand nombre de naturalistes et de philosphes se sont attachés à prouver, par les raisonnements plus ou moins concluants, l'unité de l'espèce humaine. Je crois avoir réussi à démontrer directement que non seulement cette unité existe, mais encore que notre espèce admet un type or module dont on peut facilement determiner les différentes proportions.'

23 ibid., p. 83. 'tout tend à établir, au contraire, que le type humain, dans nos climates, est identique avec celui qu'on déduit de l'observation des statues anciennes les plus regulières ....' The source used by Quetelet was C. Audran, *Les proportions du corps humain mesurées sur les plus belles statues de l'antiquité*, Paris, 1683.

24 Topinard, *Anthropology*, p. 316.

25 P. Topinard, *L'Homme dans la nature*, Paris, 1891, p. 125: 'L'art de sa nature est idéaliste, unitaire; il n'admet qu'un canon, qu'un type humain et autour de lui de simple variations, tandis que l'anthropologie, nécessairement réaliste, accepte des types et des canons multiples.' The idealist–realist opposition is frequently adduced in defence of anthropology.

26 Harvey, op. cit. Neo-Lamarkian precepts lay behind the belief 'that physical and cultural evolution were intimately tied, and that any cultural hierarchy was paralleled by an organic hierarchy'.

27 Charles Rochet, erstwhile professor at the Ecole des Beaux-Arts, was among the first to promote anthropometry as a useful aid to artists. See his *Cours d'anthropologie appliqués à l'enseignement des beaux-arts*, Paris, 1869 and *Traité d'anatomie d'anthropologie et ethnographic appliquées aux Beaux-Arts*, Paris, 1886.

28 Topard, *Anthropology*, p. 12.

29 The intersections of art and medicine in the work of Richer (1849–1933) are complex and deserving of a separate study in their own right. See Nadine Simon-Dhouailly, *La Leçon de Charcot*, exh. cat., Musée de l'Assistance Publique, Paris, 1986. Included among his writings on anthropology and artistic proportion are *L'anatomie dans l'art. Proportions du corps humain. Canons artistiques et canons scientifiques*, Paris, 1893 and *Anatomie artistique. Descriptions des formes extérieures du corps humain au repos et dans les principaux mouvements*, Paris, 1890.

30 The source was identified by John Golding. See L.D. Henderson, 'Xrays and the Quest for Invisible Reality in the Art of Kupka, Duchamp, and the Cubists', *Art Journal*, Winter 1988, pp. 331–2.

31 See *Les Demoiselles d'Avignon*, vol. 1, exh. cat., Musée Picasso, Paris, 1988, pp. 182–5. The image reproduced here was drawn on a loose sheet. The studies have been assigned to April–May 1907 coinciding with the dates of the Daumier exhibition which was held at the Rosenberg Gallery in Paris. Hence they immediately precede work on the *Demoiselles* itself and are integrally related to its primitivist project, even though the bilateral symmetry of the studies is ultimately rejected.

32 Y.-A. Bois, 'Painting as Trauma', *Art in America*, June 1988, p. 140.

33 P. Daix, 'L'Historique des *Demoiselles d'Avignon* révisé à l'aide des carnets de Picasso', in *Les Demoiselles d'Avignon* vol. 2, op. cit., pp. 505–06. There are several paintings which are clearly offshoots of this exercise in proportion, including *Woman with Clasped Hands* (Z.II 2,662), *Woman with Yellow Blouse* (Z.II 1,43), and *Male Nude with Clasped Hands* (Z.XXVI,284).

34 Picasso was already looking to Iberian sculpture for such a model. Zervos, in an unpublished manuscript based on conversations with Picasso in the spring of 1939, writes: 'In the essential elements of this art he found the necessary support to transgress academic prohibitions, to exceed established measures, and to put all aesthetic rules into question.' ('Dans les éléments essentiels de cet art il trouvait l'appui nécessaire pour transgresser les prohibitions académiques, dépasser les mesures établies, remettre toute légalité esthétique en question.') Cited in J.J. Sweeney, 'Picasso and Iberian Sculpture', *Art Bulletin*, 23, 1941, who relates the figure pose of the proportional studies to a

particular Iberian votive bronze from Despenapperos.

35 M. Golberg, *La Morale des lignes*, Paris, 1908. p. 28: 'ce qu'on appelle la deformation est le principe même de la création humaine, notre anima Dei!' Interestingly, Golberg demonstrates his awareness of an anthropometric discourse on physiognomy by referring at one point (p. 16) to the 'science anthropométrique de M. Bertillon'; the crimonologist Alphonse Bertillon pioneered a system for identifying criminals based on a profile of physiognomic features — see note 48 below. The interrelations of Goldberg and Picasso are explored by Neil Cox in La Morale des lignes: Picasso 1907–10: Modernist Reception; the Subversion of Content; and the Lesson of Caricature, Ph.D. thesis, University of Essex, 1991.

36 M. Raphael, *Proudhon, Marx, Picasso. Trois études sur la sociologie de l'art*, Paris, 1933. Quotations are taken from the English translation by John Tagg — the first two from p. 129 and the last from p. 138. Raphael anticipates the more recent discussion of caricature and primitivism in the work of Picasso by Adam Gopnik, in 'High and Low: Caricature, Primitivism, and the Cubist Portrait', *Art Journal*, Winter 1983, pp. 371–6.

It was mentioned above that some of the studies of proportion were made on the catalogue of a Daumier exhibition held at the Rosenberg Gallery from 15 April to 6 May 1907. This fact assumes added interest in the light of Raphael's remarks, made without any possible knowledge of the drawings' existence.

37 See Harvey, op. cit., pp. 115–16 and 128ff. on the Société d'Anthropologie and colonialism. The Société would pronounce on the inherent capacity for progress among native inhabitants of French colonies (p. 115). Harvey remarks that in the case of Clémence Royer, a female member of the Société, a serial 'ranking of racial groups explicitly served a vision of colonization' (p. 146). But the Société was far from unanimous in its views on this matter. See also Banta and Hinsley, *From Site to Sight*, op. cit., pp. 101–02.

38 See S. Gould, *The Mismeasure of Man*, New York, 1981.

39 R. Verneau, 'Les caractères physiques de la femme dans les races', in vol. 1 (1908) of *La femme. Dans la nature, dans les moeurs, dans la légende, dans la société* (4 vols.).

There were equivalent German and English texts: H.H. Ploss, *Das Weib in der Natur und Volkerkunde. Anthropologische Studien*, Leipzig, 1884, which was reprinted in numerous editions and translated into English in 1935, and T.A. Joyce and N.W. Thomas (eds.), *Women of all Nations. A Record of Their Characteristics, Habits, Manners, Customs and Influence*, London, 1908.

40 ibid. p. 511: 'on tire la conclusion que les variétés que l'on rencontre dans les groupes éthniques correspondent à autant de stades de l'evolution humaine.' Gould, op. cit., p. 32 also remarks upon the blithe intrusion of highly subjective aesthetic judgements into the descriptions of physical anthropologists.

41 R. Nye, *Crime, Madness and Politics in Modern France. The Medical Concept of National Decline*, New Jersey, 1984, chapter 5. Nye states succinctly that by the turn of the century 'the German menace was regarded as the sign of French decadence.'

42 See R. Harris, *Murders and Madness, Medicine, Law, and Society in the Fin de Siècle*, Oxford, 1989. The fortunes of degeneration were not confined to medicine alone, as the arrival on the literary scene of the Decadents attests. The impact of notions of degeneracy on culture and politics as well as science are explored in S.L. Gilman, J.E. Chamberlain (eds.), *Degeneration. The Dark Side of Progress*, New York, 1985. A more recent survey of the concept of degeneration in its wider European dimension is D. Pick, *Faces of Degeneration. A European Disorder, c. 1848–c. 1918*, Cambridge, 1989.

43 P. Tarnowsky, *Etude anthropométrique sur les prostituées et les voleuses*, Paris, 1889, p. 36: '*Les anomalies du visage* se traduisaient fréquemment par de l'asymétrie, du prognatisme, une disproportion sensible des diverses parties de la figure.'

See in addition Dr E. Laurent, 'Prostitution et dégénérescence', *Annales médico-psychologiques* t.X, November 1899, pp. 353–81. This article makes frequent mention of Tarnowsky whose study was also the source used by Lombroso (noted 53 below).

44 Nye, op. cit., p. 65.

45 Carlo Ginzburg traces this back to the system of connoisseurship proposed by Morelli. In 'Morelli, Freud and Sherlock Holmes: Clues and Scientific Method', *History Workshop*, 1980, p. 25.

46 Tarnowsky, op. cit., p. 25: 'Les prostituées professionnelles accusent en moyenne un amoindrissement des principaux diamètres de l'encéphale de plusieurs millimètres [. . .] L'amoindrissement de la boîte crânienne est en relation directe avec un amoindrissement de son contenu, ce qui permet de supposer une différence relative dans la quantité du cerveau [. . .] différence tout au détriment du developpement intellectuel et surtout moral des prostituées.' This is further discussed in A. Corbin *Les filles de noce. Misère sexuelle et prostitution (19e et 20e siècles)*, Paris, 1978, part C: 'Prostitution, Folie et dégénérescence'.

47 A cartoon in the popular satiric journal *L'assiette au beurre* in 1905 which William Rubin rightly compares with *Les Demoiselles d'Avignon* encapsulates the worst of these stereotypes (*Les Demoiselles d'Avignon* vol. 2, op. cit., p. 477).

The caption reads LA MEILLEURE GARANTIE and it depicts the madam of a brothel greeting two prospective bourgeois clients: 'I wouldn't say to you that these girls have their "O" Levels, but they've all been to the Pasteur Institute.' A wall poster in the background states that the women have been vaccinated for venereal disease, which is one meaning of her remark. But it is also a malicious commentary on the feeble intellect of her charges who bear unmistakeably simian features. By laughing at this *double entendre* a male reader of the journal could ventilate his own anxieties about contracting syphilis, rife during the Belle Epoque and no joke if you got it. The comic mechanism entails a fusion of meaning and displacement of affect: anxiety is transformed into hostility toward the prostitute, couched in the guise of a joke at her expense. Science, with the theory of *dégénérescence*, just as insidiously channelled fears about syphilis into a scapegoating of the prostitute. And to glance from the cartoon back to the *Demoiselles* it is evident that high art was not immune to this either.

48 Though Pierre Daix later moderated the stance adopted in his article 'Il n'y a pas d'art nègre dans *Les Demoiselles d'Avignon*', *Gazette des Beaux-Arts*, vol. 76, 1970, the most recent essay by Rubin concurs that the influence of tribal art on the mask of the seated demoiselle is minimal. Cf. W. Rubin, 'La genèse des *Demoiselles d'Avignon*', in *Les Demoiselles d'Avignon* vol. 2, op. cit, p. 486.

49 Rubin, 'Picasso', op. cit., p. 265.

50 Captions clearly identify them all as malignant tumours. See *Les Demoiselles D'Avignon*, vol. 2, op. cit., p. 421. These photographs are reproduced from an article by L. Jacquet, 'Epithéliome développé sur une cicatrice de lupus' in E. Besnier, A. Fournier et al., *Le Musée de l'Hopital Saint-Louis. Iconographie des maladies cutanées et syphilitiques avec texte explicatif*, Paris, 1895–97, pp. 191–6. None of the syphilitic lesions illustrated elsewhere in the text are associated with the gross deformity of these advanced cancers.

It is important for my argument to clear up the confusion caused by this misidentification. While degeneration most certainly was perceived as a cause of deformity, Tarnowsky is emphatic that 'acquired syphilis plays no role in malformations of the head', op. cit., p. 34 ('la syphilis acquise ne jouait aucun rôle dans la malformation de la tête.').

51 Daix, op. cit., p. 530.

52 Tarnowsky, op. cit., pp. 36–7. Whilst discounting *aquired* syphilis as a cause of facial deformity, Tarnowsky allows that *congenital* syphilis may be a cause in some cases. Since the degeneracy hypothesis lumped together causes and effects these may then be included as stigmata of degeneration. She writes: 'As for hereditary syphilis, it is very probable that a certain number of cranial defects were of this origin. From this point of view parental syphilis joins those other pernicious influences transmitted by parents to their descendants, such as alcohol abuse, consumption, nervous and mental illness etc.' (p. 35) ('Pour ce qui est de la syphilis héréditaire, il est très probable qu'un certain nombre de ces crânes défectueux lui devaient leur provenance. Mais sous ce rapport, la syphilis des parents rentre dans le nombre des autres influences pernicieuses transmises par les parents à leur descendance, telles que l'abus de l'alcool, le phtisie, les maladies nerveuses et mentales etc.')

53 Quotations are from C. Lombroso, G. Gerrero, *The Female Offender*, London, 1895, p. 85. A French translation from the original Italian was made in 1896. It is worthy of note that, unlike Tarnowsky and Lombroso, earlier authors such as Parent-Duchatelet had tended to conclude that the female prostitute could *not* be distinguished by her physical traits from other women (Corbin, op. cit., pp. 23–4).

54 ibid., p. 102.

55 'tendance au retour atavique vers la période de l'hermaphrodisme'. Cited by Alain Corbin who remarks that Tarnowsky and Lombroso were both very influential in France: 'Bien qu'ils aient été l'objet de sévères critiques, leurs travaux, rapidement traduite en français, ont fortement influencé le discours prostitutionnel entre 1890 et 1914.' Corbin, op. cit., p. 441.

56 G.M. Soularue, 'Recherches sur les dimensions des os et les proportions squelettiques de l'homme dans les différentes races', *Bulletins de la société d'anthropologie de Paris*, 18 May 1899, p. 346. '[. . .] Il y a entre les différentes races une sorte de sériation qui correspond à peu près à l'ancienneté de civilisation de chacune d'elles. La race qui présente la plus grande différence entre l'homme et la femme est la race jaune, la première civilisé; puis vient la race européene, puis les Américains. Les Nègres et les Arabes, qui présentent le degré de civilisation le moins avancé, où la femme travaille avec l'homme à d'aussi durs labeurs, présentent la plus petite différence sexuelle. Nous avons vu [. . .] que la femme nègre et l'homme nègre avaient des indices des sections d'os égaux, ce qui vient confirmer l'idée que nous énonçons.'

57 Quoted in D. Silverman, 'Nature, Nobility, and Neurology: The Ideological Origins of "Art Nouveau" in France, 1889–1900', Ph.D. Princeton, 1983, chapter 3.

58 Lecture at the Royal Academy, London, November 1988. Note an interesting point of comparison with H. Meige, 'Deux cas d'hermaphrodisme antique', *Nouvelle iconographic de la Salpêtriére*, 1895, pp. 56–64. Meige believes that antique sculptures of hermaphrodites are based on natural prototypes (see below) the

most common forms of which he describes, adding that 'more rarely it is a case of a muscular male body with narrow hips, a large and strong chest upon which the artist has applied two voluminous breasts.' ('Plus rarement, il s'agit d'une forme mâle aux muscles accentués, aux hanches étroites, à la poitrine large et fort sur laquelle l'artiste a appliqué deux seins volumineux.')

59 See *Les Demoiselles d'Avignon* vol. 1, op. cit., cat. 36.

60 See, for example, Dr R. Verneau, *Les Bassin dans les sexes et dans les races*, Paris, 1895.

61 T. Laqueur, 'Orgasm, Generation, and the Politics of Reproductive Biology', *Representations* 14, Spring 1986, pp. 1–41. Laqueur comments that in eighteenth-century France feminist and anti-feminist writers alike increasingly endeavoured to find 'in the facts of biology a justification for cultural and political differences between the sexes' p. 18.

62 H. Meige, 'L'Infantilisme, le féminisme et les hermaphrodites antiques', op. cit. The distortion of the word feminism by these authors evidently packed a reactionary political punch.

63 Dr F. Heckel, *Culture physique et cures d'exercise (myothérapie)*, Paris, 1913. 'La seule excuse réelle que l'on puisse trouver aux hommes à qui incombe la réorganisation que je prévois ici, c'est qu'ils sont imbus des idées des plus fausses sur la dégénérescence physique inélectuable et héréditaire. Ils ignorent à quel point la matière vivante est plastique et ardente vers la régénérescence.'

64 ibid. 'Donner dans un Etat un développement égal à l'éducation physique et intellectuelle, c'est accroître le rendement individual et le rendement économique; c'est augmenter la richesse nationale; c'est donner à tous les meilleures garanties de bonheur par la santé; c'est aussi accroître les possibilités de l'expansion hors de la métropole, et c'est remédier, en donnant à chaque homme confiance en soi et en l'avenir de sa descendance, à la dépopulation qui n'est en réalité que l'expression d'un état mental opposé.' (p. 494.)

65 Nye, op. cit., p. 319.

66 ibid., p. 327.

67 G. Apollinaire, 'La danse est un sport', *La Culture physique*, February 1907 and 'Guy de Maupassant athlète', *La culture physqiue*, March 1907. Reprinted in *Oeuvres complétes de Guillaume Apollinaire* vol. 4, N. Décaudin (ed.), Paris, 1966, pp. 665–79.

68 'L'alcoolisme et la dépopulation, ces plaies de la France, trouveraient dans la multiplication des bals et soirées dansantes un remède certain, sinon absolu. Et cela suffit, je pense, à montrer l'importance morale d'un exercise à la fois sain et divertissant.' *Oeuvres complètes*, op. cit., p. 668.

69 Reason — like classicism — was regarded in contemporary discourse as a defining French characteristic: '[...] par certains côtés de son talent, se rattache à la tradition la plus française sinon la plus classique'; '[...] une importante partie de son existence à son développement physique'; '[...] il mourut la raison obscurcie.'

70 See also the Basel study reproduced as catalogue number 22 in *Les Demoiselles d'Avignon* vol. 2, op. cit.

71 The reading based on Picasso's presumed phobia about syphilis is due to Rubin. The other suggestions are made by Steinberg.

72 John Golding, 'The Triumph of Picasso', *The New York Review of Books*, 21 July 1988, p. 21.

73 K. Arnold, 'The Introduction of Poses to a Peruvian Brothel and Changing Images of Male and Female', in J. Blacking (ed.), *The Anthropology of the Body*, London, 1977.

74 Specifically, the Andalusian culture from which Picasso originated. See D. Gilmore, *Aggression and Community. Paradoxes of Andalusian Culture*, New Haven, 1987, chapter 7: 'Machismo'.

75 Arnold, op. cit., p. 187.

76 S. Freud, 'Medusa's Head', 1940 [1922], in *The Standard Edition of the Complete Psychological Works of Sigmund Freud*, London, 1960, vol 18, pp. 273–4. I am very much indebted to John Nash for allowing me to read his unpublished essay on the *Demoiselles* in which he considers the picture in terms of castration anxiety and the strategies by which this is allayed. 'Pygmalion and Medusa. An Essay on Picasso's *Les Demoiselles d'Avignon*', 1983 — this paper is a longer version of a BBC Radio 3 broadcast of 24 June 1970.

77 'Il faut une règle même si elle est mauvaise, parce que la puissance de l'art s'affirme dans la rupture des tabous. Supprimer les obstacles, ce n'est pas la liberté.' Cited by G. Scarpeta, 'Picasso après-coup', in *Le Dernier Picasso*, exh. cat., Musée National d'Art Moderne, Paris, 1988, p. 120.

Art History Vol. 16 No. 3 September 1993 0141—6790 pp. 447–469

PICTURES FIT FOR A QUEEN: PETER PAUL RUBENS AND THE MARIE DE' MEDICI CYCLE

GERALDINE A. JOHNSON

Peter Paul Rubens devoted a significant portion of his artistic career to painting images either for or of women. He painted his two wives on many occasions and he was commissioned to paint religious works and portraits for important female patrons such as Archduchess Isabella, ruler of the Spanish Netherlands, and the Countess of Arundel.[1] At the same time, in his mythological-allegorical works created almost exclusively for male patrons, Rubens painted innumerable nymphs and goddesses, often nude or only partially clad. Indeed, Rubens's development of a pictorial rhetoric based primarily on the display of the bare female body is so closely tied to his artistic identity that the adjective 'Rubensian' is still current to this day. It was only in the twenty-four canvases he painted for one of the two long galleries of Marie de' Medici's newly built Luxembourg Palace in Paris, however, that Rubens combined these two aspects of his art: a female patron and his usual visual language.[2] The Medici cycle is the only major example in this period of a large-scale, semi-public cycle dedicated exclusively to glorifying the life of a contemporary woman. When Rubens fulfilled this unusual commission by using a visual rhetoric of exposed female bodies to represent history-as-allegory or myth, he inadvertently created a situation in which the cultural presuppositions of the cycle's contemporary viewers — mainly members of the French court and important visitors from abroad — ran headlong into the personal and political messages the Queen had hoped the cycle would project.[3] It is precisely the uniqueness of the Medici cycle in terms of what is represented as well as how it is represented that acts to reveal the gender-specific nature of Rubens's strategies for visual representation in general.

The Medici cycle's tensions are particularly well illustrated by one of the most interesting images in the series, the *Presentation of Marie de' Medici's Portrait to Henri IV*.[4] This painting demonstrates the consequences of Rubens's decision to use his usual visual rhetoric in the special case of a woman who is both the patron and the portrayed, the viewer as well as the viewed (plate 30). In this image, the French King, Henri IV, gazes adoringly at the portrait of his bride-to-be, Marie de' Medici, proffered to him by a group of heavenly deities. Marie de' Medici, meanwhile, stares out directly at the outside viewer. The Queen is circumscribed

30 P. P. Rubens, *The Presentation of Marie de' Medici's Portrait to Henri IV*, 1622–5. Louvre Museum, Paris. (Cliché des musées nationaux, © Photo RMN)

by the black, painted frame around her image which serves to turn her presence into a 'mere' work of art which can be scrutinized at leisure by the outside beholder, by Henri IV, and by the gods and goddesses. At the same time, Marie de' Medici breaks out of being 'merely' artificial and decorative through her confident and unflinching outward gaze which gives her the power of direct communication with the audience, a power denied most of the other figures in the image including the King himself. Male and female, subject and object, levels of reality and artifice: the complexities of the *Presentation of the Portrait* can serve as an introduction to the ambiguities which exist between the representation of women and women as representation in seventeenth-century culture.

Ever since the seventeenth century, viewers of Rubens's Medici cycle have commented on the contrasts between the artist's imagery and the historical circumstances surrounding his patron, Marie de' Medici. In the later part of the century, Félibien lamented: 'For, I beg you, just what do Cupid, Hymen, Mercury, the Graces, Tritons, [and] Nereids have to do with . . . Marie de Médicis?'[5] More recent critics have also remarked on the disjunctions between Rubens's rhetoric of allegory and the historical realities of Marie de' Medici's life.[6] Even Rubens himself complained that some visitors to the Medici gallery had 'not grasped the true meaning' of some of the paintings and had 'taken amiss' certain subjects.[7] One important factor in these problems, indeed, an important factor in the cycle's lack of immediate influence both artistically and politically, is the inherent conflict between Rubens's visual language and the fact that his patron was a woman.[8] Although some scholars have explored Marie de' Medici's role as a female patron, most of the extensive research on the cycle has concentrated on deciphering what its individual images mean. The personal and political references of the allegorical figures, the links to classical texts and emblem books, and the relationship to traditional 'female' iconographies have all been assessed, but even recent studies have largely ignored how Rubens's language of visual representation was itself also affected by his patron's history and gender and how this in turn might have affected contemporary viewers of the cycle.[9] In other words, deciphering *what* the images mean is not enough; one must also explore *how* they mean.[10]

The Medici cycle, completed in 1625, falls roughly at the midpoint of Rubens's artistic career.[11] The apparent contradictions between Rubens's representational strategies and the special demands of having a female patron can be explained in part by the history and circumstances of the commission. The surviving contracts and correspondence suggest that the project was to a certain extent a commission by committee.[12] The Abbé Maugis, Richelieu, Peiresc, Rubens and Marie de' Medici herself as well as others at the French court all played at least some role in the final choice of subjects.[13] In addition, the fact that much of the planning and execution had to be done in two different places, Paris and Antwerp, over more than three years (January 1622 to May 1625), further explains some of the cycle's inconsistencies. Even more importantly, over the course of the project, the delicate political situation between Marie de' Medici and her son, Louis XIII, was in constant flux, and her aims and tactics for personal propaganda through the Medici cycle were repeatedly adapted to the changing political climate.

Following the assassination in 1610 of her husband Henri IV, Marie de' Medici had ruled as Regent for her minor son for four years until he gained his majority.

At first, Louis XIII had been content to allow his mother to continue to exercise her power and he readily praised the 'widow who happily governs the people, . . . sends the armies, . . . chooses the captains, . . . goes on campaign, . . . [and] directs the triumphs.'[14] By 1617, however, relations between mother and son had deteriorated to the point that Marie de' Medici had been banished to Blois and in 1619 she was openly supporting the grandees who were trying to start a rebellion against the King. By 1620 Louis XIII and his mother were reconciled and in 1621, Marie de' Medici was asked to rejoin the King's council. It was during this truce that the Queen Mother commissioned Rubens to paint his series of large canvases for the main west gallery of her new Parisian palace, the Luxembourg, a space which was to serve as a grand approach and waiting area for visitors to her state apartments.[15] She chose this prominent setting in order to impress upon visitors from the French court and especially upon her son, the King, the veracity of her carefully selected and edited version of her life's main events, an important part of her attempts to regain her son's trust and hence some of her former power and influence.[16] The reconciliation of mother and son was only temporary, however, for by 1631 Marie de' Medici was forced to flee permanently from France and had to live out her days in exile.[17] In terms of solidifying her personal and political position in France, the Medici cycle had not been effective or, at least, not effective enough as an act of visual propaganda.[18]

Before the cycle and continuing after its completion, Rubens developed a pictorial language for allegory which was ultimately based on the symbolic display of nude female bodies. When he adapted this rhetoric to the Medici cycle commission in which the primary heroic subject was a woman, Rubens's deployment of nude female bodies as allegorical figures inevitably created friction between the messages he and his patron intended the paintings to project and the visual language used to represent them. In the *Education of Marie de' Medici*, for example, Rubens used the instantly recognizable image of the nude Three Graces as an attribute of the Queen's childhood education (plate 31). The instrument-playing male god, Orpheus,[19] assumes the role of the implied heterosexual male viewer by gazing directly at the nude women, whose bare flesh is highlighted all the more by the sharp contrast between their brightly lit, pale skin and the much darker surrounding space.[20] One of the Graces looks coyly out to the viewer and thus it is she alone, the only one implying an awareness of the presence of the beholder standing before the painting, who teasingly tries to hide her nudity.[21]

The *Education of Marie de' Medici* seems to illustrate the relationship found in many of Rubens's mythological-allegorical works in which a male viewer (implicitly standing before the work and, in many cases, explicitly depicted within the work) scrutinizes a female nude. Unlike Rubens's many versions of the *Judgement of Paris* or his *Nymph and Satyr* or *Shepherd* paintings intended primarily for the decoration of the private apartments of male patrons, however, the projected audience for the *Education of Marie de' Medici* included two very different categories of viewers, namely, the Queen herself as patron of the cycle and, equally importantly, the male courtiers of the French court who made formal visits to the Luxembourg Palace. The inclusion of the Three Graces was a means of asserting the Queen's femininity. At the same time, the young Marie de' Medici is depicted turning her back on these women and instead concentrating intensely on the lessons of

31 P. P. Rubens, *The Education of Marie de' Medici*, 1622–5. Louvre Museum, Paris. (Cliché des musées nationaux, © Photo RMN)

32 P. P. Rubens, *Marie de' Medici as Queen Triumphant*, 1622–5. Louvre Museum, Paris. (Cliché des musées nationaux, © Photo RMN)

the goddess of Wisdom, Minerva, dressed in armour. It is the figure of Orpheus who summarizes the inherent problems of using nude female bodies in conjunction with a message about a woman pursuing the then still primarily masculine arts of learning:[22] like the implied heterosexual male viewers of the painting as envisioned by Rubens, Orpheus can only concentrate his gaze on the enticing nude Graces, not on the young Marie de' Medici who should be the work's main focus. Thus, by using his usual visual rhetoric of the allegorical female nude and by including a viewer in the person of Orpheus who acts out the normative heterosexual male response to this visual language, Rubens has unwittingly demonstrated how distracting his representational strategy based on the nude female body can be to the painting's viewers. Rather than proving to the French courtiers that Marie de' Medici's primary interest lies in learning the art of wise government, Rubens's nude female allegorical figures act instead as distractions from the Queen's intended message by reminding male viewers of the dangers associated with female sexuality in seventeenth-century culture in general.[23]

The motif of the exposed female body, especially the exposed breast, occurs in several other paintings in the Medici cycle. In the *Meeting of Marie de' Medici and Henri IV in Lyons*, Marie de' Medici looks down submissively and presents her bare breast to her husband as a sign of her acceptance of her role as wife and mother subservient to her King.[24] The composition echoes a Coronation of the Virgin and, in fact, Marie de' Medici's exposed breast is Virgin-like, the ultimate symbol of woman as nurturer and procreator in an ordered, male-dominated universe.[25] Indeed, this image is one of several in the cycle which explicitly link Marie de' Medici to her namesake, the Virgin Mary.[26] In the *Peace of Marie de' Medici and Louis XIII Confirmed in Heaven*, the allusion is to an Assumption of the Virgin. Like the Virgin, Marie de' Medici becomes both the mother and mystical bride of her son, her bare breast acting as a sign of this dual role. Rubens in fact used the bare breast as an attribute of the Virgin in several paintings he produced on the theme of the Virgin and Child.[27] In both the *Meeting in Lyons* and the *Peace Confirmed in Heaven*, the Queen Mother's bare breast emphasizes her feminine and motherly qualities. Rubens used these attributes to depict Marie de' Medici as powerful precisely because of her gender, because of her ability to bear and nurture the King's children, thereby ensuring the continuation of the dynasty.[28] This image of a woman defined, empowered and sanctified through the attributes of her gender appears in other works painted by Rubens throughout his career which also accentuate the nurturing breast as the principal attribute of such a woman. In the Dulwich *Mars, Venus and Cupid* or the Rijksmuseum *Cimon and Pero*, a woman's breast gives life to both a young male child and an old male prisoner. In paintings such as the *Allegory of Peace and War* in London or the *Origins of the Milky Way* in Madrid, the mother's breast is the symbol of the establishment (or re-establishment) of an ordered world, indeed, an ordered universe.

In other paintings by Rubens, however, bare breasts carry much more negative associations. Instead of being positive symbols of the submissive and nurturing wife and mother, bare breasts allude to the dangers of female seduction. This is seen perhaps most powerfully in Rubens's London *Samson and Delilah*.[29] In this painting, Delilah's provocatively bared breasts, emphasized by the luminously painted flesh tones which are highlighted all the more by the contrast with the much darker surrounding space, are symbols of a woman's ability to use her sexuality to incapacitate and emasculate an unwary man. Delilah uses her passive female sexuality symbolized by her bare breasts in order to exercise vengeance and control, traits associated in this period primarily with active male heroes and a very different type of meaning for the exposed female breast than that associated with the Virgin as wife and mother.[30]

Seventeenth-century culture in general seems to have held similarly ambiguous views about the significance of the bare female breast.[31] The bare breast was depicted as a positive attribute in images of the Virgin Mary as well as in the tradition of heroic female portraiture. Moralizing works such as Juvernay's *Discours particulier contre la vanité des femmes de ce temps*, on the other hand, stressed the horrible fate which awaited any woman who dared to bare her breasts in public.[32] The frontispiece of this book shows a woman baring her breasts in a low-cut dress about to be attacked by a devil rising up out of the mouth of Hell. Other works such as Polman's 1635 sermon on *Le Chancre ou Couvre-sein féminin* viciously attacked women who displayed their bare breasts in public, calling them whores who 'fling out carnal thoughts between those two mounds of flesh; they let villanous desires lodge in the trough between those bare breasts.'[33] This type of vitriolic assault on the bare female breast crops up in French texts published throughout the seventeenth century.[34] In addition to the textual evidence provided by sermons and pamphlets, the pervasive notion in this period that the female breast was something powerful and potentially dangerous can be detected in the widespread practice of putting babies out to nurse, often to wetnurses in the country, thereby keeping even the nursing breast of middle- and upper-class women controlled by husbands and hidden from public view.[35] Thus, although Rubens and his patron certainly intended the Queen's bare breasts in paintings such as the *Meeting at Lyons* and the *Peace Confirmed in Heaven* to be viewed positively as signs of her submissive and nurturing role as wife and mother, seventeenth-century culture in general and Rubens in works such as his *Delilah* in particular would have conditioned male viewers to see this attribute as potentially negative in its dangerous associations with female seduction, sexuality and power.

The problems contemporary visitors to the Medici gallery faced in trying to interpret Marie de' Medici's bare breasts are intimately related to the question of context: if the Queen was clearly portrayed as exclusively Virgin-like when exposing her breasts, the cycle's viewers would have understood this display in a positive context. In several of the images, however, Rubens and his patron chose to pair bare female breasts with attributes normally associated in the seventeenth century with male power, a combination which would have reminded viewers instead of the well-known topos of the dangerous power of women.[36] In the *Felicity of the Regency* and the portrait of *Marie de' Medici as Queen Triumphant*, for example, the Queen's exposed breast is juxtaposed with attributes usually associated with male rulers (scales of justice, sceptre, orb, throne chair) in the case of the former and with male warriors (helmet, armour, cannon, guns) in the latter (plate 32). Although Rubens and his patron clearly wanted these paintings to act as positive affirmations of the Queen's abilities, in spite of her gender, to govern wisely and lead France to glory, the seventeenth-century view of women as potentially dangerous temptresses like Delilah who used their femininity to gain power over men meant that these images at the same time inadvertently allowed for very negative interpretations of Marie de' Medici's intentions.

In France, the Salic law specifically prohibited women from inheriting the throne.[37] The fact that this law was circumvented three times in less than a century — for the regencies of Catherine and Marie de' Medici and for Anne of Austria later in the seventeenth century — simply confirmed male courtiers' fears of women gaining power at their expense.[38] A text published at the same time that Rubens was working on the Medici cycle made clear allusion to the perceived dangers of Marie de' Medici's assumption of power when it condemned the

> . . . true trickery [of] that superb Assyrian Queen Semiramis, who massacred her husband and son . . . in order to rule over men and, so much did she want to imitate men's actions, she even dared to renounce woman's dress and clothe herself in the royal mantle.[39]

The combination of bare female breasts with the clothing and attributes normally associated with male rulers in paintings such as the *Felicity of the Regency* or the *Queen Triumphant* would thus have reminded contemporary viewers of the then-current topos of the Queen as a woman trying to usurp traditional male power. The fact that some of the cycle's images could easily have been (mis)interpreted in this way points to a fundamental problem: as an unusual, indeed, unique type of project in this period, the Medici cycle as a whole was unable to provide its seventeenth-century viewers with a sufficiently stable or unambiguous context which would prevent such negative readings of its images and its patron's intentions.

This friction between Marie de' Medici's desire to regain political power and the suspicion seventeenth-century patriarchal culture had of powerful women is reflected in the conflicting portrayals of women in printed books of the period. A popular literary genre in the seventeenth century was the so-called 'gallery' of famous women, biographical compilations of the lives of female 'worthies' from the Bible, mythology and history which served as positive examples for contemporary women.[40] At the same time that authors such as Pierre Le Moyne in *La gallerie des femmes fortes* (1647) and Jacques Du Bosc in *La femme héroïque* (1645) used women of the past as heroic examples for the female sex, other texts of the period afforded much more negative readings of many of these same exemplary women. In works such as the anonymous *Les Singeries des femmes de ce temps descouvertes* and the *Tableau historique des ruses et subtilitez des femmes*, both published in 1623 while Rubens was designing the Medici cycle, famous women from the past were presented as dangerous figures whose deceitful seductions allowed them to tempt and then triumph over men.[41] Thus, while the biblical Susanna or Judith or the ancient Queen Semiramis could be praised as worthy models in some (con)texts, they could also serve as dire warnings of the dangers of female sexuality and power in other (con)texts. By combining images of female nudity with images of female power on behalf of a female patron, the Medici cycle therefore inevitably created a context which evoked many of this period's complicated and often contradictory notions of the nature of female sexuality and its relationship to power.

This wide range of meanings associated with female nudity can be further illustrated by another project undertaken by Rubens shortly before he began the Medici cycle. In about 1620 Rubens designed an engraving of *Susanna and the Elders* which he dedicated to Anna Roemer Visscher, an important member of Dutch humanist literary circles who was also particularly admired for her virtue.[42] The dedication included an appropriately chaste and moralizing inscription calling Susanna, whose nude body forms the focal point of the composition, a 'Pudicitiae exemplar'. Originally, however, Rubens had planned to dedicate a different *Susanna* print to Anna Visscher. This print was finally executed in 1624 but, instead of a chaste dedication to Anna Visscher, it had a rather bawdy inscription which would have been much less appropriate for association with a highly respected woman even though the nude figure of Susanna remained basically the same in both prints (plate 33).[43] Instead of a comment about female chastity and virtue, this latter print was inscribed with the motto 'Turpe Senilis Amor', a warning about the absurdity of old men being tempted to lust after pretty young girls.[44] The heterosexual male viewer, included symbolically within these images in the figures of the lecherous old men about to assault the cowering Susanna, could have interpreted either depiction of female nudity as potentially dangerous. It was only thanks to the prints' different inscriptions that a viewer was able to determine whether Susanna's nudity was to be understood as a sign of innocent virtue or as a sign of seductive vice. Rubens was able to use very similar compositions for

33 P. P. Rubens (design), *Susanna and the Elders*, engraved by Pontius, 1624. Courtesy of the Fogg Art Museum, Harvard University Art Museums, Cambridge, Mass., Gift of Belinda L. Randall from the Collection of John Witt Randall

quite different purposes only because a text was included in order to provide the interpretive context necessary for a 'correct' reading of the significance of each image's nudity.

In other instances, even the presence of an inscribed text was inadequate for ensuring that an exposed female body was understood 'correctly'. This appears to have been the case in Rubens's title-page design for Balthasar Cordier's edition of commentaries on St Luke's Gospel, the *Catena sexaginta quinque graecorum patrum in S. Lucam*, published in Antwerp in 1628. Here, even the context provided by the title-page's text was not enough to prevent Cordier from misreading the exposed legs and breasts of the figure of Truth negatively and demanding that the figure be covered up.[45] With neither a single, authoritative text to accompany it, nor previous painted examples of this type of project to refer to, the context for interpreting the entire Medici cycle was inevitably much less clear than in the case of the title-page of a religious treatise. The ever-changing personal and political situation of Marie de' Medici, as evidenced by the continuous modifications made to the list of subjects she wished to have painted, meant that a certain degree of ambiguity in the cycle was probably willed by both patron and painter. Nevertheless, the volatility inherent in using a visual rhetoric based on the nude female body in a cycle commissioned by a woman seeking to regain power meant that the positive context in which the Queen wished her cycle to be framed could easily have been misunderstood by contemporary male viewers conditioned to view female nudity as something potentially dangerous and threatening.

In creating the Medici cycle, Marie de' Medici and Rubens must have been aware to a certain degree of the possible problems involved in developing a series of paintings which would extol the Queen's abilities to govern France without suggesting that she was a dangerously aggressive woman intent on seizing traditional male power. The original plans for both the Marie de' Medici gallery and the never-executed parallel gallery planned for Henri IV called for the 'heroic deeds' of the Queen and the 'triumphs' of her dead husband to be the main themes of the cycles.[46] This theme of triumph is made more explicit in the second plan of April 1622, when the most prominent position on the far end wall of the Queen's gallery was reserved for Marie de' Medici's *Triumph at Jülich*, a painting in the tradition of the quasi-historical royal equestrian portrait.[47] This initially clear focus on Marie de' Medici as a triumphant Queen, however, became increasingly obscured as modifications were made to the subjects and their placement in the gallery in response to changing political circumstances. For instance, the ignoble *Flight from Paris* (which, in the end, was never executed), the *Escape from Blois* and the *Full Reconciliation of Hostilities* were subjects suggested for the cycle later in 1622 which depicted the recent low points in the Queen's relations with her son followed by the current truce.[48] These subjects were unlikely to enhance the theme of the Queen Triumphant, but signalled instead a new, perhaps less aggressive approach by the patron to regaining the King's confidence. As the Queen's political aims and tactics changed, Rubens modified his original plan to represent Marie de' Medici as a clearly heroic and triumphant ruler and instead added scenes which would have been less threatening to the cycle's most important male viewer, Louis XIII.

The essence of the problem facing both Marie de' Medici and Rubens in creating a gallery dedicated to a Queen seeking to regain her lost powers can be reduced to a single question: over what could and should Marie de' Medici be shown to be triumphant? In the course of the Medici cycle project, answers to this question fluctuated, leading to a sense of uncertainty in the message being projected by the gallery as a whole. In scenes such as the *Triumph at Jülich*, the *Consignment of the Regency*, or the *Exchange of Princesses* (a painting of Marie de' Medici's carefully arranged political marriages for her children), the triumphs of the Queen were clearly military or political. Like any male ruler, Marie de' Medici demonstrated through these paintings her ability to soldier, govern and negotiate marital alliances. In other paintings in the cycle, the Queen's triumph was over her own gender and its limitations in the eyes of seventeenth-century patriarchal culture. As previously discussed, Marie de' Medici turns her back on the nude Graces in the *Education of Marie de' Medici* and focuses instead on the lessons of the armour-clad Minerva. Similarly, in the *Disembarkation at Marseilles*, Marie de' Medici not only symbolically walks away from her earlier political attachments to Tuscany but also literally walks over the frothy nude Nereids frolicking in the sea below (plate 34). In the *Apotheosis of Henri IV and the Assumption of the Regency*, the dishevelled nearly nude female Victory in the centre of the long rectangular canvas is a sign of the disordered world which Marie de' Medici's enthronement as Regent on the right-hand side of the painting is meant to reorder.[49] The violently abducted nude female figure of Truth in the *Triumph of Truth* and the bare-breasted female Virtues

34 P. P. Rubens, *The Disembarkation of Marie de' Medici in Marseilles*, 1622–5. Louvre Museum, Paris. (Cliché des musées nationaux, © Photo RMN)

who row the symbolic ship of state in the *Majority of Louis XIII* are literally depicted beneath the person of Marie de' Medici, thus signalling that, like any male ruler, she too can use the visual rhetoric of the nude female allegorical figure to signify her power over her sex as well as over truth and virtue.[50]

Unlike a man, however, Marie de' Medici's use of nudity in the context of a series dedicated to returning a woman to a position of power left her open to highly critical interpretations of her intentions by the male courtiers from the French court who came to visit the Luxembourg Palace and who were used to equating certain kinds of female nudity and seductiveness with a dangerous loss of male potency and power. Even without reading the paintings in such a negative context, the implied heterosexual male viewers, like Orpheus gazing at the nude Graces, could have been distracted altogether from the personal and political messages the Queen was trying to put forth in the cycle by the repeated display of nude female bodies in one painting after another. This emphasis on female nudity was heightened by the formal strategies used by Rubens, strategies which were particularly important when one considers the fact that these canvases, measuring nearly 4 m in height, would have been viewed mainly from below by the gallery's visitors.[51] Many of the nude women in the Medici cycle are either near the centre or in the forwardmost plane of the image as, for example, in the *Education of Marie de' Medici*, the *Disembarkation at Marseilles*, the *Apotheosis and Assumption of the Regency*, and the *Triumph of Truth*. Rubens further accentuated the bare female bodies he painted in luminous shades of pink and white by contrasting them with often much darker surrounding spaces. By using these types of compositional and colouristic tactics, Rubens in effect was privileging a reading of these nudes as merely seductively painted bodies prominently displayed for visual consumption rather than as essential figures in a complex iconography devised to vindicate the Queen.

This problematic relationship between female subject and male viewer, between art and beholder, is made most explicit in the Medici cycle in the *Presentation of Marie de' Medici's Portrait to Henri IV* discussed briefly above. It is in this scene that the problems of viewing, and, in particular, of viewing a woman who is both subject and patron, are brought most clearly to the surface. In the *Presentation of the Portrait*, the two opposed ends of the spectrum of the woman as object of the male gaze are condensed into a single image: woman as seductive Venus and woman as chaste Virgin. Even Rubens's formal approach stresses this duality with the restrained colour and composition of Marie de' Medici's portrait contrasting sharply with the exuberantly painted, bare-breasted figure of Juno floating directly above the Queen's image. Unlike earlier allusions in the cycle to Marie de' Medici's sacred namesake, the portrait within the painting recalls not the historical events associated with the Virgin Mary's life but rather refers specifically to other depictions of the Virgin in works of art, namely, in icons. Rubens's painting for the Roman church of S. Maria in Vallicella, for instance, is one of several works by him which are actually paintings about paintings of the Virgin (plate 35).[52] In this image, putti hold up a painting of the Virgin and Child for both the outside viewer and the angels within the composition to adore. The Medici cycle's *Presentation of the Portrait* echoes this type of painting: winged deities hold up the portrait of Marie de' Medici-as-Virgin Mary to be admired from below by the outside viewer as well as by the figures within the image including her future husband, Henri IV.

Besides the references to Marian prototypes, the *Presentation of the Portrait* also recalls traditional depictions of the Virgin's pagan opposite, Venus. In Rubens's *Venus at her Mirror* in the Prince of Liechtenstein's collection, for instance, the mirror reflection of the goddess looks out directly at the viewer with a knowing and almost challenging gaze, much as Marie de' Medici looks out from her portrait (plate 36).[53] The allusions to the dangers of feminine vanity and the seductiveness of the female gaze which are implicit in such depictions of Venus and her mirror are somewhat lessened in the *Presentation of the Portrait* by the fact that the person who looks into the mirror-like painting is not a woman but the King of France, Henri IV.[54] Indeed, the composition may well allude to the literary genre known as the 'Mirror of the Prince', a type of book devoted to describing appropriate royal conduct. The title-page of one such book published in Brussels in 1655, Belluga's *Speculum Principum*, in fact depicts a prince looking into a black-framed mirror in which he sees a reflection of himself accompanied by Virtues (plate 37).[55] By seeing Marie de' Medici in the painting-as-mirror, the implication is that Henri IV sees himself in her, a point which the Queen was eager to stress in her claims to be her husband's legitimate successor. While paintings such as the *Consignment of Government*, the *Coronation*, and the *Apotheosis and Assumption of the Regency* all overtly sought to legitimize Marie de' Medici's claims to the regency, it is only in the *Presentation of the Portrait* that she is transformed into the mirror-image of the King, a somewhat subtler but perhaps even more effective plea for the legitimacy of her

35 P. P. Rubens, *Icon of the Virgin and Child Adored by Angels*, 1608. S. Maria in Vallicella, Rome. (Photo: Alinari/Art Resource, New York)

rule than the depiction of any single historical event could ever be.

Early seventeenth-century texts and images took up this notion of Marie de' Medici as the mirror-image of her husband, the King, and made it explicit. Even before the death of Henri IV, emblems were designed which emphasized this mirror-like relationship. An emblem of 1609, for example, shows a sun reflected in a rectangular framed mirror with a somewhat later description explaining that this scene

> Allegorically represents the [Queen's] ... wise recognition that all her lustre comes from that of the King ... [who] planned to make her Regent in his absence and to give her all the honours which she could hope for (plate 38).[56]

36 P.P. Rubens, *Venus at her Mirror, c.* 1616. Collections of the Prince of Liechtenstein, Vaduz Castle

37 (left) Title page for P. Belluga's *Speculum Principum*, anonymous engraving, 1655. Harvard Law School Library, Special Collections, Cambridge, Mass.

38 (above) Sun and mirror emblem (1609) from J. De Bie's *La France metallique*, 1636. By permission of the Houghton Library, Harvard University, Cambridge, Mass.

In the 1615 *Harangue panegyrique a la reine sur l'heureux succez de sa regence*, the author Balzac wrote that it 'seems to us that he [Henri IV] reigns still under a face of a woman and such that we must call him Queen in you, or call you King'.[57] A pamphlet extolling the Queen's virtues which was published in 1612 assets that

> ... our King is not dead, but seeing himself decaying, he wanted ... to take new life ... in order to lengthen the stretch of his years ... [therefore] you [Marie de' Medici] seeing him before your eyes, only hav[e] ... changed of degree.[58]

And Jean Prévost's 1613 text on the *Apothéose du très chrestien Roy de France et de Navarre Henri IIII* says that Henri IV has built his mausoleum in the very person of Marie de' Medici.[59]

At the same time that the King seems to search for a mirror-image of himself in the portrait of his bride-to-be, Marie de' Medici's own gaze in the *Presentation of the Portrait* is self-consciously directed outwards: she is a woman who is fully aware of being looked at both from within the painting and from without by the outside viewer. In one sense, as the patron of the cycle, the represented Marie de' Medici's outward gaze acts as a kind of mirror reflection of the real Marie de' Medici standing before the painting. As importantly, however, her unflinching gaze serves to acknowledge the other key viewers of the cycle, namely, the male courtiers on official visits to her palace and especially her son, the King. It is through her awareness of her position as the object of the male gazes of her courtiers and King (Henri IV as well as Louis XIII) that Marie de' Medici gains power. By calmly and steadily returning the outside viewer's gaze, Marie de' Medici adopts a position which is equal to that of the men who view her. Indeed, as the only figure in the scene (besides the putto directly beneath her) who seems to be aware of the presence of an outside viewer, it is she who communicates most powerfully and directly with the spectator, like an icon of the Virgin whose outward gaze allows her to affect directly the worshipful viewers gathered before her image.[60] The force of Marie de' Medici's gaze should have played an important role in her attempts to use the Medici cycle in her quest to regain the personal and political authority which she had recently lost.

In fact, the theme of Marie de' Medici's powerful and empowering gaze was developed in several texts published during her regency. The Queen is described as the 'Beautiful regent of our lands/Whose rich gazes of female charms/... Gives life or death' and 'Her favourable gaze is all powerful/May it pour over us a saintly influence.'[61] But, in the same way that seventeenth-century culture could read the biographies of famous women of the past or could view bare breasts in negative as well as in positive terms, Marie de' Medici's gaze was also described very critically by some contemporary writers, especially after her first fall from power. *Les Singeries des femmes de ce temps descouvertes*, published in 1623, says in a passage which alludes to Marie de' Medici that

> ... the woman hides under a deceitful face all that one can imagine in this world which is perfidious and evil ... there is nothing more inconstant than her face ... the head of Medusa turns all things to stone ... [including] men.[62]

In an anonymous text published while Marie de' Medici was still in power, she is described as

> This beautiful French Astraea [who] has totally changed: She has removed her blindfold, *she now sees clearly* . . . her [outer] dress is . . . chameleon-like in order to allow her to take on whatever colours her passion demands.[63]

The gaze of the powerful woman could be threatening as well as life-giving in the opinion of seventeenth-century writers.

One must assume that both Rubens and Marie de' Medici intended her assertive outward gaze in the *Presentation of the Portrait* to be interpreted in a positive manner. One of the problems faced by contemporary viewers of the painting, however, was trying to determine the appropriate context in which to place the portrait of the bride-to-be who eventually ruled as Regent. Marie de' Medici's portrait collapses within itself two quite distinct portrait traditions: depictions of beautiful women intended to be admired by their male lovers as well as portraits commemorating male patrons who wanted a visual affirmation of their worldly fame and power which would impress their peers.[64] This ambiguity about how to understand the Queen's portrait in terms of its implied function and audience could, of course, be seen as a felicitous combination of the dual roles — loving wife and mother as well as powerful ruler — Marie de' Medici wished to adopt at the time of the cycle's commission. Once again, however, the patron's lack of control over her audience's actual responses could just as well have led contemporary male viewers to regard very negatively her attempts to mask her quest for power under the guise of the seductive female gaze. It is perhaps ironic, then, that Marie de' Medici's empowering gaze out towards the male viewers before the painting is only affected through the mediation of artifice: like the painting of the *Icon of the Virgin and Child* in S. Maria in Vallicella or the Liechtenstein *Venus*, the Queen's assertive gaze seems to be possible only when it issues forth from a painting within a painting, from a mirror within art's mirror.[65]

The ambiguities associated with the female gaze, with the role of art in depicting female sexuality and power, are also part of the broader issue of Rubens's understanding of visual representation in general. The fact that the black frame around the Queen's portrait in the *Presentation of the Portrait* echoes the black frames which encased the entire Medici cycle allows this particular image to function even more explicitly as a painting which mirrors the painted cycle as a whole.[66] Like Gide's 'mise en abyme', the text which includes within itself a representation of itself, or Schlegel's notion of a 'poetry of poetry', Rubens's *Presentation of the Portrait* recapitulates in the painting within the painting some of the artist's ideas on the nature of visual representation.[67] While the 'mise en abyme' is usually used to highlight the internal structure of a text or other work of art, in the case of the *Presentation of the Portrait* it also acts to bring to the surface the gender-specific tensions inherent in Rubens's strategies of visual representation and in seventeenth-century culture in general.

Rubens produced other images which illustrate his on-going interest in thematizing the problems of representing representation and of exploring the relationship between art and the viewer. One of these is the title-page he designed for Blosius's *Opera* in 1632 (plate 39). Like the painting within the painting in the *Presentation of the Portrait*, this engraving depicts an open book on the title-page of the book which the reader holds in his or her hands.[68] It too includes an active viewer-reader within the composition who looks up to the book held aloft by heavenly beings, a book which echoes the larger opus the reader is about to peruse. In the *Christ and Doubting Thomas* triptych painted for Nicolaas Rockox in *c*. 1613–15, Rubens used a sacred narrative to represent the ideal relationship between image and spectator (plate 40).[69] At the same time, this work could also be interpreted as a comment on the relative positions of male versus female viewers. St Thomas and the other apostles gathered around Christ have direct physical as well as visual access to the subject itself, while secular viewers, both those standing implictly before the painting and the two donors depicted explicitly in the side panels, are relegated to a space clearly outside the sacred scene. The apostles' gazes and gestures demonstrate the properly reverential viewing relationship the spectator should have to Christ's sacred body. The viewers before the painting, however, are also made aware of the distance between themselves and this image by the separated figures of Nicolaas Rockox and his wife Adriana Perez. The spectator is both drawn into the work by Adriana Perez's inviting outward gaze as well as simultaneously excluded from the sacred central core to which only Nicolaas Rockox, intensely gazing at Christ's body, seems to have visual access. Adriana Perez is empowered by her direct visual communication with the outside viewer, but at the same time she remains excluded from the true centre of power, the sacred body of Christ, which is accessible only to the male gazes of her husband and the apostles.

In projects such as the Rockox triptych or the Blosius title-page, as Frank Stella has accurately observed, 'Rubens came to believe that he could make painting about painting.'[70] The crucial difference between such images and the *Presentation of the Portrait*, however, is that in the latter work, Rubens creates a painting not about representation in general but about a very particular problem, namely, how to depict a woman seeking power in seventeenth-century France. As the first (and only) example in this period of a large-scale series dedicated to glorifying the life of a contemporary woman, the Medici cycle had no precedents. Its viewers, therefore, had no frame of reference, no clearly defined context in which to interpret the cycle. Indeed, the ever-varying combinations of female imagery, from the Queen's assertive gaze and occasionally bared breast to the nude Graces and Nereids, could easily have been misinterpreted by seventeenth-century male visitors to the gallery conditioned to assess the female gaze as well as the female body in highly ambiguous ways. To understand the elusive relationships between gender and representation brought to the surface by the Medici cycle, one must go beyond deciphering its Classical and Christian iconography, beyond trying to determine *what* individual images mean, and instead focus on *how* they mean, that is, on the mechanisms which create meaning. Rubens's essentially patriarchal visual rhetoric encompasses not just iconography but also the dynamic interaction of allegory, myth and history, the tactical use of colour and composition, and references to the repertoire of female images available to his contemporaries. It is only by dissecting these strategies for visual representation and analysing them within the context of seventeenth-century culture that one can begin to understand the

39 P. P. Rubens (design), Title page for L. Blosius's *Opera*, engraved by C. Galle, 1632. Teylers Museum, Haarlem

40 P. P. Rubens, *Christ and Doubting Thomas* (Rochox triptych), *c.* 1613–15. Koninklijk Museum voor Schone Kunsten, Antwerp

inevitable problems which arose when Rubens applied this rhetoric to the project of depicting a once-powerful woman trying to regain her influence in a male-dominated society.

Geraldine A. Johnson
Harvard University

NOTES

I would like to thank Joseph Koerner and Simon Schama for invaluable advice and encouragement in preparing this article. I am also grateful for the comments provided by R. Stanley Johnson and Ursula Johnson on an earlier version of this essay.

1 Rubens served Archduchess Isabella as artist, diplomat and confidant. On his diplomacy on her behalf, see C.V. Wedgwood, *The Political Career of Peter Paul Rubens*, London, 1975, and *Rubens Diplomate*, Elewijt, 1962. On Rubens and the Countess of Arundel, see Christopher White, *Peter Paul Rubens: Man & Artist*, New Haven, 1987, p. 138.

2 The Medici gallery was a well-lit and richly decorated space measuring 58 × 7.60 m. Rubens's paintings would have towered over the gallery's visitors: most are nearly 4 m high with the bottom edges of the frames originally at least 1.30 m above the floor. Twenty of the canvases were hung between the windows on the long sides of the gallery with the remaining four on the two short ends of the space. See Deborah Marrow, 'The Art Patronage of Maria de' Medici', Ph.D., University of Pennsylvania, 1978, pp. 66–9; Marie-Noëlle Baudouin-Matuszek, et. al., *Marie de Médicis et le Palais du Luxembourg*, Paris, 1991, pp. 220 and 225; and Jacques Thuillier and Jacques Foucart, *Le storie di Maria de' Medici di Rubens al Lussemburgo*, Milan, 1967, pp. 65–6, and the illustrations on pp. 33, 35 and 68–9.

3 On seventeenth-century visitors to the gallery, see Baudouin-Matuszek, ibid., pp. 218–22, and Thuillier and Foucart, ibid., pp. 10, 120, 122–6 and 130 ff. Except for the Queen herself and the female members of the court mentioned in a description of the gallery's opening in 1625, only male visitors are recorded in the surviving documents. One assumes, however, that female members of the court continued to visit the cycle as well. In any case, the Queen's primary concern would have been to impress the male courtiers who, in a highly patriarchal culture, wielded the most power and influence. On the women in the Queen's entourage and her relationship to the male grandees, see Baudouin-Matuszek, pp. 125–30.

4 Portraits of potential brides were often sent to kings and noblemen in this period. Marie de' Medici herself requested such works for her second son. See Marrow, op. cit., pp. 107–111. Ronald F. Millen and Robert E. Wolf, *Heroic Deeds and Mystic Figures: A New Reading of Rubens's Life of Maria de' Medici*, Princeton, 1989, pp. 49–50, mention portraits of Marie de' Medici sent to Henri IV during marriage negotiations. Some portraits of the Queen similar to the one in the *Presentation of the Portrait* survive. See Karla Langedijk, *The Portraits of the Medici: 15th–18th Centuries*, vol. 2, Florence, 1983, pp. 1245 and 1250–1.

5 Marrow, ibid., p. 105. See also Susan Saward, *The Golden Age of Marie de' Medici*, Ann Arbor, 1982, p. 5, and Thuillier and Foucart, op. cit., pp. 40–2.

6 For example, Svetlana Alpers, 'Manner and Meaning in some Rubens Mythologies', *Journal of the Warburg and Courtauld Institutes*, vol. 30, 1967, p. 295, feels that Rubens 'cannot devise a satisfactory relationship between the real Queen and the world of allegorical figures which surround her'. Thuillier and Foucart, ibid., p. 36, also comment on the compromises found in the incessant mixture of history and allegory throughout the cycle.

7 From letters to Jacques Dupuy in 1626 and to Peiresc in 1625, respectively. See Ruth Saunders Magurn, *The Letters of Peter Paul Rubens*, Evanston, 1955, pp. 149 and 109.

8 Alpers, op. cit., p. 295, calls the cycle a 'striking failure'. Politically, the series was unable to solidify Marie de' Medici's precarious position at the French court. Millen and Wolf, op. cit., p. 13, suggest that if the Queen's '... fall can be attributed to any single misstep, it would be the overconfidence with which she commissioned and conceived the Luxembourg paintings.' Thuillier and Foucart, op. cit., pp. 38–40; Marrow, op. cit., p. 105; and Anthony Blunt, *Art and Architecture in France 1500–1700*, London, 1982, p. 361, all comment on the cycle's failure to inspire any contemporary artistic imitations.

9 For instance, Millen and Wolf, ibid., and Saward, op. cit., have seen emblems and

classical literature, respectively, as the iconographic keys which will unlock the cycle's meaning. Beverly Heisner, 'Marie de Medici: Self-Promotion through Art', *The Feminist Art Journal*, vol. 6, no. 2, Summer 1977, pp. 21–6; Marrow, ibid., and 'Marie de' Medici and the Decoration of the Luxembourg Palace', *Burlington Magazine*, vol. 121, no. 921, December 1979, pp. 783–91; Elaine Rhea Rubin, 'The Heroic Image: Women and Power in Early-Seventeenth Century France, 1610–1661', Ph.D., The George Washington University, 1977; and Mary D. Garrard, *Artemisia Gentileschi*, Princeton, 1989, pp. 157–9, have analysed the Queen as a female patron and her use of 'female' iconographies. The role of gender in strategies of representation — in the processes of creating meaning — as well as in iconography has been examined in greater depth by Stephen Greenblatt, Louis Montrose and Roy Strong in the art and literature produced under Elizabeth I, the period's most powerful female ruler.

10 See Joseph L. Koerner, 'The Mortification of the Image: Death as a Hermeneutic in Hans Baldung Grien', *Representations*, no. 10, Spring 1985, pp. 52–101, on the notion of *how* images mean as opposed to *what* they mean.

11 There is a vast literature on Rubens. Two recent overviews of his career are White, op. cit., and Michael Jaffé, *Catalogo completo: Rubens*, Milan, 1989. See also the on-going *Corpus Rubenianum Ludwig Burchard*, parts 1–26, Brussels, 1968 ff. On Rubens's artistic formation in Italy, especially important in relation to his Medici patron, see Jaffé, *Rubens and Italy*, Oxford, 1977, and Mina Gregori (ed.), *Rubens e Firenze*, Florence, 1983.

12 The project is well documented by Thuillier and Foucart, op. cit., especially pp. 131 and 91ff. See also Ewald M. Vetter, 'Rubens und die Genese des Programms der Medicigalerie', *Pantheon*, vol. 32, no. 4, 1974, pp. 355–73, and Marrow, *Art Patronage*, op. cit., pp. 92–9.

13 On the important role played by Marie de' Medici as a patron, see especially Marrow, ibid.

14 Rubin, op. cit., pp. 84–5.

15 On the function of the gallery as a waiting area for visitors, see Marrow, *Art Patronage*, op. cit., p. 66, and Thuillier and Foucart, op. cit., p. 31.

16 Rubens describes Louis XIII's first visit to the gallery in a letter to Peiresc on 13 May 1625. See Magurn, op. cit., p. 109; Baudouin-Matuszek, op. cit., p. 218; Thuillier and Foucart, ibid., pp. 120–1; and Millen and Wolf, op. cit., p. 11.

17 On Marie de' Medici's relationship to Louis XIII, see Victor-L. Tapié, *France in the Age of Louis XIII and Richelieu*, Cambridge, 1984, and Geoffrey Parker, *Europe in Crisis: 1598–1648*, Ithaca, 1979, pp. 128 ff. On Louis XIII's childhood, see Elizabeth Wirth Marvick, *Louis XIII: The Making of a King*, New Haven, 1986. Recent biographies of the Queen include Baudouin-Matuszek, ibid., pp. 37–163; Michel Carmona, *Marie de Médicis*, Paris, 1981; and Françoise Kermina, *Marie de Médicis: Reine, régente et rebelle*, Paris, 1979. Louis Batiffol, *Marie de Médicis and the French Court in the XVIIth Century*, New York, 1908, also remains a useful source.

18 Millen and Wolf, op. cit., in note 8 above, suggest that the Medici cycle may have actually contributed to the Queen's final and permanent fall from favour at the French court.

19 Although early guides to the cycle call this figure both Apollo and Orpheus, a text possibly dictated by Rubens himself calls him by the latter name. See Jacques Thuillier, 'La "Galerie de Médicis" de Rubens et sa genèse: un document inédit', *Revue de l'art*, no. 4, 1969, p. 56.

20 The 'male gaze' has been discussed extensively by scholars such as Griselda Pollock, Linda Nochlin, Marina Warner, Mary Garrard, Mary Ann Doane and Laura Mulvey. See Edward Snow, 'Theorizing the Male Gaze: Some Problems', *Representations*, no. 25, Winter 1989, pp. 30–41, for a recent critique of feminist theories of the male gaze.

21 Rubens's interest in exploring the nuances of the female gaze is suggested by the preparatory oil sketches for the *Education of Marie de' Medici* and the *Presentation of the Portrait* which do not yet show either the Grace or the Queen looking outwards. See Rüdiger an der Heiden, *Die Skizzen zum Medici-Zyklus von Peter Paul Rubens in der Alten Pinakothek*, Munich, 1984, and Julius Held, *The Oil Sketches of Peter Paul Rubens*, Princeton, 1980.

22 Although Marie de' Medici had a relatively liberal education for a woman of her time, the emphasis was mainly on the visual arts and skills such a precious stone connoisseurship rather than on history, literature or politics. On her education and cultural formation in Florence, see Thuillier and Foucart, op. cit., p. 13; Marrow, *Art Patronage*, op. cit., pp. 7–13; Baudouin-Matuszek, op. cit., pp. 38–84; and Sara Mamone, *Firenze e Parigi: due capitali dello spettacolo per una regina: Maria de' Medici*, Milan, 1987. On female education in general, see Ian Maclean, *Woman Triumphant: Feminism in French Literature 1610–1652*, Oxford, 1977, pp. 53 ff, and *The Renaissance Notion of Women*, Cambridge, 1980.

23 Seventeenth-century attitudes towards female nudity, sexuality and seduction will be discussed in greater detail below.

24 The Queen's interest in emphasizing her position as wife as well as mother is demonstrated by her commissioning numerous images of marriages and mothers. See Marrow, *Art Patronage*, op. cit., pp. 48–9, 71–3, and 155–9.

25 John B. Knipping, *Iconography of the Counter Reformation in the Netherlands*, Leiden, 1974, vol. 2, pp. 258 and 263 ff, and Margaret R. Miles, 'The Virgin's One Bare Breast: Female Nudity and Religious Meaning in Tuscan Early Renaissance Culture', *The Female Body in Western Culture*, edited by S.R. Suleiman, Cambridge, Mass., 1986, pp. 193–208, explore the sometimes ambiguous meanings associated with the Madonna's bare breast in art.

26 The *Birth of Marie de' Medici*, the *Education of Marie de' Medici*, the *Marriage by Proxy*, the *Birth of Louis XIII*, the *Coronation*, and the *Apotheosis of Henri IV and Assumption of the Regency* which shows the Queen enthroned all recall a traditional iconography of the Virgin. On the cycle's Marian imagery, see Heisner, op. cit., pp. 23–4; Marrow, *Art Patronage*, op. cit., pp. 149–55; F. Hamilton Hazlehurst, 'Additional Sources for the Medici Cycle', *Bulletin: Musées royaux des beaux-arts de Belgique*, vol. 6, 1967, p. 114; Millen and Wolf, op. cit., pp. 34, 61–2, and 217–18; and Robert W. Berger, 'Rubens and Caravaggio: A Source for a Painting from the Medici Cycle', *Art Bulletin*, vol. 54, no. 4, December 1972, p. 473–7. Kristine Weber and Justus M. Hofstede, ' "Non si fa niente contra la verita": Historischer Schauplatz und ikonographische Inszenierung im Vermählungsbild von Rubens' Medici-Zyklus', *Wallraf-Richartz-Jahrbuch*, vol. 51, 1990, p. 152, argue rather unconvincingly against the importance of Marian allusions in the cycle.

27 See, for example, Rubens's *c.* 1635 painting of the *Virgin and Child* in Cologne.

28 It is ironic but not unexpected that the Queen was never the principal wetnurse or caretaker of her son. On Louis XIII's childhood, see Marvick, op. cit.

29 See White, op. cit., pp. 99–102, for a summary of this commission.

30 A similarly dangerous display of female breasts is seen in Rubens's *Judith* in Braunschweig. Knipping, op. cit., vol. 1, p. 47, discusses the popularity of the theme of 'the fatal influence of women'; H. Diane Russell, *Eva/Ave: Woman in Renaissance and Baroque Prints*, Washington, DC, 1990, pp. 147 ff, examines prints illustrating the power of women; and Simon Schama, 'Wives and Wantons: Versions of Womanhood in 17th century Dutch Art', *Oxford Art Journal*, vol. 3, no. 1, April 1980, p. 9, analyses the portrayal of women in Dutch art as 'deceitful and vengeful women leading heroes to their ruin'. On the notion of the passive female versus the active male hero, see Rubin, op. cit., *passim*.

31 Anne Hollander, *Seeing Through Clothes*, New York, 1978, pp. 187–99, suggests that bare breasts went from alluding primarily to virtuous maternity in fifteenth-century art to being increasingly associated with sexual pleasure and desire by the seventeenth century. On the ambiguous connotations of exposed breasts in the case of Elizabeth I, see Louis A. Montrose, 'A *Midsummer Night's Dream* and the Shaping Fantasies of Elizabethan Culture: Gender, Power, Form', *Rewriting the Renaissance*, edited by M.W. Ferguson, et. al., Chicago, 1986, pp. 65–8.

32 First published in 1635. See Maclean, *Woman Triumphant*, op. cit., p. 218. This book was so popular that a third edition had been printed by 1637 with a different title, *Discours particulier contre les femmes desbraillees de ce temps*, which focused even more clearly on the dangers of female nudity.

33 'Les mondains . . . lancent des pensées charnelles entre ces deux mattes de chair; ils logent des désirs vilains dans le creux de ce sein nud.' Pierre Darmon, *Mythologie de la femme dans l'ancienne France, XVIe–XIXe siècle*, Paris, 1983, p. 42.

34 For example, see the anonymous 1617 texts *Discours nouveau de la mode* and *La Courtisane déchiffrée* or the 1675 books by Père Louis de Bouvignes, *Le Miroir de la vanité des femmes mondaines*, and Jacques Boileau, *Abus des nudités de gorge*, which all continue to harangue women who bare their breasts. Darmon, ibid., pp. 41–3. Although it is unclear whether Marie de' Medici or Rubens knew the specific texts cited here, the fact that a work like the *Discours particulier* had three editions in as many years, as mentioned in note 32 above, does imply a relatively widespread interest in such tracts. In addition, the Queen's active promotion of the Catholic reform and her links to Catholic devotional politics in Paris speak to an interest on her part in the kinds of issues raised by these types of religious sermons and moralizing works. On the Queen's religious habits and pro-Catholic policies, see Baudouin-Matuszek, op. cit., pp. 108–109, 112–13, 121–2, 134–6 and 139–45.

35 On the use of wetnurses by even the artisan class in the early modern period, see Christiane Klapisch-Zuber, 'Blood Parents and Milk Parents: Wet Nursing in Florence, 1300–1530', *Women, Family, and Ritual in Renaissance Italy*, translated by L. Cochrane, Chicago, 1985, pp. 132–64, and Jacques Gélis, 'L'individualisation de l'enfant', *Histoire de la vie privée: De la Renaissance aux Lumières*, vol. 3, edited by P. Ariès and G. Duby, Paris, 1986, pp. 315 and 320–1. See also note 28 above.

36 See note 30 above on the theme of the power of women in seventeenth-century culture.

37 On the Salic law in France, see Rubin, op. cit., pp. 8–10, and Maclean, *Woman Triumphant*, op. cit., pp. 58–62. On England and female inheritance of the throne, see Marie Axton, *The Queen's Two Bodies: Drama and Elizabethan Succession*, London, 1977.

38 On earlier French female rulers, see Marian F.

Facinger, 'A Study of Medieval Queenship; Capetian France 987–1237', *Studies in Medieval and Renaissance History*, vol. 5, 1968, pp. 1–48, and Claire R. Sherman, 'Taking a Second Look: Observations on the Iconography of a French Queen, Jeanne de Bourbon (1338–1378)', *Feminism and Art History*, edited by N. Broude and M. Garrard, New York, 1982, pp. 100–117. Marrow, *Art Patronage*, op. cit., pp. 159–160, discusses Marie de' Medici's interest in earlier French Queens.

39 '... une vraye singerie [de] ... ceste Royne superbe des Assiries Semiramis, laquelle massacra son mary & son fils ... pour regenter sur les hommes, & osa bien mesme, tant elle avoit le coeur d'imiter les actions des homes, quitter les habits de femme & se revestir du manteau Royal.' *Les Singeries des femmes de ce temps descouvertes*, 1623, p. 12. See Rubin, op. cit., pp. 105–106, and Garrard, *Artemisia*, op. cit., pp. 156–7.

40 On this literary genre and its popularity in this period, see Maclean, *Woman Trimphant*, op. cit.; Rubin, ibid.; and Marrow, *Art Patronage*, op. cit., pp. 160–1. Some of these texts included engravings which depicted each woman in a full-length portrait. Several painted galleries dedicated to women 'worthies' were also commissioned in this period but, despite their 'female' iconography, they differed from the Medici cycle which alone focused on the life of a contemporary woman rather than on virtuous women from the past. On these galleries, see Maclean, pp. 210–211; Marrow, pp. 162–5; Garrard, ibid., p. 158; and Bernard Dorival, 'Art et politique en France au XVIIe siècle: la galerie des hommes illustres du Palais Cardinal', *Bulletin de la société de l'histoire de l'art français*, 1973, pp. 43–60.

41 See Rubin, ibid., pp. 104–109 and *passim*; Maclean, ibid., and Darmon, op. cit., on seventeenth-century 'anti-feminist' texts.

42 See Simon Schama, *The Embarrassment of Riches*, Berkeley, 1988, pp. 408–410, on Anna Roemer Visscher.

43 Susanna is placed a bit further back in space and her crouching pose is reversed in the later engraving, but the overall compositions of the two prints are quite similar.

44 See Elizabeth McGrath, 'Rubens's "Susanna and the Elders" and Moralizing Inscriptions on Prints', *Wort und Bild in der Niederländischen Kunst und Literatur des 16. und 17. Jahrhunderts*, edited by H. Vekeman and J.M. Hofstede, Erftstadt, 1984, pp. 81–5, on these inscriptions. See also Paola della Pergola, 'P.P. Rubens e il tema della Susanna al bagno', *Bulletin: Musées royaux des beaux-arts de Belgique*, vol. 6, 1967, pp. 7–22.

45 Cordier's condemnation of Truth's nudity is known from a letter to him by his publisher, Moretus. See J. Richard Judson and Carl van de Velde, *Book Illustrations and Title-Pages (Corpus Rubenianum Part XXI)*, Philadelphia, 1978, vol. 2, p. 382, and vol. 1, pp. 249–53, figs. 199–200. See also Knipping, op. cit., vol. 1, p. 63.

46 See Thuillier and Foucart, op. cit., pp. 95–6 and 68–70, for the first contract of February, 1622, and for the plans for the Henri IV gallery. See also Ingrid Jost, 'Bemerkungen zur Heinrichsgalerie des P.P. Rubens', *Nederlands Kunsthistorisch Jaarboek*, vol. 15, 1964, pp. 175–219, and Baudouin-Matuszek, op. cit., pp. 222–3.

47 Thuillier and Foucart, ibid., pp. 85–6; Millen and Wolf, op. cit., pp. 155–9; Marrow, *Art Patronage*, op. cit., pp. 166–74; and Otto von Simson, 'Politische Symbolik im Werk Rubens', *Rubens: Kunstgeschichtliche Beiträge*, edited by E. Hubala, Constance, 1979, pp. 26–7, discuss this painting and the theme of triumph throughout the cycle.

48 See Thuillier and Foucart, ibid., p. 12, and the chart on p. 131.

49 On the 'disorderly' or 'misused' woman as a sign of societal disarray, see Natalie Zemon Davis, 'Women on Top', *Society and Culture in Early Modern France*, Stanford, 1975, pp. 124–51, and Griselda Pollock, *Vision and Difference: Femininity, Feminism and Histories of Art*, London, 1988, p. 32.

50 On the violently-abducted or 'rapt' woman in seventeenth-century culture, see Sarah Hanley, 'Family and State in Early Modern France: The Marriage Pact', *Connecting Spheres: Women in the Western World, 1500 to the Present*, edited by M.J. Boxer and J.H. Quataert, New York, 1987, pp. 58–61, and Margaret D. Carroll, 'The Erotics of Absolutism: Rubens and the Mystification of Sexual Violence', *Representations*, no. 25, Winter 1989, pp. 3–30.

51 See note 2 above on how the paintings were originally displayed in the gallery.

52 The icon of the Virgin and Child within the larger composition was painted on a removable copper plate beneath which was kept a miraculous fresco of the Madonna. The literature on the Vallicella Madonna is reviewed by Fernanda Castiglioni, '"Non sono, dunque, si' mala cosa le immagini" (C. Baronio). Stato degli studi, considerazioni e ipotesi sui Rubens della Vallicella', *Annuario dell'Istituto di Storia dell'Arte, Università degli Studi di Roma*, n.s. 2, 1982–83, pp. 14–22. See also Michael Jaffé's important article on 'Peter Paul Rubens and the Oratorian Fathers', *Proporzioni*, IV, 1963, pp. 209–241, as well as White, op. cit., pp. 50–1; Kerry Downes, *Rubens*, London, 1980, pp. 68–72; Pierre Georgel and Anne-Marie Lecoq, *La peinture dans la peinture*, Dijon, 1983, p. 63; and Hans Belting, *Bild und Kult: Eine Geschichte des Bildes vor dem Zeitalter der Kunst*, Munich, 1990, pp. 541–5.

53 Snow, op. cit., pp. 32–4, emphasizes the male

viewer–female object relationship in the Liechtenstein *Venus*. G.F. Harlaub, *Zauber des Speigels: Geschichte und Bedeutung des Spiegels in der Kunst*, Munich, 1951, pp. 79–80 and 107–108, examines the role of mirrors in this and other images of Venus. On mirrors in art, see also Bialostocki, 'Man and Mirror in Painting: Reality and Transcience', *Message of Images*, op. cit., pp. 93–107, and Heinrich Schwarz, 'The Mirror in Art', *Art Quarterly*, vol. 15, no. 2, Summer 1952, pp. 96–118.

54 Interestingly enough, a mirror which once belonged to Marie de' Medici is now in the Louvre. Although its frame is more ornate than the one around the Queen's portrait, it too has an upright rectangular shape. See Baudouin-Matuszek, op. cit., p. 98.

55 On this genre, see J. A. Emmens, 'Les Menines de Velasquez: Miroir des Princes pour Philippe IV', *Nederlands Kunsthistorisch Jaarboek*, vol. 12, 1961, especially pp. 60–2.

56 'Cela rapporté par un sens allegorique à ... la Princesse [Marie de' Medici], qui recognoit avec grande prudence, que tout sont lustre procede de celuy du Monarque ... [qui] projetta de laisser la Reinne Regente en son absence, & luy deferer tous les Honneurs qu'elle pouvoit esperer.' Jacques De Bie, *La France metallique*, Paris, 1636, p. 309. Illustrated as medal IX (Marie de' Medici section). See also Millen and Wolf, op. cit., p. 141. Another emblem in De Bie on the theme of the King's reflection in a mirror is medal LXXXV (Henri IV section), described on p. 292. The Queen is said to reflect her son, Louis XIII, in medal XXXI (Marie de' Medici section), described on p. 321.

57 Rubin, op. cit., p. 75.

58 From the anonymous pamphlet *Prosopopée historique et alitographie du bon heur de regente de Frances*, Rubin, ibid., p. 71.

59 Rubin, ibid., p. 79. In François de Rosset's 1612 text, *Le Romant des chevaliers ...*, Morpheus appears before Marie de' Medici's eyes as Henri IV. See Rubin, pp. 71–2.

60 See Belting, op. cit., *passim*, on the intercessory functions of Madonna icons and on the power of the Virgin's gaze.

61 The first passage is from the 1614 *Vers divers sur le ballet des dix verds*; the second is from the 1615 *Ballet de Madame, soeur aisnée du roi*. Rubin, op. cit., pp. 76 and 87.

62 '... la femme sous un visage trompeux cache tout ce qui se peut imaginer au monde de perfide & de meschant ... il n'y a rien de plus incostant que sa face ... la teste de Meduse corvertissoit toutes choses en pierre ... [aussi] l'homme.' *Les singeries des femmes*, op. cit., pp. 9–10. See Rubin, ibid., pp. 104–105.

63 'Ceste belle Astree Françoise est toute changee: Elle a quitté son bandeau, elle voit clair ... sa robbe est ... de Cameleon pour pouvoir recevoir les couleurs que sa passion luy demande.' *La Cassandre françoise*, 1615, pp. 14–15, with emphasis added in the translation. See also Rubin, ibid., p. 88.

64 Elizabeth Cropper, 'The Beauty of Woman: Problems in the Rhetoric of Renaissance Portraiture', *Rewriting the Renaissance*, op. cit., pp. 175–90, and Patricia Simons, 'Women in Frames: the gaze, the eye, the profile in Renaissance portraiture', *History Workshop*, issue 25, Spring 1988, pp. 4–30, explore issues of gender in Italian portraiture.

65 On paintings within paintings, see Hartlaub, op. cit.; Georgel and Lecoq, op. cit.; Andre Chastel, 'Le tableau dans le tableau', *Fabres, Formes, Figures II*, Paris, 1978, pp. 75–98; Francis H. Dowley, 'French Portraits of Ladies as Minerva', *Gazette des Beaux-Arts*, pér. 6, vol. 45, May–June 1955, pp. 266–9; John F. Moffitt, 'Francisco Pacheco and Jerome Nadal: New Light on the Flemish Sources of the Spanish "Picture-within-the-Picture"', *Art Bulletin*, vol. 72, no. 4, December 1990, pp. 631–8; and Jean Wirth, 'La représentation de l'image dans l'art du Haut Moyen Age', *Révue de l'art*, no. 79, 1988, pp. 9–21.

66 Unlike the present frames, the original black wood frames also had some decorative motifs in gold painted on them. See Thuillier and Foucart, op. cit., pp. 131–2.

67 On Andre Gide's theory of the 'mise en abyme', see Lucien Dällenbach, *The Mirror in the Text*, Cambridge, 1989, who also quotes Friedrich Schlegel on poetry, pp. 175–6. See also Tadeusz Kowzan, 'L'art en abyme', *Diogène*, no. 96, 1976, pp. 74–100. The problem of the representation of visual representation has been repeatedly addressed in essays on Velázquez's *Las Meninas*. See especially Michel Foucault's influential chapter in *The Order of Things*, New York, 1970, pp. 3–16.

68 Julius Held, 'Rubens and the Book', *Rubens and His Circle: Studies by Julius Held*, edited by A. W. Lowenthal, et. al., Princeton, 1982, p. 179, says that 'the very book ... has become its own title page.' See also Judson and van de Velde, op. cit., vol. 1, pp. 260–5, and vol. 2, figs. 208–211.

69 See White, op. cit., pp. 102–106, on this commission. Rockox also owned Rubens's *Samson and Delilah*. Both works are shown in an imaginary view of Rockox's collection by Frans Franken the Younger. Gerard Thomas included the triptych's central panel in another imaginary gallery with an artist pointing at Christ, thus further supporting a reading of this work as a paradigmatic image on the relation between art and the viewer. See Zirka Z. Filipczak, *Picturing Art in Antwerp: 1550–1700*, Princeton, 1987, pp. 58–9, figs. 30 and 94, and White, pp. 99–100, fig. 115.

70 Frank Stella, *Working Space*, Cambridge, Mass., 1986, p. 40.

REVIEW ARTICLES

THE WOMAN WHO MISTOOK HER ART FOR A HAT

Mary Jacobus

Berthe Morisot's Images of Women by *Anne Higonnet*, Cambridge, Mass., and London: Harvard University Press, 1992, 311 pp., 12 col. plates, 111 b. & w. illus., £35.95

'Berthe Morisot made a painting the way you make a hat' — or so Degas is reputed to have said.[1] Gendered tributes like this were often affectionately and admiringly bestowed on Morisot by her friends and relations. Paul Valéry (who married Morisot's niece) represented her as a domestic diarist, whose paintings kept step with her developments as a girl, wife and mother, while her grandson, Denis Rouart, wrote that 'with her to love was to paint'.[2] But Morisot, whose reserve was as striking as her privileged domestic life, was also capable of affecting her friends as '*l'amicale méduse*' (in Mallarmé's memorable phrase) — as an intimidating, even chilly presence, whose painting functioned like a cold but divinatory pane of glass.[3] We are invited to view her as a painter whose art sprang naturally from her femininity, or whose personal distinction was inseparable from the aesthetic transformation she wrought on the *quotidienne*.

An art of personal relations (Morisot as sister, mother, aunt) or the distilled expression of an enigmatic personality? Either way, such tributes imply that Morisot lived her art as she lived her life — elegantly, in the bosom of her family, and with the exemplary privacy that made her comparatively unknown at the time of her death in the mid-1890s. More insidiously, we are also asked to believe that Morisot's painting was the artistic expression of her femininity — a form of love, turned like an irradiating light or Mallarméan '*divination*' on the persons and settings of the late nineteenth-century *haute bourgeoise* family. But how effortlessly did a woman make a hat (and in what ways did it announce the *ensemble* of a woman's social and economic class, her sexuality and style)? Feminist critics have been quick to point out that Morisot's much-praised femininity and spontaneity, her seeming domesticity and loving attention to what she painted, are the very qualities which were also said at the time to characterize the Impressionist movement as a whole.[4] Rather than seeing in her painting the phases of a woman's life, we should see them in terms of the major periods of a painter's development — a trajectory that leads from Morisot's early days as a student of Corot and Oudinot, to her artistic dialogue with her future brother-in-law Edouard Manet, her adherence to Impressionist doctrines during the 1870s and 1880s, and her experiments with new themes and styles during the 1890s, when Renoir and Mallarmé had become her closest colleagues and friends.

Thanks to recent writing on Morisot, we now know much more about her artistic ambitions and professional activities, her anxiety to exhibit and sell her painting, and the intensity of her engagement in the avant-garde movements of her time — whether as an ardent supporter of Manet, an active participant in successive Impressionist exhibitions, or a constant innovator in her own work.[5] But Degas's millinery metaphor, however mistakenly, offers a means of broaching the cultural and aesthetic status of femininity in Morisot's painting. Did Morisot aestheticize women in her painting, much as she herself was aestheticized by Manet's fascinated portraits of the 1870s (often with a hat), or by Mallarmé's impenetrable tribute on the occasion of her posthumous retrospective? Linda Nochlin has pointed to the ways in which cosmetic art in a painting like *Lady at her Toilet* (1875) can be read as a sign for Morisot's own art.[6] If Morisot tacitly endorsed the analogy between the labours of feminine self-beautification and the work of painting, does that make her art an unselfconscious reflection of the ideological linkage between images of women, beauty, and art during the latter part of the nineteenth century?

Anne Higonnet's *Berthe Morisot's Images of Women* provides an answer of sorts: yes and no. Griselda Pollock's 'Modernity and the Spaces of Femininity' has analysed the way in which recent definitions of Impressionistic modernity work to marginalize women painters because of their subject matter.[7] Morisot's paintings (like Cassatt's) represent the missing, modern 'spaces of femininity'. As Higonnet has concluded in her sympathetic biography of Morisot, 'In her images we now find the secluded and almost invisible world of women's values and women's lives, of femininity as it was perceived and experienced from within.'[8] Morisot's seclusion is redefined as a space of femininity evoked by the studied interiority of her luminous paintings, where women or children avert their gaze from public life in the privacy of their own rooms, *robes d'intérieur* or *déshabillé* indicate that women are either at home or not at home except to each other, and a flurry of paint-strokes create the shimmering effects of filtered, indoor light — equally suggestive of technical spontaneity and the atmospherics of intimacy.[9]

Like Higonnet's earlier biography, *Berthe Morisot's Images of Women* celebrates what Caroll Smith-Rosenberg calls 'the female world of love and ritual'.[10] But this second book, copiously illustrated and resourcefully argued, focuses specifically on the feminine visual culture which, according to Higonnet, enabled Morisot to redefine the terms of her art, whilst revealing 'femininity' to be socially constructed rather than innate. The possibility of introducing feminine visual culture into the context of high (and by definition, masculine) art, Higonnet argues, allowed Morisot to become a woman painter. Amateur women's pictorial production, with its emphasis on women's social roles and on the diffusion of ideals of social harmony via a feminized familial circle, and the fashion plate images of a burgeoning consumer culture (the commodification of art in an age of mechanical reproduction) function for Higonnet not simply as the context of Morisot's painting, but as an explanation for her achievement.

Higonnet states at the outset: 'Berthe Morisot became a painter despite being a woman. She painted the way she did because she was a woman' (p. 1). She ends by asserting that 'She did become a painter despite being a woman and despite a lifelong commitment to the representation of femininity' (p. 258). The recurrence of Higonnet's 'despite' signals an unresolved tension. Is Morisot's representation of femininity achieved *despite* or *because of* (the conditions of) her (historically specific) situation as a woman painting at the end of the nineteenth century? Was she at once disempowered and enabled by her gender? Higonnet wants to have it both ways. Disrupting the categories of public and private, masculine and feminine, marginal and dominant cultures, Morisot, she suggests, defied the constraints on women that prevented them from becoming great artists, whilst deriving strength from the feminine visual culture on which she drew. Morisot becomes a heroine of the *salon*-studio — the dual-purpose room where, in fact, she chose to paint.

Higonnet's enterprise bears the marks of a version of American feminist criticism originating in the 1970s. For the most part non-psychoanalytic, often naïvely affirmative, such feminism saw a positive value in what Higonnet herself calls, approvingly, 'a visual sense of self' ('However fragmentary, marginal, or ephemeral, women's pictures gave them a visual sense of self' p. 256). Higonnet's is a long way from the old 'images of women' approach (the quest for portrayals of women, hitherto believed to be, or treated as, invisible in cultural representation and cultural production). But it does have in common with this earlier brand of feminist criticism the belief that a (positive) self-image and its relation to representation are relatively uncomplicated entities — enabling mirrors in which women can find cultural validation for their experience.

Berthe Morisot's Images of Women uncovers a wealth of material to connect nineteenth-century women with their mirrors. But although Higonnet invokes '*ce Narcisse féminin*' in her concluding epigraph (p. 253, citing Lou Andréas-Salomé rather than Freud), she remains uninterested in the possibility that such narcissism might be viewed, less transparently, from a psychoanalytic perspective. Nor, in the end, does she choose to investigate the ways in which consumer culture may have related to women's changing economic status or shaped their desires. As Rachel Bowlby puts it, 'Consumer culture transforms the narcissistic mirror into a shop window, the glass which reflects an idealized image of the woman (or man) who stands before it . . . Through the glass, the woman sees what she wants and what she wants to be.'[11] 'Just looking', the shopper's apology, loses its innocence. Loving and painting may, after all, turn out to be connected in this narcissistic mirror where a self comes into being in relation to an image and as a refraction of the desire of the other. It is never just a matter of a woman and herself (or her positive self-image).

As Higonnet concedes, a woman's self-representation remained subject to nineteenth-century conditions of possibility for feminine self-representation. She argues persuasively that Morisot managed to contest as well as negotiate these conditions of possibility. But was it really the legacy of feminine visual culture that gave her the means to do so? Higonnet's discussion of amateur women's painting prompts her to say that whereas Morisot's sister Edma was 'trapped by amateur values' (she gave up painting when she married), 'Berthe was empowered by them' (p. 59). The evidence for this empowerment involves a narrative of feminist resourcefulness: '[Morisot's] recognition of the amateur tradition's strengths was her first great asset. The second was her ability to outwit its limitations' (p. 60). Morisot's appropriation of the fashion plate for the images, poses and settings of her paintings in the 1870s is adduced as similar evidence of proto-feminist resourcefulness: 'If images like fashion plates did offer mid-nineteenth-century women some kind of escape from past gender constraints . . . then Impressionism's attention to the fashion plate offered Morisot the — slim — possibility of salvaging those meanings while at the same time exercising the privileges of painting' (p. 103). How slim can a privileged possibility get? As Higonnet lets slip, 'fashion plates and Morisot's paintings look alike because they share the same attitude' (p. 106). But 'attitude' (well-dressed women looking preoccupiedly into mirrors, or turning their backs to stand by cradles) is just about all they share.

Morisot's paintings differ from fashion plates not only because (most obviously) their socio-economic function and conditions of production differ radically — not only because one originates in the *salon* or studio and the other in the workshop; not only because in one nothing can be bought while in the other everything is advertised for sale. They differ because a well-known painting like *The Cradle* (1872), for instance, is a study in the slight but significant differences between what is darkly material and what is light, what is diaphanous and what is solid — a study, above all, of an act of looking displaced from the acquisitive gaze of the potential shopper to the absorption of a woman in the sleeping baby whose pose mirrors hers. If indeed, as Higonnet speculates, Morisot did while away her time by leafing through the pages of the *Moniteur de la Mode* during the upheavals of the civil war of the Commune in 1871 (when she and her family were trapped in their Paris suburb), we still cannot help seeing that her paintings involve formal and compositional choices, artistic concerns and ambitions, that could never arise in the context of the fashion plate. As Higonnet admits, 'Morisot's paintings do something more' (p. 115). What is that something?

It would be doctrinaire to see the diaphanous drapery and graceful symmetries of *The Cradle* as a mystification. And yet the power of Morisot's paintings to make the economics of labour disappear permits their strategic deployment by the advertising industry (in a recent campaign for Renault cars), where Impressionism itself has become a culturally approved export. If women's proper 'work' in paintings like these is to disguise the fact that leisure and beauty, like the upper-class home (or car) depend on someone else's labour, where does that leave the invisible work of painting in Morisot's *oeuvre*? I want to explore this question by way of two examples — shifting the terrain from the economics of production and consumer desire to a psychic economy, whilst at the same time returning to the issue of Morisot's relation to high, and allegedly masculine, culture. Two chapters of Higonnet's book — 'Mirrored Bodies' and 'A Mother Pictures her Daughter' — direct our attention particularly to Morisot's struggles with the female nude (the classical *topos* of a masculine artistic tradition) and to her portrayals of the adolescent daughter, Julie Manet, through whom, Higonnet suggests, Morisot renewed herself much as Renoir renewed himself through the classical nude during the same period. Both the female nude and the *jeune fille* pose the question of narcissism — loving (one's own) images — in the context of feminine difference.

Morisot's *At The Psyché* (1891), for instance, can be read as an almost punning statement about the relation between visual pleasure, the female nude and the woman painter. Morisot (as Higonnet has pointed out) installs herself obliquely in this painting by means of an allusion to one of Manet's striking portraits of her as a young woman (fully clothed, needless to say), faintly reflected in the mirror that also holds the reflection of the half-naked model.[12] Higonnet — who chooses to emphasize the relative lack of success of Morisot's painting of the female nude, and the tensions involved in confronting a self seen through masculine eyes — reads the painting as a *mise en abyme*; Morisot was confronted by the uncanny return of her own past, 'the ghost of her past as a man's [i.e. Manet's] model' (p. 247). For Higonnet, it was the collaboration with Cassatt in her parallel studies for 'The Coiffure' that freed Morisot to attempt the female nude and contest the masculinity of the *topos*. Complicated by Morisot's ownership of Manet's *Nude Arranging Her Hair* (1879), which hung in the room where she worked, and by her admiration for Renoir's nude paintings and drawings of the late 1880s, the Cassatt/Morisot pairing is seen by Higonnet as the story of the introduction of a crucial feminine difference.

Higonnet insists that both Morisot and Cassatt were blocked from going further in their exploration of the female nude by 'the ineluctably gendered relationship between the masculine artist and the female body' (p. 186). But it seems equally possible to read *At the Psyché* as evidence of Morisot's sensuous pleasure in, and meditation on, the female body as an icon of meaning in her own painting. The subtly insistent doublings in the composition of *At the Psyché* in any case work to complicate any simple paradigm of the desirous masculine gaze focused voyeuristically on a female model. The imaginary gaze becomes that of the woman painter (the model's own eyes are averted) whose portrait redefines the invisible space of the painter-onlooker; the nude is at once the subject and the object of her own and Morisot's *rêverie*. The gender-meaning of the painting, if it lies anywhere, is to be found in a syntax diffused across its entire compositional range — in all possible subject positions. The image of a woman paired with, but not identical to, her reflection(s) inserts a diacritical mark into the painting's representational scheme, making the relation between image and mirror-image at once a source of pleasure and an interpretive crux.

If we are to see Morisot's own reflection in her art, it is not simply as a refraction of other (artists') images of women, but in the interplay of light, colour, illusion and allusion, and in the formal and spatial relationships that give a painting like *At the Psyché* its distinctive rhythms. At the risk of being overly allegorical, one might also suggest that for Morisot, the *psyché*, or cheval glass, may itself have functioned as the site, not only for introducing sexual difference into the traditionally masculine *topos* of the female nude, but for differentiating between degrees of representational illusion — here, between the volume of the material body that is already an image, and the airy immateriality of its reflection. The story of Psyche involves both Eros and Psyche; pleasure is produced by the play of mind on body. Such possibilities for '*divination*' (Mallarmé's term), or even Baudelairean '*correspondances*' — the exacting aesthetic ideals and Symbolist practice of her contemporaries — remain half-glimpsed, yet tantalizingly immanent, in Morisot's painting.

The darkened mood and evolving technique of Morisot's intriguing series of portraits of her daughter during the 1890s are a case in point. Whether as the adolescent mourner in *Julie Manet and her Greyhound Laertes*, or as the musician in *Julie Playing the Violin* (both belonging to 1893), or as the subject of her own *rêverie* in the coolly languorous *Julie Daydreaming* (1894), Julie functions as a symbol of the diffused, unfocused, unrepresentable state that the Symbolist movement identified most closely with music and creativity in general. G. Stanley Hall's classic book, *Adolescence: Its Psychology and its Relations to Physiology, Anthropology, Sociology, Sex, Crime, Religion, and Education* (1904), lists 'inner absorption or reverie' at the start of its catalogue of adolescent malaises (with a potential for both poetry and pathology). To Hall, adolescence marked the treacherous threshold of sexual difference, just as, for Freud, it marked the intensification of feminine narcissism. Although not herself a feminist (or, for that matter, associated with the union of women painters that emerged in the early 1880s), Morisot seems to have become interested in women's rights and particularly in the contemporary debate about the nature of the *jeune fille* provoked by the adolescent journals of Marie Bashkirtseff, published in the late 1880s.[13]

More importantly, Morisot found in Julie a symbol of the self-absorbed *rêverie* that had characterized her own painting from the start (the early *Study: At the Water's Edge* of 1864, for instance, where a thoughtful female Narcissa contemplates her reflection). If we find ourselves saying, with Denis Rouart, that 'with her to love was to paint', it may be because, in paintings like these, maternal narcissism takes as its pleasurable object the only partially split-off aspect of self represented by a daughter. What better image of non-identical self-difference could there be? Questions such as: What does she know? What does she want? What is she about to become? seem to exercise Morisot's portraits of the adolescent Julie (much as they exercised Freud in his encounters with young female hysterics at the same period). Mallarmé alludes to Morisot's '*ardente flamme maternelle, où se mit, en entier, la créatrice*'.[14] But Morisot's paintings of her daughter testify not only to her maternal regard, or even to the hidden ideological labours of producing the *jeune fille*, but also to the opportunity Julie provided for artistic self-reflection.

In *Julie Playing the Violin*, Julie is flanked by Manet's painting of Morisot (the same one glimpsed in the mirror of *At the Psyché*) and a slice of Degas's portrait of her father Eugène Manet. But Morisot is surely inscribing her own lines of artistic filiation as well as the impeccable pedigree of a *jeune fille*. Like the Japanese print behind Julie in *Julie Manet and her Greyhound Laertes* (or the dog itself — a gift from her guardian, Mallarmé), objects have at once a personal and a cultural meaning.

But the light-reflecting surface of a Chinese jar also suggests Morisot's fascination with transforming the surface of the *quotidienne*. Even the long line of Julie's violin bow can be read as an allusion to the lines of the painter's own brushstrokes, which have become elongated and flowing where once they were short and leaping. A painting about music-making becomes a painting about painting; a portrait of Julie in her familial frame gestures beyond it to Morisot's own cultural *milieu*. It becomes a summation of her own artistic past and present.

Morisot's painting is the product of her privileged and intimate relation to the high avant-garde culture of her time. Avant-garde art occupies the same ambiguous relation to tradition and modernity, the marginal and the mainstream, popular and high culture, that Higonnet attributes to feminine visual culture. Arguably, Morisot's commitment to the contemporary (paradoxically expressed also in her allegiance to the past) was as much, if not more, instrumental in her emergence as a woman painter. This may have to do with the unexpectedly favourable conjunction between Morisot's social class, her gender and the cultural status of high art at the time; the distinctly non-bohemian Morisots hoped Berthe would marry (or not marry a Manet), but they actively encouraged her artistic career. The existence of an extraordinary group of painters and writers around Manet, Mallarmé and Morisot herself gave her access to discussions about art and poetry — and, indeed, femininity — scarcely provided by the fashion plate even if Mallarmé did once edit a ladies' magazine).

Anne Higonnet's accomplished, informative and thought-provoking book acknowledges that Morisot never abandoned *haute bourgeoise* woman's proper place, the *salon*, whilst also recognizing the disturbing challenge her career poses to such definitions. But an investigation into femininity and the cultural power of its association with high artistic practice in *fin de siècle* France remains to be undertaken. What did it mean for Morisot to occupy a milieu where the culture and aestheticization of the feminine had become so closely identified, not only with the mirror, but with art? The exact terms of Morisot's accession to her deservedly central place in the history of Impressionism and women's painting remain open to debate. *Berthe Morisot's Images of Women* does not exhaust the possibilities of Morisot's self-reflexive modernity, or open up the psychic spaces of femininity. But it does pay tribute to a previously neglected aspect of Morisot's painting — to the art of self-fashioning implicit in Degas's millinery metaphor.

Mary Jacobus
Cornell University

NOTES

1 See A. Higonnet, *Berthe Morisot's Images of Women*, p. 77.
2 Arts Council of Great Britain, *Berthe Morisot*, exh. cat., London, 1950, p. 5.
3 'Berthe Morisot', *Oeuvres complètes de Stéphane Mallarmé*, Editions Gallimard, Paris, 1945, p. 534.
4 See, for instance, K. Adler and T. Garb, *Berthe Morisot*, Oxford, 1987, pp. 64–5; *Berthe Morisot: The Correspondence*, Denis Rouart (ed.), intro. K. Adler and T. Garb, London, 1986, pp. 6–8; and T. Garb, 'Berthe Morisot and the Feminizing of Impressionism', *Perspectives on Morisot*, T. J. Edelstein (ed.), New York, 1990, pp. 57–66.
5 See, for instance, S. Glover Lindsay, 'Berthe Morisot: Nineteenth-Century Woman as Professional', *Perspectives on Morisot*, op. cit., pp. 79–90.
6 See L. Nochlin, 'Morisot's Wet Nurse: The Construction of Work and Leisure in Impressionist Painting', *Perspectives on Morisot*, op. cit., p. 99.
7 See G. Pollock, *Vision and Difference: Feminism, Femininity, and the Histories of Art*, London and New York, 1988, pp. 50–90.
8 Anne Higonnet, *Berthe Morisot: A Biography*, London, 1990, p. 222.
9 For the significance of costume in Morisot's paintings, see A. Schirrmeister, 'La Dernière Mode: Berthe Morisot and Costume', *Perspectives on Morisot*, op. cit., pp. 103–115.
10 See C. Smith-Rosenberg, 'The Female World of Love and Ritual: Relations between Women in Nineteenth-Century America', *Signs*, vol. 1, no. 1, Autumn 1975, pp. 1–29.
11 R. Bowlby, *Just Looking: Consumer Culture in Dreiser, Gissing and Zola*, London, 1985, p. 32.
12 See also A. Higgonet, 'The Other Side of the Mirror', *Perspectives on Morisot*, op. cit., p. 75.
13 See A. Higonnet, *Berthe Morisot: A Biography*, p. 203, and *Berthe Morisot: The Correspondence*, pp. 177, 233. Julie Manet, who kept her own journals read Marie Bashkirtseff sympathetically in 1897; see Julie Manet, *Journal 1893–1899: sa jeunesse parmi les peintres impressionistes et les hommes de lettres*, Paris, 1979, pp. 130–1, 138.
14 *Oeuvres complètes de Stéphane Mallarmé*, p. 535.

MUTE SIGNS AND BLIND ALLEYS

Martin Kemp

Pieter Saenredam, The Painter and his Time by *Gary Schwartz* and *Marten Jan Bok*, London: Thames and Hudson, 1990, 356 pp., 259 plates, £38.00

Perspectives: Saenredam and the Architectural Painters of the 17th Century, exhibition catalogue, Museum Boymans-van Beuningen, Rotterdam, 1991, essays by *Jeroen Giltaij, J. M. Montias, Walter Liedtke, Rob Ruurs*, catalogue entires by *Jeroen Giltaij* and *Guido Jansen*, 326 pp., 64 col. plates, numerous b. and w. illus., Dfl 99.50

Why have so many art historians gone to such enormous trouble to document the careers of artists?

The traditional impulse to document the circumstances of an artist's life — in terms of professional activities, family, social situation, contacts and even daily doings — is still very much alive, as is vividly shown by the burst of renewed attention devoted to the circumstances of the careers of a number of Dutch seventeenth-century painters, including Rembrandt and the elusive Vermeer. Now the life of the great master of the Dutch church interior, Pieter Saenredam, has been subjected to an astonishingly detailed treatment by Schwartz and Bok. If we want to know all there is to be discovered about Saenredam's uncles and cousins (first, second and variously removed), all is here. But why bother?

The answer given by Schwartz and Bok is that they are rejecting 'as the essential subject of art history' the understanding of 'stylistic development and influences, qualitative judgements, comparisons between one master and another, one school and another, chains of imagery and iconography, ties between style and meaning, style and culture'. Rather, by concentrating 'on a fairly thorough reconstruction [the 'fairly' is a notable understatement] of Saenredam's background, connections, finances, associations and artistic production', including a fascinating study of his patrons, the authors assure us that 'we are discussing true seventeenth-century issues'. If we could all share this confidence that by concentrating solely on the available documention we can be certain of focusing on the 'issues' that are 'true' to the period in question, how much easier art history would become.

The authors seem unaware — or at least leave the reader unaware — that what is considered relevant documentation in the historian's quest to reconstruct the essential features in the production of a painting is ultimately dependent upon what *we* consider the issues to be. If we consider, as the authors do, that 'perspective, space, colour, technique' are 'secondary considerations', and that the reading of pseudo-narratives, symbolic motifs and other bearers of meaning within Saenredam's church interiors reveal his fundamental 'scale of values', then we will revel in Schwartz's and Bok's meticulous documentation of the religious attitudes and social interests of Saenredam's patrons and immediate circle. The authors make neat cases as to why individual patrons might have favoured a concentration on a particular motif in the church, or even encouraged the introduction of fictitious church furniture, such as a bishop's tomb or a Catholic altar in the great church of St Bavo in Haarlem. What they then assume is that the *motif* they identify in the painting — often a small detail such as a man pointing at an organ — is the all-embracing *motivation* for the making of that painting. This method seems all too reminiscent of studies of Impressionist paintings that seem to be interested exclusively in smoking chimneys in the far-distant background.

The authors do show, beyond reasonable doubt in a number of cases, that Saenredam's visual pointing (often very unemphatically) to a real or imagined feature in a church interior was purposely directed to or by the patron's concerns. Through the welter of documentation of people, organizations and places we start to become so naturalized in the functions and associations of the parts of the churches as to understand more of the considerations that contemporary viewers could have brought to the images. For example, the presence of one of Saenredam's characteristically perky dogs or stumpy children in St Bavo's, where there was a special chapel for the 'dogwhipper' (who was briefed to prevent transgressions by both canines and minors), would have carried an immediacy of resonance for those contemporary viewers who were well acquainted with the running of the great church — a resonance that readily eludes the modern viewer. By reconstructing such resonances, our reading of the pictures is undoubtedly enriched. But are such motifs what the pictures are really 'about'? The presence and behaviour of dogs and kids in churches was certainly a seventeenth-century Dutch issue — as was the behaviour and education of children in general — but do the motifs within the pictures explain why they were made and why patrons wanted them? Does the fact that we can construct a daunting body of information about the immediate social circumstances of the artist and the customers, in contrast to the meagre pickings in contemporary literature about the nature of the visual qualities of the works, mean that the motifs are primary and the visual characteristics secondary? I do not think we can confidently answer yes. Not only is there the problem that an art history restricted only to commenting on what can be documented in written sources for the period is dependent upon the vagaries of survival, but more profoundly such a procedure limits a study of the visual to the same parameters as was possible in verbal culture in the same period. Indeed, I think there is a case to be made for saying that visual images begin to assume their special potency for a given society at the very point where the parameters of the verbal are too limiting — and *vice versa*.

Oddly enough, Schwartz and Bok actually go a long way to acknowledge that they have failed to deal with the question as to why Saenredam's art still warrants our attention — and, by reasonable extension, why it warranted the special enthusiam of his patrons. Near the beginning of their book they confess that

> In the final analysis what has brought us to devote years to the study of Pieter Saenredam is our conviction, which we share with a gratifyingly large number of people, that he was important for the quality and significance of his art. However, we do not feel that the historical discipline we practice is equal to explaining that quality and significance.

At the very end, having subjected us to a minutely detailed exposition of contingent documentation, they disconcertingly admit that

> The eye of the draftsman stays where it was, in the head of a human being conditioned by his birth, background, surroundings and circumstances. No one would pretend that knowledge concerning the person of the artist allows us to form a picture of what his work looks like. Neither does the appearance of the work form a trustworthy guide to understanding the person who created it. Independent study of both is needed to arrive at a balanced judgement concerning what happens when an artist, a social being of flesh and blood, puts part of himself onto paper and into paint. We have tried to do half this job.

This vision of the two independent and apparently incommensurate means for the study of art can at best be seen as sensible temporizing which permits the cautious historian to tackle concrete 'history' rather than nebulous 'art'. But to me this avoiding action represents a form of visual timidity, which results in little more than saying, in the manner of the popular cliché, 'I know what I like' (and 'what lots of other people like') but I cannot tell you why. It ultimately results in a failure to tackle head-on the way in which form and content are integrated and profoundly reciprocating components in the making and reading of works of art in their historical and modern contexts.

Even relying upon the kind of period evidence championed by Schwartz and Bok, there is good reason to think not only that Dutch spectators regarded the visual skills of the perspectivists and the significance of their subjects as all of a piece but also that Saenredam's particular patrons were sensitive to the integrated wholeness of his art with respect to visual means and labelled motif. As Montias shows in a fine study in *Perspectives*, Saenredam's patrons were likely to be prominent in society, predominantly Calvinist (by a ratio of 4:1 in Amsterdam), wealthy and especially concerned with collecting pictures (in that a disproportionate amount of their wealth resided in their collections). Saenredam's pictures were expensive — up to five times the cost of a landscape — and were available on commission rather than off the peg. They seem to have appealed to those who were prepared to pay for visual 'quality'. A pleasingly early acknowledgement that Saenredams were the in-taste for connoisseurs is provided in 1662 by Cornelius de Bie's *Het Gulden Cabinet* in which we learn that

> about the year 1628, he [Saenredam] turned completely to the painting of perspectives, churches, halls, galleries, buildings and other things, from the outside as well as the inside, so true that life and nature can display no greater perfection than he is able to express very skilfully with his brush. This can be attested by the city of Utrecht, where he spent a period twenty weeks, practising this art with great industriousness, as can be

> observed in his drawings and paintings (depicting very beautiful perspectives, churches and halls), which are very highly esteemed by all connoisseurs and are judged to be most exceptional.

Some hint of what Cornelius meant by the perfection and beauty which appealed to the connoisseurs can be gleaned from the poem he subsequently cites, which speaks glowingly of the painter's mathematics and the way in which the vertical and horizontal members speak of the formal and structural properties of each building — what might be called the building's rectitude. The fact that we have to rely upon such slight verbal hints to understand what visual properties were found especially appealing by a select group of connoisseurs does not mean that they were of slight importance to artist or patron. It simply means that contemporary spectators did not have (and presumably did not feel the need to have) an elaborate vocabulary of critical categories or genres of literary production with which to articulate their responses for subsequent generations. In fact, what evidence does survive about the viewing of his pictures nowhere directly supports the idea that they were read primarily for their pseudo-narrative or symbolic motifs. Rather, the great bulk of contemporary testimony suggests that they were appreciated as *perspectives* of notable buildings painted with remarkably high skill and special visual appeal. There is not one contemporary account which articulates a reading in terms of the specific details advocated by Schwartz and Bok.

Contemporaries do not seem to have experienced much difficulty in knowing what images of Dutch church interiors were 'about'. They were 'perspectives', as the title of the Museum Boymans-van Beuningen exhibition acknowledges, and there is every sign that the leading artists took their competence in the science of perspective very seriously. A series of quite sophisticated books, most notably by Marolois and Hondius, were published in numerous editions to meet the demand for knowledge. I strongly suspect that Saenredam would have been shocked to hear that perspective was a 'secondary' feature of his paintings, and that 'space and colour in his works may interest us a great deal, but Saenredam did not work on them actively'. He may also have been surprised to learn that 'geometry as such did not interest him', when his library of books testifies to an unusually strong collection of geometrical texts, including three Euclids in Dutch, which are themselves testimony to the burst of publication of major works of science in the vernacular in Holland in the early seventeenth century. When we also read that Saenredam's unusually wide variety of formats for pictures was one of a series of technical 'idiosyncrasies' that 'hardly affect the appearance of his paintings', we may begin to wonder whether the authors' self-confessed lack of visual acumen is not so much a cunning limitation as a dangerous liability.

Their treatment of Saenredam's perspective is little more than a lame re-hash of the analyses published by Rob Ruurs.[1] The strength of Ruurs's analyses resides in the detailed scrutiny of how the artist actually went about making his construction drawings, using as one of his central techniques a 'distance point' coupled with precise horizontal and vertical scales. Ruurs also convincingly infers a close relationship with the surveyor Pieter Wils. Unfortunately, the authors make little of Ruurs's telling treatment of individual constructions whilst accepting in a schematic manner his uncertin treatment of where Saenredam stands in relation to the artistic and mathematical traditions of perspective. Their statement that 'none of the existing printed books of the time, including Stevin's, was pedagogically or typographically sufficient as a stand-alone manual for learning to use perspective the way Saenredam did' stands in need of serious qualification and does not appear to be founded on an adequate technical knowledge of the full range of texts available. They are also wrong to attribute Saenredam's obstinate attachment to a planar orientation for the primary forms in his pictures to the difficulty of doing otherwise. The so-called 'distance-point method' could, as Cousin, Danti, Marolois and others had shown, be used conveniently for forms at any angle to the picture plane. Above all, it is profoundly misleading to argue that Saenredam's perspectival methods and achievements were those of a bread-and-butter perspectivist, merely concerned with the pragmatics of a working construction. His method of working from precise measurements of existing buildings, and the plotting of the equivalent measures in perspective projection on the receding orthogonals in vertical and horizontal planes, was utterly exceptional, requiring a powerful feeling for perspectival projection and a devotion to long-winded perspectival duty that few artists (Piero della Francesca is the most conspicuous exception) have been prepared to countenance. His penchant for unexpected station points within the buildings and his wide-angle views — lying well outside the upper limits recommended by the theorists — confirm the exceptional nature of his visual proclivities.

Looking at the evidence of the drawings and paintings, including the artist's own notably detailed inscriptions, it is possible to build up a picture of Saenredam's working method which is quite remote from the model implicit in Schwartz's and Bok's book. Typically, the painter selected a building of established interest and reputation. He made one or more detailed on-the-spot drawings, noting his 'eye point' (equivalent to our 'vanishing point') as an essential marker for any future coordinates he might wish to use. He also took or obtained precise measurements of the overall dimensions and details of the building. This raw material was then filed away, sometimes for a number of years, until contacts with a patron indicated that it might be exploited as the basis of a painting. The motif and the point of view (both literal and attitudinal) were agreed, and he embarked on the painstaking labour of translating the raw data (sketched and measured) into a constructional drawing which integrated motif and mathematics in a seamless manner. The construction was then transferred as a flat, linear projection to the panel by the blacking of the back of the drawing and the pressing through of the main outlines on to the prepared panel. Preparing his pigments involved unusual admixtures of gold dust, with rose and yellow added to the whites. The final act of painting was conducted with astonishing delicacy of tonal touch and linear refinement, to create a coolly poised image which is both unexpected and yet apparently inevitable. In this scenario, the motif may serve as the circumstantial trigger for the commission, but it hardly acts as an adequate explanation of the visual attention his paintings have warranted.

What the setting of Saenredam in the broader context of Dutch architectural painters of the century serves to show, as was splendidly accomplished in the Rotterdam exhibition, is how little shared or comparable motifs actually result in different painters making similar pictures. There can be little doubt that both artists and audience prized the way that the major masters of the relatively exclusive and apparently constrained genre of church interiors exhibited their own manner. There was, to be sure, some of the inevitable borrowing which invariably occurs when someone invents a new trick, such as the Plinian device of an illusionistic curtain suspended in front of the picture plane, but there was also a sense of conscious individuality in the production of painters like Houckgeest and de Witte that was calculated to attract Cornelius de Bie's 'connoisseurs'. Collectively, the interpretative essays in the catalogue, by Jeroen Giltaij, J. M. Montias, Walter Liedtke and Rob Ruurs, strike a reasonable balance between historical data and visual acumen, and the catalogue entries by Jeroen Giltaij and Guido Jansen deal effectively with the history of the individual works. On matters of perspective, however, the catalogue entries are not entirely to be trusted. There is a consistent confusion of the 'distance point' with the vanishing point for any set of parallel lines at any given orientation. The so-called 'distance point' is properly defined as the point at which the diagonals through a normally oriented, square-tiled floor meet on the horizon, or, alternatively, as the vanishing point for all horizontal lines oriented at 45° to the picture plane. Technically speaking, in the asymmetrically angular views favoured by Houckgeest and de Witte, there is no 'central vanishing point' and lateral 'distance point', as the authors consistently infer, but a series of separate vanishing points distributed along the horizon.

Not the least of the problems which accrues from faulty analyses of the varied bases on which the perspectives were created is a failure to deal with the question of the extent to which the tiled floors of the churches were regularized for the sakes of constructive convenience and visual effect. If we look, for example, at the images of the tomb of William the Silent in the Nieuwe Kerk, Delft, by Houckgeest and de Witte (nos. 31, 34 and 38), it appears that Houckgeest has produced a chequerboard spread of an extent, consistent pattern and optical impact not present in the church itself. By contrast, de Witte has deliberately set off the regular tiles immediately around the monument by the patchwork irregularity of the more-or-less rectangular stones which had over the years come to comprise the main pavement of the church. Although de Witte's perspectival competence comes in for rather rough treatment in the catalogue, it seems to me that a proper analysis would reveal that in his handling of less than perfectly regular elements from unexpected angles he is accomplishing something no less sophisticated than Saenredam — though with different visual priorities.

In a sense, it would be easy to characterize these two publications as representing the new and the old: one a book on Saenredam as a producer in a social market, playing strongly to those who believe that works of art are essentially 'deposits of social relationships' (to adapt Baxandall's phrase); the other a traditional exhibition catalogue, directed to the explication of master-works (and lesser master-works) as objects of aesthetic contemplation. There is an element of truth in this characterization, but it is too facile. The introductory essays in the catalogue begin to demonstrate that there might be a way out of the blind alleys signposted, respectively, 'art' and 'society'. At present I feel rather like the traveller in the old joke, who asks someone for directions to somewhere, and is duly told 'I wouldn't start from here'. Reading the heroic monograph on Saenredam, I am increasingly convinced that we should not be starting from the authors' visually constricting premise, and that we should have the courage to combine visual and historical intuitions in such a way as to produce a genuine history of the visual.

Martin Kemp
University of St Andrews

NOTES

1 R. Ruurs, *Saenredam: the Art of Perspective*, Amsterdam and Philadelphia, 1987.

OF WAR, DEMONS AND NEGATION

David Anfam

Jackson Pollock: An American Saga, by *Steven Naifeh* and *Gregory White Smith*, New York: Harper Perennial, 1989 (reprinted 1991), 934 pp., 16 col. plates, 200 b. & w. illus., $16.95

Jackson Pollock, by *Ellen Landau*, New York: Harry N. Abrams, Inc., 1989, 283 pp., 211 col. plates, 159 b. & w. illus., £45.00

Reconstructing Modernism: Art in New York, Paris and Montreal 1945–1964, edited by *Serge Guilbaut*, Cambridge, Mass. and London: The MIT Press, 1990, 418 pp., 74 b. & w. illus., £29.25 (hdbk), £15.25 (pbk)

Abstract Expressionism, by *David* and *Cecile Shapiro*, Cambridge: Cambridge University Press, 1990, 442 pp., 19 b. & w. illus., £16.95

Abstract Expressionism: Creators and Critics, by *Clifford Ross*, New York: Harry N. Abrams, Inc., 1990, 304 pp., 12 col. plates, 57 b. & w. illus., $49.50

Benton, Pollock, and the Politics of Modernism: from Regionalism to Abstract Expressionism, by *Erika Doss*, Chicago: The University of Chicago Press, 1991, 445 pp., 137 b. & w. illus., £31.96

Abstract Expressionism and the Modern Experience, by *Stephen Polcari*, Cambridge: Cambridge University Press, 1991, 408 pp., 32 col. plates, 290 b. & w. illus., £40.00

> But if response must be directed to the social circumstances of 'cultural production' then the identification of self must be found in a relation to such circumstances. The culture of the past becomes a set of documents that define modern men not as the inheritors of the secret imagination of the past but the guilty heirs of the social inequalities that are 'inscribed' on its art forms. (George Hunter)[1]

What tales will Abstract Expressionism unfold about America, nationalist politics, modernism and even the human psyche? These are big questions. They vex much of the recent literature that addresses this most contentious 'movement' of the twentieth century. It is no longer prudent to write accounts, such as Irving Sandler did almost twenty-five years ago with his classic *Abstract Expressionism: The Triumph of American Painting*, which aspire to seemingly transparent recording, to an art history beyond bias or complicities. Battle-lines have long since been drawn; covert agendas unmasked, or at least flung between the various factions; and the ground churned by ideological manoeuvres, attacks, counter-denials and retrenchment. Whoever takes the kind of 'objective' approach manifest, for instance, by Ellen Landau's eminently reasonable monograph on Pollock risks — rightly or otherwise — the charge of being not quite *au courant*. To sit on the fence is to become a target. Scholarship may be a casualty of these theoretical wars. Certainly, they attest at the least to partisan motives. For there is of course a lot at stake: not just tenures, ambition and intellectual status, but also the broader empowerment that attaches to narratives themselves. The Authorized Version of Abstract Expressionism is the story that, *ipso facto*, exposes the fictiveness of its rivals. Some fables, nevertheless, are more equal than others. The 'truest' representations are often the most feigning.

Abstract Expressionism is not a field likely to be transformed in the near future by any sudden abundance of new facts. Indeed, the subject has been so well researched that the archaeology of our knowledge is starting to look comparatively replete. To be sure, hindrances persist, but they are islands on a charted map: the apparent absence of a corpus of significant earlier works by de Kooning beyond the canon already known and shown, the ongoing inaccessibility of Clyfford Still's huge pictorial legacy and a dearth of fully informative correspondence by several leading figures all come to mind (Newman and Motherwell apart, Pollock was notoriously terse, and Rothko, among others, just seems to have often chosen the telephone). An outcome of this situation has been to escalate subsidiary issues, set on by academic pressures to garner 'new' research and, especially in the United States, to publish doctoral theses. Whether the plight of an interesting, if decidedly minor, Afro-American gesturalist painter or the relevance of yet another sub-genre of Jungian or Freudian literary popularization in the 1940s is at stake, these constitute footnotes to a larger text. At the present moment what counts most revolves around the long view, the relation of part to whole and the very procedures of the revisionist enterprise. Hermeneutics is basic to making sense of how sense is made of Abstract Expressionism.

No greater gulf could exist than that between Stephen Polcari's grand treatise, *Abstract Expressionism and the Modern Experience*, and the selection of essays entitled *Reconstructing Modernism*. The former is the fruit of more than a decade's research; the latter grew from papers given at a University of British Columbia symposium at Vancouver in September 1986 dealing with artistic production and the Cold War. As memorialized in this volume, the event was apparently an ingrown affair, to the extent that little real dissension surfaced among the participants; for that, the audience was necessary. Nor is there at root much substance, let alone a great deal to engage with, underlying most of the essays tackling Abstract Expressionism. (The rest are in general far more valuable, notably Thomas Crow's 'Saturday Disasters: Trace and Reference in Early Warhol' and Larry May's analysis of Hollywood politics, though unfortunately outside the scope of the present discussion.) Contrary to the best traditions of radical thought, self-criticism was in short supply. Instead, an ideological framework to which revisionism has too easily fallen hostage fossilizes the debate: the editor Serge Guilbaut's notion that American art of the 1940s and early '50s is altogether explicable by reference to cultural hegemony and the economic bases of imperialism. As set forth in *How New York Stole the Idea of Modern Art* (1983), and present like a *doxia* that wafts through the interstices of *Reconstructing Modernism*, this critique is compromised less by its proximity to vulgar Marxism or even on factual grounds (few can dispute the fact that certain Cold Warriors indulged in promotional chicanery and manipulation), than for its unrelenting narrowness. What might Marx himself have made of these foreclosed horizons whereon bad faith masquerades as acuity? Firstly, the art is turned into a cipher because it receives little serious attention. Once effaced, its features then mirror solely those of the original Cold War climate and its ambient political strategies. Secondly, Guilbaut slips his own Gallic chauvinism into any residual gaps. While his distaste for American abstraction is obvious enough, he is at once coy to present an alternative canon, yet keen to recuperate all manner of artists. In itself this is praiseworthy and provides for an introductory memoir by the Franco-American painter John-Franklin Koenig which is refreshing in its modesty. By comparison, Guilbaut does duty 'in the trenches of critical discourse', the title of the climactic section of his essay 'Postwar Painting Games'. There, such predictable recruits as Fougeron, Wols, Fautrier and Soulages hold the fort — already manned (as the editor's Introduction suggests) by a group of Montreal Automatists which includes Riopelle, Barbeau and Borduas. Although he promises to stage a 'confrontation' with 'the Western aesthetic' (presumably thereby denoting the 'New York School'), it never materializes. In answers to questions from the floor, Guilbaut claims to be 're-injecting' into artworks the 'sort of urgency they had when first produced' (p. 81). If only saying could make it so.

T. J. Clark's contribution, 'Jackson Pollock's Abstraction', evinces a far more seriously theorized standpoint. Here, something of what Charles Altieri has elsewhere alluded to as the 'liberating force of demystification' can at last be felt.[2] With several *aperçus* en route, Clark discourses at length along two subtly intertwined paths. On the one hand, he employs Mikhail Bakhtin to argue that the fortunes of Pollock's abstraction — a signal instance being their hijack by Cecil Beaton's lens in 1950 as a backdrop for *haute-couture* models — re-inscribe themselves into a total pattern of significance (pp. 176–7). On the other, Clark seeks to reconstruct Pollock's autonomy, his decision-making processes (pp. 183ff.). Between them, the two approaches try to avoid a dilemma elsewhere most plainly encapsulated in the interpretive controversy between E. D. Hirsch and Hans-Georg Gadamer (and of course replayed in infinite variations throughout post-structuralist theory). Hirsch has argued for meanings rooted in the stable domain of authorial origins, whereas Gadamer favours a concept of semantic autonomy according to which 'textual meaning can somehow exist independently of individual consciousness' so that 'understanding is not a reproductive but always a productive activity.'[3] Clark aims to synthesize both yet, somewhat like Gadamer and Hirsch, in the end seems to orbit the so-called 'hermeneutic circle': the contradiction that understanding part of a text/image requires knowledge of the whole, while comprehension of the whole assumes a purchase upon every part. Perhaps in order to break free, Clark has recourse to a catalyst that propels his logic and also, or so he believes, Pollock's: 'negation'. As first applied to avant-gardism in Clark's 'Clement Greenberg's Theory of Art', negation does explain important aspects of earlier modernist practice.[4] At a pinch, it might still fit a subsequent maverick such as Ad Reinhardt, though in his case negation truly falls under the sway of *différance* (even before Derrida so much as explicated the idea), being continually delayed in that play of opposites between which Reinhardt's statements and his final 'black' paintings oscillate. But Pollock and negation? All the evidence available suggests otherwise.

Among the almost one thousand pages of Pollock biography by Naifeh and Smith one observation strikes a novel (at least for this reader) and tantalizing note. It amplifies pointers little more than implicit in the photographs and films of the artist painting, or pretending to do so. The authors cite several sources indicating how, during the 'drip' phase, Pollock 'began to work in the air above the canvas, tracing the unwinding images in three-dimensional space' (p. 539). If true, this accords with the canvases' complex mixture of indexical *and* mimetic processes, itself another outgrowth of Pollock's all-embracing, at times even hopelessly overwrought involvement, above all, with the aesthetics of 'presence'. 'Presence' might mean Nature, *One*-ness, raw pigment, the imaging of masculine force, the body pictorially encoded or indulgence in an obsessive figuration itself. But whatever the guise, its suasions for Pollock were intense. Clark asserts the very reverse. In his view, the 1947–50 pictures display 'renunciation' and are 'the *opposite* of figuration, the outright, strict negative of it' (p. 191). Elsewhere, Clark's watchwords are 'high negativity', emptiness, effacement, 'discomposure', cancellation and even 'disappointment' (p. 225).[5] And there, faintly, the motor beneath the model can be heard. Regardless of how sophisticated the superstructure becomes, movements down below bespeak an urge to narrativize. Revealingly, neo-Hegelianism bulks large in Clark's account and this, in turn, depends heavily on two-tiered paradigms, patterns of dialectical causation and intentionality driven by the desire for concordance, or despondency at its imaged lack.[6]

As Barbara Herrnstein Smith has observed, the split-level view of narrative may bespeak 'a lingering strain of naïve Platonism' which is predicated upon a dualism of surface and content, *histoire* and *récit*. To illustrate the premise she recalls the folklorist who found that 345 different tales were at bottom all variants of the Cinderella story (in turn a theologian friend of Smith's thought them 'really' to be allegories of Christian redemption).[7] Inadvertently, *Jackson Pollock: An American Saga* lays bare the Platonism that generates this distinction in its soured, latter-day form and so poses a moral for art history whose resonance goes beyond the journalistic frame of the biography.

Good journalists that they are, Naifeh and Smith offer a racy read. They have conducted over 800 interviews yielding 1,800 pages of typescript, testament to a peculiarly American positivism which associates quantification with qualitative results. A life already quite well chronicled is fleshed out in exhaustive detail, particularly in the initial sections covering Pollock's family background and the years out West. Thereafter, the decline is long, gradual and redeemed by insightful flashes. Part of the blame might be attributable to an eye on the bestseller market responsible for a sensationalism that pesters Pollock's sexuality and foregrounds his more unsavoury exploits and bodily functions (alas, most photographs reveal a rather weedy, uncharismatic person) to few satisfactory ends. Given their physiological gossip about the artist, must his 'dripped' paintings henceforth be renamed the 'pissed' paintings? Maybe Warhol was craftier than ever when he did the 'Oxidation' series. On a less raunchy plane, the trouble lies in the authors' stealthy, psychologizing inheritance from Platonism. Everything on the surface — literally and figuratively — becomes a shadow cast by some content in the depths. Hence certain structural similarities with the detective story genre appear. Over and again, there lurks the question, 'Whodunit?'. The answers: 'the demons inside' (p. 408), the West (p. 468), aberrant draughtsmanship (p. 220), repressed homosexuality (p. 301), the void (p. 254), even Stella Pollock herself (p. 300). To rephrase Auden, what huge imago could have made a psychopathic painter? Causality enfolds any loose temporal ends, signified by a preference for the future perfect tense; the non sequitur cuts off other stray signals. Abstraction is deemed duplicitous, a cloak concealing psychic discourse below (p. 455). As Clark equivocates over individual works and everywhere scents (historical) contradiction, so Naifeh and Smith over-determine most of the compositions, sure that they represent (psychological) alter egos. Are these not poles of a similar narrativity, the one rooted in a materialism turned doubtful, the other in its philistine double?

Abstract Expressionism and the Modern Experience leaps boldly over these problems. Its thesis is clear. Crudely stated, the most seminal artists were children of their time. The times were out of joint (World War II being only the most climactic, awesome symptom of that malaise) and the artworks woven on a loom geared to the blueprint of historical crisis: one that entailed fear, hope, the recuperation of the past to redeem the present, an aspirant spirituality to counteract social ruin or war-time devastation and recourse to myths of vitalism, regression and renewal. Detractors will probably claim that Polcari's agenda remythologizes Abstract Expressionism. They will be wrong because he has brought such a wealth of scholarship to bear that any requisite deconstruction can be done by readers themselves and by future scholars, now in the position to see whatever ideological work the fictions of the 1940s had to serve. In this respect, the two most recent anthologies of statements by artists and critics will also be handy adjuncts. Between them, that of David and Cecile Shapiro is the more reasoned package, while David Ross's is the more attractive. To balance the scales further, the Shapiros do not trim their documents to the extent that Ross does, although the former miss out by excluding Gorky, Reinhardt and Still from their range. Inverted snobbery (Abrams have also done an excellent production job on Landau's monograph, which includes six gatefold colour plates) should not obviate the fact that Ross culls some unfamiliar texts: the alert will discover 'working notes' by Rothko (on p. 173), for example, which, albeit brief, are virtually unkown.

Whereas other 'revisionists' have mistaken the margins for the centre, foundering upon the art's historical distance from us, Polcari mostly bridges that distance by a close reading of the cultural and intellectual matrix in which Abstract Expressionism was embedded. He gives short shrift to the supposition that the concinnity among at least five or six of the artists grew from mere chance or avant-garde jockeying, and thus reasserts a canon. At its head, and quite rightly so, stand Still, Pollock, Rothko and Newman. Lest canonicity stop an élite vanguard from being recontextualized, Polcari cast his net widely. Forgotten artists such as Benton Spruance, an array of Jungian proselytizers, William Wyler's film *The Best Years of Our Lives* and the choreographer Martha Graham are alike typically examined for the light they shed on the mythic rendition of the collapsing societal constructs of 'human nature' and individual 'destiny', especially under the impact of war. That Gottlieb and Baziotes should figure centrally in Polcari's canon (while Guston, strangely, does not) seems less due to intrinsic artistic merits than to this focus upon the two world conflicts and their iconographic heritage as the very types of modern Western crisis. A possible reservation here again concerns the dangers of totalizing narratives which discern the universal beneath many particulars. The archetypal can overwhelm the ectypal. In sum, if war and the Spenglerian *Zeitgeist* are added to the suspects in the 'whodunit' drama, no victim is beyond its scope.

As Northrop Frye's example proved, decoding mythopoeic configurations risks standing back so far that parts blur into awesome wholes and everything points to a transcendental signified. Interpretation of art that avoids a fixed centre altogether is rare — perhaps even impossible, unless an art-historical analogue to Robbe-Grillet is welcome — although Rosalind Krauss's endeavours count among the best in that direction. Moreover, catastrophe, war and a sense of ruptured temporality have long been recognized as ingredients in the current broth.[8] Doing art history as the history of ideas can gain its own momentum and needs to be slowed down by anchors cast into causes specific to a particular moment, place, person or class, rather than universal motives. Why should the concept of psychic recapitulation (caught in the phrase, 'ontogeny recapitulates phylogeny') that Polcari believes governs Still's development take hold when and where it does? In fact it is not unique to the 'modern experience' and occurs at least as far back as Sir Thomas Browne's *Religio Medici* (*c.* 1642). Was it a symptom in Still's case of new beginnings that were pandemic in 'modern culture' (p. 95), or rather indexed to the social realities of life in south-western Canada during the 1920s and early '30s?[9] Or perhaps both?

Grand schemes of cause and effect are bought at a certain didactic expense. This is where Polcari transacts with Erika Doss's *Benton, Pollock, and the Politics of Modernism* and Landau's *Pollock* to his ultimate profit, despite minor losses en route. Doss plots another broad scenario. Pollock is seen here as the rightful heir to Thomas Hart Benton's art of producerist optimism thrust, nonetheless, into a conflicted no-man's land when the vision of social contract that had spurred regionalism abruptly ceded to post-war consensus and alienation. Benton himself, incidentally, emerges less as the rabid fascist dog that modernist demonology requires than as a decent old stick at heart who was mired in a hopelessly naïve Jeffersonian world-view. That there is no passionate engagement with individual pictures in this book reflects Doss's preference for a standpoint that regards them as pedagogical set-pieces. In thus capturing Benton's one-dimensional aesthetic — but not Pollock's — the argument succeeds in an almost self-defeating kind of way.[10] By contrast, the empirically minded Landau tends to abjure theory. She instead summarizes in one volume most of the leading strains of Pollock scholarship. The imperatives are those of the monographic format. Apart from a temporary lapse at the close into a remythologized subject ('an American Prometheus'), this is therefore a sensibly eclectic, no-nonsense account. For anything more analytical, we must still await publication of William Rubin's lengthy research on Pollock.

Abstract Expressionism and the Modern Experience scores above its rivals most highly when it combines breadth of outlook with an investigative intensity that presents a plethora of fresh knowledge to which scholars will be indebted for a long time ahead. The sections devoted to the movement's intellectual roots, and to Rothko, Gottlieb and Baziotes are outstandingly good. On Pollock, within a cogent overall discussion of the artist's relation to surrealism and primitivism, there is an instructive example of how different interpretations negotiate, and diverge from, the same nexus. As is well known, Pollock spoke in a December 1950 interview about modernity:

> My opinion is that new needs need new techniques. It seems to me that the modern painter cannot express this age, the airplane, the atom bomb, the radio, in the old forms of the Renaissance or of any other past culture. Each age finds its own technique. . . . The modern artist is living in a mechanical age . . . expressing the energy, the motion and other inner forces.[11]

Polcari correlates Pollock's ideology here with a 'vitalism' in the interwar years that expressed a desire to regenerate the world (pp. 251, 255), an apt enough conclusion, though it could be a bit more site-specific. Landau takes no sides and places the quotation within the scheme of fitting Pollock 'into the matrix of his times' (pp. 240–1). Doss wants to see the statement as 'intertwined' with a post-war political culture utterly changed from that of Benton's era (pp. 331–2). For Guilbaut at an earlier moment, Pollock's was The Atomic Age: indeed *Shimmering Substance* (1946) expresses the 'energy' of which the artist later spoke, but its source is destructive (negation again) and he claims, without a shred of evidence, that the picture shows 'the atomic bomb, transformed into myth'.[12] Almost perhaps more striking than these inferences, however, is the simple continuity of Pollock's ideology with a 1930s populist agenda; so seamless, that it might even, surprisingly, be Stuart Davis talking, or a Minnesota schoolgirl writing in 1937:

> Different time and different countries have their own art. Modern is only a relative term. Things may be old-fashioned today and in the future be modern. . . . Art of today must be created today. It must express the life about us. Ours is a complex age. It is much more complex than any previous age. Invention, machinery, industry, science, and commerce are characteristic of today. . . . These new ideas demand new materials.[13]

Throughout, Polcari moves tellingly from contemporary cultural documents such as posters and war-time records to the iconography of Abstract Expressionism, so that its picturing of the space of the 1940s emerges in sharp relief. In fact, a leaner book can be sensed lurking within these 400 pages which would possibly not treat de Kooning, Motherwell and Kline at all, but rather focus on the interaction at mid-century of modernism with war, alienation and cultural despair or anti-materialism. On those themes Polcari adduces such rich findings that they are ripe for further study. Hence, his canny analysis of the ties between the Abstract Expressionist figuration of bestiality and the psychology of war opens new vistas for research. Namely, how the affirmation of 'Man' partly contingent upon war (which calls for stereotypes of heroic masculinity) meshed with an ongoing reconstitution of 'Woman' as Other: Man, Heroic and Sublime, becomes the antitype to an eternal Feminine, bestial and destructive. If I am correct in seeing the first state of Picasso's 1930 etching *Orpheus Killed by the Maenads* as one primary inspiration behind de Kooning's epochal *Excavation*, then what might appear as mere personal misogyny or angst in an artist not directly affected by the war filters back into a larger sociological and, ultimately, political matrix.[14] Both Landau and, especially, Polcari excel at unearthing new sources anyway. It reflects less on their acumen than upon the extreme layering of Abstract Expressionist practice that neither remark on the obvious dependency of Pollock upon Picasso in two important instances. The first concerns the manifest horizontal proliferation of schemata derived from the latter's *Girl in Front of a Mirror* (1932, Museum of Modern Art, New York) across Pollock's germinal 1943 *Mural*. The second is an even blunter point of inspiration for Pollock's *Moon-Woman* (1942) in a 1927 *Bather* crayon drawing by Picasso.[15] These relatively mundane origins surely condition both images and, in so doing, curtail some of the more imaginative elaborations of Pollock's motives and mentality. But they are minor considerations withal, as are the typographical and editorial slips that Cambridge University Press happen shamefully to have let stand in Polcari's text, the more so because it belongs to an endangered species. Besides being a major contribution to the area, *Abstract Expressionism and the Modern Experience* represents that rare achievement, a work of intellect which plunges into a treacherous field — where revisionism and revanchism too frequently rhyme nowadays — yet manages not to fall foul of Susan Sontag's old, if still sadly topical, apothegm: 'Interpretation is the revenge of the intellect upon Art.'[16]

David Anfam
Washington DC

NOTES

1 George Hunter, 'The History of Styles as a Style of History' in Margaret Tudeau-Clayton and Martin Warner (eds.), *Addressing Frank Kermode*, Urbana, 1991, p. 76.

2 Charles Altieri, *Canons and Consequence*, Evanston, 1990, p. 8. Altieri makes trenchant observations apposite to 'revisionists' who currently claim to be dismantling canons — mostly meaning, however, that they wish to wrest control of them.

3 See E. D. Hirsch, *Validity in Interpretation*, New Haven, 1967, pp. 248–9.

4 T. J. Clark, 'Clement Greenberg's Theory of Art', *Critical Inquiry*, vol. 9, no. 1, September 1982, pp. 139–56.

5 Cf. Michael Fried, 'How Modernism Works: A Response to T. J. Clark' in ibid., pp. 217–34: 'At the centre of Clark's essay is the claim that the practices of modernism in the arts are fundamentally practices of negation. This claim is false.'

6 Hence, perhaps, the special stress Clark sets upon absence, shortcomings, velleity, disillusion, aimlessness, dissonance and exclusion in Pollock. Hegel has also of course recently come to the aid of neo-conservatism, witness Francis Fukuyama's *The End of History and the Last Man* (1992).

7 Barbara Herrnstein Smith, 'Narrative Versions, Narrative Theories', *Critical Inquiry*, vol. 7, no. 1, Autumn 1980, pp. 213–36.

8 Apart from Sandler's chapter 'The Imagination of Disaster' in his *Abstract Expressionism: The Triumph of American Painting*, London, 1970, one can point to their customary appearance in one article among multitudes such as Steven Henry Madoff, 'What is Postmodern About Painting: The Scandinavia Lectures', *Arts*, vol. 60, no. 1, September 1985, pp. 116–21.

9 See my '"Of the Earth, the Damned and of the Recreated": Aspects of Still's Earlier Work', *Burlington Magazine*, vol. 135, no. 1081, April 1993, pp. 260–9.

10 Simplistic or even dubious generalizations such as the following are not uncommon: 'The spidery webs of Jackson Pollock's abstract expressionist paintings also reflect disaffection and anxiety' (p. 339). But the book is also thorough and scrupulously fair in its treatment of Benton.

11 Francis V. O'Connor and Eugene V. Thaw (eds.), *Jackson Pollock. A Catalogue Raisonné of*

Paintings, Drawings and Other Works, New Haven and London, 1978, vol. 4, pp. 249–50.

12 Serge Guilbaut, *How New York Stole the Idea of Modern Art*, Chicago, 1983, p. 97.

13 Quoted in Martin Grief, *Depression Modern: The Thirties Style in America*, New York, 1977, p. 32.

14 The Picasso etching was reproduced early on in Bernhard Geiser, *Picasso: Peintre–Graveur*, Berne, 1933, no. 173.

15 Zervos VII, no. 104; reproduced in *Cahiers d'Art*, nos. 3–10, 1938, p. 85. Correspondingly, Pollock's *Moon-Woman* is one of the few works by a fellow Abstract Expressionist that perhaps inspired Clyfford Still, as it shares several key features with Still's 1943 *Unititled* oil on paper (itself a prototype for several of Still's large later canvases such as *Untitled*, 1946, in the Menil Collection, Houston), reproduced in Robert Hobbs and Gail Levin, *Abstract Expressionism: The Formative Years*, Ithaca, 1978, p. 132.

16 Susan Sontag, *Against Interpretation and Other Essays*, London, 1967, p. 7.

AMERICAN CULTURE WARS: PRISONERS OF THE PAST

Francis Frascina

Culture Wars:Documents from the Recent Controversies in the Arts, edited by *Richard Bolton*, New York: The New Press, 1992, 363 pp., 20 b. & w. illus., $19.95

> 'Those who ignore the past will be forced to relive it.' (H. Cruz); 'Not to know is bad; not to wish to know is worse.' (Nigerian Proverb)[1]

Since 1989 there have been intense battles in the USA about economics and power as they are encoded in public questions of ethnicity, sexuality, morality, obscenity and freedom of artistic expression. Although the past tells us that such battles are nothing new, it is important to be aware of contemporary ideological struggle manifest in cultural forms and debates. The major merit of Richard Bolton's *Culture Wars* is precisely this: as a resource for those who wish to know about the constituent parts of recent instances of permissibility and control. With a substantial introduction and over a hundred documents from a wide political spectrum, detailing the three years up to 1991, he focuses on issues and debates raised by a particular controversy centred on government funding of the arts in the United States.

One major side in these 'culture wars' represents a brand of puritanism which has been a substantial strand in the paradoxes and contradictions of the 'American experience'. Since World War II the various strands of this experience have been woven within an umbilical cord connecting the elements of US imperialism abroad and at home: no Cold War without McCarthyism, no Vietnam War without segregation, no CIA foreign intervention without Watergate and J. Edgar Hoover's FBI, no Gulf War without what Chomsky calls cultural commissars. It is now widely accepted that all of these elements necessitated assumptions, unconscious and conscious, about the production and/or use of cultural forms as strategic resources and symbols. These range from the worldwide distribution of Hollywood movies to MoMA's international travelling exhibitions, from the CIA's funding of, for example, a tour of the Boston Symphony Orchestra to Paris in 1952, to the activities of the United States Information Agency (USIA) and the Voice of America. For those on the Left a major dilemma has been how to produce an oppositional art which escapes the determining effect of the interests that sustain US imperialism and the powerful resentment of its representatives.

Since 1989 a newly invigorated right wing has been particularly outraged. One focus of rage has been the use of 'taxpayers' money' in grants awarded by the National Endowment for the Arts (NEA), a federal agency chartered in 1965 'to support the best of all forms that reflect the American heritage in its full range of cultural and ethnic diversity and to provide national leadership on behalf of the arts'. Its budget for 1989 was $169.09 million. In May of that year in the Senate, Republican senator D'Amato tore up a copy of the NEA Awards in the Visual Arts catalogue which reproduced Andres Serrano's *Piss Christ*, 1987. He denounced the NEA award of $15,000 to the artist and declared:

> This so-called piece of art is a deplorable, despicable display of vulgarity. ... This is not a question of free speech. This is a question of the abuse of taxpayers' money. ... If people want to be perverse, in terms of what they recognize as art or culture, so be it, but not with my money, not with the taxpayers' dollars, and certainly not under the mantle of this great Nation. This is a disgrace. (Bolton, pp. 28–9)

Besides Serrano's *Piss Christ* other works denounced in similar attacks include Robert Mapplethorpe's *X Portfolio*, 1977–8. Both represent an interest in the body, including its fluids, and sexual and social taboos. Serrano's work is a cibachrome photograph, submerged in urine, of a mass-produced wood and plastic crucifix. In April 1989 the American Family Association (AFA) sent out a letter about *Piss Christ* suggesting blasphemy and claiming that the 'bias and bigotry against Christians, which has dominated television and movies for the past decade or more, has now moved into the art museums' (Bolton, p. 27).

Mapplethorpe's photographs of intimate acts from a gay subculture formed part of an exhibition, *Robert Mapplethorpe: The Perfect Moment*, planned to be shown at the Corcoran Gallery of Art, Washington DC in 1989. In June the Corcoran trustees cancelled their plans, reportedly because of the growing controversy about Mapplethorpe's work. They were anxious that to proceed with the show would threaten congressional reauthorization of the NEA which had partly funded the exhibition. Their anxiety had been fuelled by the puritanical rhetoric and social mobilization of the forces of order and control both in the US Senate and in the network of religious, moral and political groups throughout the country. This phenomenon is not new in the cultural history of the United States. Examples include the cancellation of *Sport in Art* and *100 American Artists of the Twentieth Century* in 1956 because of claims, particularly from conservative religious groups, that some of the artists were pro-communist: MoMA's withdrawal of support for the Art Workers Coalition's (AWC) *'And Babies'* poster in 1969, based on a photo of the May Lai massacre, because the museum trustees were terrified by the poster's politics; the Guggenheim's cancellation of its Haacke exhibition in 1971 because of the political implications of his social systems pieces uncovering malpractice amongst New York landlords.

An indication of the depth and character of the Right's recent engagement can be gained from the words of a profoundly influential figure, that of the Reverend Donald Wildmon, executive director of the AFA. In the light of successful campaigns against sponsors of TV programmes and adverts, on claimed religious and sexual grounds, Wildmon says that he is

> involved in a great spiritual struggle for the heart and mind and soul of our society. It's very much a cultural battle. . . . It has taken fifty years or longer to reduce our culture to its present sorry state. We are just beginning to swing the pendulum back the other way. (Bolton, p. 9)

For Wildmon the 'other way' is 'to put into a political frame of reference the ideals of Jesus Christ' consistent with the ideological reconstruction of American values which are to the right of the Reagan and Bush administrations. The strength with which such views are held is clear from the candidacy of Pat Buchanan for the Republican presidential nomination in 1991–2. Buchanan is a syndicated journalist and television commentator who is closely linked to Wildmon and senator Jesse Helms. Helms was responsible for an amendment passed by the Senate, in 1989, designed to 'prohibit the use of appropriated funds for the dissemination, promotion, or production of obscene or indecent materials denigrating a particular religion'. This amendment had originally been designed to undermine the work of the NEA in particular.

Is there a relationship between Wildmon's and others' 'cultural battle' and the US government's aims to restore corporate profitability and impose some discipline on a turbulent world, at home and abroad? The political programme of a broad elite consensus in the 1970s and '80s produced a disciplinary process which Chomsky has analysed as 'deterring democracy':

> The natural domestic policies were transfer of resources to the rich, partial dismantling of the limited welfare system, an attack on unions and real wages, and expansion of the public subsidy for high-technology industry through the Pentagon system, which has long been the engine for economic growth and preserving the technological edge.[2]

This process was spectacularly symbolized on domestic and international TV, largely via Cable News Network (CNN), during the Gulf War, when an enormous financial investment in technological death machines provided viewers with a mega 'super-Nintendo' experience. The astounding and orchestrated tele-visual display of destruction fed the induced consumerist need for computer games and the State's long-term desire to erase the negative memory of Vietnam as 'US defeat'. The 'Holy

War' to control oil supplies, to reinvigorate the order books of the arms industry, and to confirm a 'New World Order' went hand in hand with a 'Holy War' to regain the 'heart and mind and soul' of an America supposedly corrupted by blasphemy, feminism, gays and sexual liberation. And worse, in the eyes of the 'moral majority' the NEA was funding artists such as Serrano, Mapplethorpe and Karen Finley, to produce their 'corrupting' representations. What the Pentagon was funding from 'taxpayers' money' did not get the same attention. In all of this we should not forget the power of agencies such as CNN in forging a perception of US culture as a global norm. Andrew Ross has argued that a

> perception of the national culture is the primary shaping principle behind CNN's own house style for editing and broadcasting world news across the major league of nations. Performing the global function once served by the BBC in the age of radio, CNN's decentred corporate populism has effectively replaced the voice of paternal imperialism that used to issue from Europe's metropolitan centres.[3]

Richard Bolton's *Culture Wars* is an important and useful volume of documents for anyone interested in aspects of this recent history. The fact that this book has been published so quickly is indicative of a preservation of a strand of radical protest in the US, as is the publication of Chomsky's books by small, often collective publishers, and Toni Morrison's recent anthology on the Anita Hill/Clarence Thomas event.[4] Together such publications are a mark of the progress in resources for informed dissent.

However, despite its merits I wish to argue that *Culture Wars* is symbolic of a profound dilemma in which the US Left has often found itself since World War II. The effects of forgetting and amnesia as they relate to repression are problematic and painful enough in the individual but in the body politic they have many more disciplinary consequences. It is my contention that a major element in the contradictions endemic to 'art and politics' in the US since World War II is the American Left's failure to recognize that it is caught in the repetitive syndrome of re-inventing itself. As the artist Irving Petlin, a driving force in the Los Angeles *Peace Tower* and the Art Workers' Coalition during the 1960s, recalls in an interview:

> [In France and Britain] there always was something to circulate around. There was a consistent pole or a party to rally, support and which magnetized issues of the Left. This has not been true in America at all in the post-[Second World] War world. . . . All the protest movements that have succeeded one another have had to invent themselves because there has not been this continuity. . . . It's not like politics in Europe where the Left has its continuous associations. There are no continuous associations in the United States. The Civil Rights movement, the anti-[Vietnam] war movement and even the environmental movement literally had to invent themselves, adopt methods and invent strategies that were outside traditional politics in order to attract the attention of a larger public.[5]

Without internalizing the struggles of the past, radical groups are forced to relive them, whilst believing that 'the present crisis' is somehow unique. The history of the Left cannot be understood without an awareness of this process of repetition which has contributed to the US management of its corporate public image, domestic puritanism, consumerist soma, and technological 'efficiency'. In *Culture Wars* a chronology detailing 'selected examples of major cases of censorship and controversy in American culture' (pp. 331–63) only begins in 1962 and the first example of actual censorship is the cancellation of the Haacke exhibition in 1971. To ignore the years from, for example, 1946, when 'Advancing Modern Art' was ridiculed by George A. Dondero, through to the acts of suppression and intervention in the 1950s is significant, particularly so because of the close connections between the interests which underpinned Dondero's rhetoric and those which determine utterances by Wildmon, Buchanan, Helms, D'Amato and so on. A major reason for the Left's neglect of the roots of its present dilemmas is the persistent legacy of the era of McCarthyism and the early Cold War which has encouraged the process of denying or erasing that which still acts as a determining force. The cutting away of roots and associations became a pathological process in the 1950s and subsequently was internalized as amnesia into the American experience.

Two glosses on this. At a panel discussion in New York, October 1992, the numerous collective activities of artists protesting in the late 1960s against the Vietnam War and the systems of state power were retold and illustrated by original activists. Startlingly, these marches, events and strikes were largely unknown to the audience and to representatives of the newest collective group of the early 1990s, Women's Action Coalition (WAC). A second gloss is the way in which 'views from the margin' are treated by the official culture. Terry Eagleton ironically concluded in a review of Edward Said's *Culture and Imperialism* that such views 'as he [Said] well knows are no more than the resentful whinings of those with a chip on their shoulder, when measured against the disinterested discourse of academics in the pay of the White House' (*The Guardian 2*, 9 February 1993, p. 10). Importantly, the influence of this 'disinterested discourse' has not deterred Said or Chomsky from making their lucid analyses of imperialism and totalitarianism from *within* the USA.

Bolton at the end of his excellent introduction to *Culture Wars* draws on political theorists and cultural commentators. Significantly, these are from *outside* the US: Laclau and Mouffe. He quotes their argument (p. 24), from *Hegemony and Socialist Strategy*, that the political logic of totalitarianism in the name of the 'Nation', or whatever, seeks to

> ... control all the networks of sociability. In the face of the radical indeterminacy which democracy opens up, this involves an attempt to reimpose an absolute center, and to re-establish the closure which will thus restore unity. (Laclau and Mouffe, p. 188)

Bolton rightly claims that this 'describes the logic behind the attack on NEA', as it does many other manifestations of control in nations and groups: 'Censorship of the arts reveals the failure of democratic institutions to articulate and defend the complexity and diversity of the American public.' But are these US institutions 'democratic' in any real sense? The evidence largely says no and even more so recently.

What is certain is that the moment of '1968' rattled the dominant post-1945 process influentially articulated by George Kennan in *Policy Planning Study* 23, 1948:

> We [the USA] have about 50 per cent of the world's wealth, but only 6.3 per cent of its population. ... Our real task in the coming period is to devise a pattern of relationships which will permit us to maintain this position of disparity without positive detriment to our national security. To do so, we will have to dispense with all sentimentality and day-dreaming; and our attention will have to be concentrated everywhere on our immediate national objectives. ... The day is not far off when we are going to have to deal in straight power concepts. The less we are then hampered by idealistic slogans, the better.[6]

The powerful public image of self-proclaimed democratic and progressive institutions, underpinned by the proliferation of such institutions during the post-war consumerist boom, has hidden the reality of the fragmentation of actual democratic possibilities. Again, the evidence of the 1950s is instructive, especially if we look at the cultivated liberal intelligentsia who were in positions of cultural power: such as Alfred Barr, at MoMA, Lloyd Goodrich, at the Whitney, those associated with the American Federation of Arts and regional museum directors and supporters of modernism in art. From the evidence of their correspondence and files, many of them were caught up in a dilemma which encouraged paranoid tendencies. They wished to preserve what they regarded as the progressiveness of cultural modernism (including 'the complexity and diversity of the American public') which for them largely meant the ideology of the aesthetic and autonomous art. But their ideas, and they themselves, were under attack from those licensed by Dondero's hostility to modern art in general. The attack on the Dallas Museum and its exhibition of *Sport in Art* in 1956 demonstrates the connection between Dondero-derived ideas, right-wing financial interests and a puritan fundamentalism. Barr retained comprehensive files on everything he regarded as a threat to his belief in modern art, as defined by MoMA. But equally, he and others were nervous of any support for artists who could be shown to have communist sympathies. This became translated into hostility and condemnation: Picasso, a member of the PCF who produced *Massacre in Korea*, was described as 'politically naïve' and the work of Diego Rivera was 'propaganda'. US artists with communist connections were similarly marginalized. This situation led many of the liberal intelligentsia to become members of the American Committee for Cultural Freedom, affiliated to the Congress for Cultural Freedom, later revealed as CIA-funded as part of Cold War attrition. The effect of this was a subtle confirmation of Kennan's 'real task': 'to deal in straight power concepts. The less we are then hampered by idealistic slogans, the better.'

The legacy of the dilemmas of the cultivated liberal intelligentsia, particularly those in powerful positions in supposed 'democratic' institutions, still haunt the USA and help us to understand some of the documents in *Culture Wars*. I want to split this into two related areas. The first is the example of what I will call the *Tilted Arc* problem. Serra's massive 'public' sculpture was commissioned in 1979 by the General Services Administration for New York's Federal Plaza and installed in 1981. Dominating the architectural space and that of the viewing subject, the 3.65 × 36.58 m slab of corten steel caused heated public controversy during the 1980s. Calls for its removal culminated in a public hearing where many artists, critics, curators and dealers spoke up for the integrity of the sculpture and warned against attacks on the freedom of the arts and the risks of censorship. Should critically ratified 'progressive' artists in a proclaimed free society not be left alone to produce whatever they wish in a public space, thereby preserving the autonomy of art? A problem with such a question is that in post-war USA, the concept of autonomy had been deprived of its oppositional political credentials and subsumed within a formalist aesthetic that was radically elaborated in the 1970s and '80s.

For supporters of Serra's sculpture, which he described as a 'benign, civilizing effort', the contemporary version of autonomous art overrode the interests of those who worked in and around Federal Plaza. To these supporters, social and human accountability somehow smacked of idealistic slogans and those political aspects of art which had long been institutionally suppressed. In contrast, for those who were critical of *Tilted Arc* and its rhetoric of power the reality of the curving and leaning slab cutting across the Plaza was that it destroyed and dehumanized a public space in which workers relaxed and ate their lunch. The viewing subject's body was dominated by a coldsteel slab which signified corporate masculine power and the authority of an alientating 'autonomy'. After bitter controversy, Serra's sculpture was removed in 1989. Was the art world's defence of *Tilted Arc*, from Rubin to Krauss, a continuation of the classic dilemma of the US liberal intelligentsia since the 1950s? Did the defence of autonomy in the midst of Reaganomics leave the ground open for right-wing attacks on art works such as *Piss Christ* and Mapplethorpe's *X Portfolio*? Did these attacks in turn deflect attention from and marginalize projects on social activism and multi-culturism?[7]

The second related area I want to outline connects to recent concerns with the body as a metaphor for the struggle for identity and difference. A major part of the puritan outrage contained in the documents in *Culture Wars* relates to the representation of the body, its fluids and its private parts in unratified contexts: Serrano's piss covering an image of Christ's semi-naked body; Mapplethorpe's photographs of, for example, a hooded 'Jim' pissing into the mouth of 'Tom', or of a male arm, or a bull whip, deep into the anus of another male. These images and their reception raise issues that have centred around the 'discourse of the body'. There are two sides to this. One is the development of radical approaches in the USA and Europe in which concerns with metaphor and power may coexist with an insouciance and ignorance of socialist struggles. As Eagleton has argued there 'is a privileged, privatized hedonism about such discourse, emerging as it does at just the historical point where less exotic forms of politics found themselves suffering a setback'.[8] The second side is the fascination with and fear of the body as a symbol of wholeness and power. This is profoundly masculine in the rhetoric of cultural life in the US both as a personal obsession and as a national idea. For example: 'perfectibility', signified by the enormous plastic surgery industry; 'policing', signified by the culture of political and racial surveillance and surgical strikes; 'puritanism', signified by groups dedicated to pro-life, the emphases on procreation rather than erotic pleasure and the homophobic denial of sexual difference; and so on.

Powerful aspects of control are embedded in the ideology that insists on the libido as attracted only to unities. Many of Mapplethorpe's photographs *confound* this ideology with close-ups of parts of the male body, a process conventionally devoted to the patriarchal fetishization of parts of the female body, in film and photography. The ideology of perfectibility produces a powerful anxiety in various utterances and actions, many of which are rooted in the history of post-war USA, particularly that which is erased in official representations. For example, this ideology can help to explain the repeated cases of US troops' castration of the corpses of the Vietcong. Dismemberment was a sign of a loss of sexuality and to mutilate, to ruin the oriental 'other' was to confirm the GI's notion of acceptability as 'Western man' in the eyes of his peers. This went together with the GI's fear of fragmentation — bomb wounds to every part of the body including genitals, buttocks, hands and legs. At the same time the US war machine had developed napalm and cluster bombs which dismembered and fragmented the bodies of the Vietnamese. There is also evidence that American troops cut off the ears of warm corpses stringing them around their necks as a sign of previous kills.[9] In the Gulf War dismemberment of the Iraqis, systematically devalued in media rhetoric, was mostly achieved at a technological distance. But advance fear of fragmentation led some of the US troops to place their frozen sperm in 'banks' so that a whole version of themselves could be reproduced in the unerotic process of clinical fertilization. No wonder Mapplethorpe's photographs produced a shudder of rage.

Bolton's *Culture Wars* is an important resource. It enables us to know about instances of present political struggles fought out within culture. But its value will be lost if its historical place and symbolic meaning are forgotten. As I have argued, cultural and political amnesia enables the US to police or manage dissent and at the same time to make a few more bucks by encouraging the production of commodities and media spectacles in the market of ideas. This market not only poses little actual threat to capitalism but also provides the system's guardians and cultural commissars with interesting information on what the actual and fantasized opposition are thinking. For them there is nothing better than to encourage dissent, with its novel forms ripe for commodification, when its more troublesome manifestations are contained and fragmented.

However, collections such as those by Richard Bolton and Toni Morrison and 'views from the margins' by Chomsky and Said can enable a critical and historical reflectiveness in their readers. Those who know their history can resist the process which forces them to relive the past.

Francis Frascina
The Open University

NOTES

1 Both quoted in Willie Birch, *Knowing Our History, Teaching Our Culture*, 1992, mixed media, wood, papier mâché, 4 parts, exhibited at the Arthur Roger Gallery, New York, Oct–Nov 1992.

2 *Deterring Democracy*, Vintage, London, 1992, p. 81.

3 Ross, 'The Private Parts of Justice', in T. Morrison (ed.), *Race-ing Justice, En-gendering Power: Essays on Anita Hill, Clarence Thomas, and the Construction of Social Reality*, London: Chatto and Windus, 1993, p. 41.

4 ibid.

5 Interview with the author, October 1992.

6 Quoted in Chomsky, 'Visions of Righteousness', in *The Vietnam War and American Culture*, J. Rowe and R. Berg (eds.), New York: Columbia University Press, 1991, pp. 46–7.

7 See, for example, *If You Lived Here: The City in Art, Theory and Social Activism, A Project by Martha Rosler*, Brian Wallis (ed.), Seattle: Bay Press, 1991; Michele Wallace, *Invisibility Blues: From Pop to Theory*, London: Verso, 1990; Lucy Lippard, *Mixed Blessings: New Art in A Multicultural America*, New York: Pantheon, 1990.

8 *The Ideology of the Aesthetic*, Oxford and Cambridge: Blackwell, 1990, p. 7.

9 See David Haward Bain, *Aftershocks: A Tale of Two Victims*, New York: Methuen, 1980; Maurice Berger, *Representing Vietnam 1965–1973: The Antiwar Movement in America*, New York: The Hunter College Art Gallery, 1988; Susan Jerrods, 'Tattoos, Scars, Diaries, and Writing Masculinity' in Berg and Row (eds.), op. cit.

SHORTER REVIEWS

Angelica Kauffman. A Continental Artist in Georgian England edited by *Wendy Wassyng Roworth*, with essays by *David Alexander, Malise Forbes Adam & Mary Mauchline, Angela Rosenthal, Wendy Wassyng Roworth*, Brighton and London: Reaktion Books Ltd, 1992, 216 pp., 42 col. plates, 107 b. & w. illus., £9.95

This book is to be welcomed for the serious, unsensationalized consideration given by its contributors to the question of Angelica Kauffman's success in a competitive art market, which in Georgian England was largely a man's world. Much depended on her strategies of self-presentation, both in the social space of the studio and within the picture spaces. We are left in no doubt that she was an astute business woman — one of the first to see the advantages for an artist's career of the new mechanical processes. She also understood the need to be perceived by her contemporaries as attractive woman without seeming vulnerable, and as professional artist, founder member of the Royal Academy, without being transgressive. That her portraits were perceived as having legibly 'feminine' characteristics counted in her favour. Furthermore, she saw the value of flexibility in range of production. Wassyng Roworth focuses on Kauffman's history paintings, Rosenthal on her portraits,[1] Forbes Adam and Mauchline on her decorative work, and Alexander on the prints after her creations. In all of these areas Kauffman was exceptionally accomplished and successful — which makes her relatively marginalized position in art history the harder to accept. This book and the exhibition, *Angelica Kauffman, A Continental Artist in Georgian England*, will do much to restore the recognition she enjoyed during her lifetime.

For a woman aspiring to the status of history painter, as Kauffman did, apparently from the age of sixteen, opportunity and success were harder to find than they were for a man. It was considered unseemly for women academicians to study the nude and in Zoffany's famous group portrait of the Royal Academy founder members in the life class Kauffman and Mary Moser could only be represented as painted portraits on the wall. Despite Kauffman's exclusion from this site of opportunity, her history paintings were usually favourably reviewed 'considering her sex'. It clearly mattered to her to find acceptable ways of drawing attention to her personal status of history painter, one of which was to insert her own portrait in unexpected places. She cast herself as virtuous Hercules (no less) in *Self-Portrait: Hesitating between the Arts of Music and Painting*, and as the artist working on the fictive picture within *Zeuxis selecting Models for his Painting of Helen of Troy*. She selected her subjects from history carefully, either to be innovative, or to illustrate her erudition — with *Trenmor and Imbaca*, 1773, she must surely have been one of the very first to paint a subject from Ossian — or to focus on women who represented something other than the passive victims of classical antiquity. Her Penelope series is a case in point here: it is suggested that Kauffman was almost alone to depict Penelope 'for a more positive interpretation of female virtue and strength'.

Kauffman's influence on eighteenth-century decorative arts in England is fully explored and the authors explode long-held myths of her involvement in Robert Adam interiors. We learn of the extent to which, through engravings, her designs reached a wider public 'and were given a greater diversity of use than those of any other decorative painter of her generation'. The 1770 engraving after her painting of *Maria* from Sterne's 'Poor Maria' found its way, for example, on to a pole-screen, a tea tray and a Wedgwood cameo, and the craze for Cupid designs on porcelain was fuelled by popular engravings after her work. The most important engraver for spreading her fame was William Wynne Ryland and he in turn developed a new kind of decorative print from her work — the stipple engraving.

The book worked well as an enlightening accompaniment to the exhibition held in Brighton and York. In the longer term it will remain a stimulating and informative source for anyone interested in the social production of art in eighteenth-century Britain and in understanding the success of Angelica Kauffman's innovations and interventions in that world.

Helen Weston
University College London

NOTES

1 See also A. Rosenthal, 'Angelica Kauffman Ma(s)king Claims', *Art History*, vol. 15 (1992), pp. 38–59.

The Female Nude: Art, Obscenity and Sexuality by *Lynda Nead*, London and New York: Routledge, 1992, 133 pp., 40 b. & w. illus., £9.95

> Comme un beau cadre ajoute à la peinture,
> Bien qu'elle soit d'un pinceau très-vanté,
> Je ne sais quoi d'étrange et d'enchanté
> En l'isolant de l'immense nature.
>
> Ainsi meubles, bijoux, métaux, fourrures
> S'adaptaient juste à sa rare beauté (. . .)
> Et tout semblait lui servir de bordure.

Thus Baudelaire's 'Le Cadre', 'The Frame'. The woman's rare beauty is matched to perfection by the frame of furniture, jewels, furs, which isolates her from 'immense nature' like a frame a painting. The painting may be by someone famous: the frame is what adds charm and magic to her. Everything seems to serve as a border to her.

Though Baudelaire never figures among a wonderfully suggestive list that ranges from Plato and Aristotle through to Kristeva, Mary Douglas, Said, Foucault, Eagleton and Derrida, and that analyses debates about, and representations of, the female nude from the two Clarks to Carol Duncan and from Dürer to Mapplethorpe, using an equally eclectic set of discourses, his poem could be taken as both symbol and symptom of what this nimble and economical book is about: frames — what they do and what to do with them.

The nude, Lynda Nead argues, is about the containment of nature through art. By means of it, through a tradition rooted in the Kantian category of the aesthetic, and perpetuated by Kenneth Clark and beyond through the distinction between contemplation and arousal, art and the obscene, the intrinsic and the extrinsic, boundaries are established. From the Renaissance to modernism to the lessons of the life class, the female nude demonstrates 'that art originates in and is sustained by male erotic energy' (Duncan). It is an icon of Western subjectivity, that securely classifies the male artist/spectator as the one who creates or perceives form, establishing his subjectivity in the process, and the female body as nature, mother, that to be elevated to the status of art must be purified of its imperfections or excess. Thus does Kenneth Clark praise the slim Cycladic doll over the ample body in parturition of the Willendorf Venus.

The originality and strength of Lynda Nead's approach is in the resolutely post-modernist and sharply illustrated way that, through a combination of examples and theory, she forges compact little icons of her own to demonstrate the paradox at the heart of the iconic female nude, and to show how, through the subversion and questioning of the boundaries, patriarchal forms of representation may be opened, and more diverse, less power-ridden forms of identity made possible. There is thus a fascinating use of the suffragette Mary Richardson's slashing of the Rokeby Venus, and media interpretations of her act, to show how the language of connoisseurship, social discourse (she is portrayed as a male 'Ripper'), and political metaphor (the Venus is 'a perfect image of not only womanhood but the nation, under attack at the hands of iconoclastic subversives' — later she is used in cartoons about Home Rule) all hinge upon particular gender constructions.

The paradox: the nude is both at the centre (as icon) and at the margins, forever threatening excess: excess flesh, excess matter, vulgarity, sexual excitement, obscenity. High culture polices it. In so doing (following Bourdieu's analysis), it helps maintain distinctions between high and low, elite and popular, unique and mass-produced, 'pure gaze' and commodity exchange, that serve the interests of the dominant group. Lynda Nead demonstrates how smudged are the borders between the artistic and the pornographic, and endorses Linda Williams's contention that 'hard core' is about investigating (in fear?) 'the visible truth of female pleasure'. She also endorses (and this in a way is the crux of the book) a feminist policy of using precisely those shaky borders to question patriarchal mastery. She argues for a feminist aesthetic of the sublime, relates it to Cixous's and Irigaray's 'écriture féminine' aesthetics of excess. She precisely and eloquently shows how the work of artists such as Judy Chicago, Carole Schneeman, Chila Kumari Burman, Lesley Sanderson, Mary Duffy and Jo Spence subvert the proper–improper, erotic–pornographic, artist–model, disabled–beautiful distinctions. They 'do' rather than let things be done with or to them. 'Write or be written off', a notice above a morgue-like foreshortened (Mantegna-like?) Jo Spence photograph admonishes. By challenging the boundaries of the aesthetic, such artists make room for diversity, and more access to the real. 'The coy play of eroticism and artistic experience is replaced by a direct address to relationships of desire, representation and the female body'.

Having myself recently become immersed in the fierce feminist debates about pornography, I admire the deftness with which Nead enlarges and displaces the questions. I applaud the way she highlights how women artists have worked to alter perceptions of the nude, taken the initiative, carnivalized the icons. I am not convinced that this is enough, nor that raiding the 'sacred frontier' is in itself going to yield greater subjecthood. In the 'real world', however 'constructed' that may be, so-called pornography entails subjection, exploitation, physical and emotional and economic exploitation. I do not need to be persuaded that censorship is not the answer. But just as there is a spectrum with important degrees, degrees that make for life and death, between aggression and violence, and it is important to distinguish between the acceptable and the unacceptable, is there not a similar question of limits in the aesthetic–erotic–soft–hard–pornographic? And does subversion necessarily lead to the uncovering or positing of desire? I note that in all the female artists represented (with the arguable exception of Mary Duffy), the only one who makes 'positive', celebratory images of the female nude is Judy Chicago, who comes in for heavy criticism on socio-political grounds. Would the truly liberating representation not be one that made women, precisely, feel sublime, joyfully excessive about their bodily self-images? Where are they?

For me, the most exciting and challenging strand in the book is what it suggests about re-integrating what has been excluded from the female nude: the maternal body, the pregnant body, the active, desiring body. Janine Chasseguet-Smirgel labels as 'sexual monism' psychoanalytic accounts that make the penis/phallus into the only sexual organ (e.g. Freud, or Lacan). This is in fear of the archaic mother, in frustration at the boy-child's inability to possess the mother as the father does. Denial of the existence of the womb, or dreams of being its kingly, or queenly occupant, are compensatory or self-protective. Woman must be represented in as different a way as possible from the mother. Is the female nude at one and the same time the perfect representation of the desired (unmotherly, young) female and of the penis/phallus revelling in the womb/decor? Baudelaire's 'Le Cadre' ends with the woman voluptously 'drowning' her nakedness 'in the kisses of satin and linen', with the 'child-like grace of the monkey'. Is that monkey the mistress or is she an icon for another little monkey? 'Une Géante' explores a dream of the poet being a cat cavorting in the mountainous shadow of a young Giantess's body. ... Is it because Gossaert's *Neptune and Amphitrite* so clearly suggests a primal scene, the couple's arms so relaxedly and companionably round each other's shoulders, the shell on Neptune's cock so pointed, that Kenneth Clark found it obscene? If so, let us now praise famous male artists for daring to express their desires and fear. Let women artists, as well as questioning the power implications of these representations, and above all the discourses about those representations, continue to explore and express their own.

Nicole Ward Jouve
University of York

Watteau's Painted Conversations: Art, Literature, and Talk in Seventeenth- and Eighteenth-Century France by *Mary Vidal*, New Haven and London: Yale University Press, 1992, 236 pp., 53 col. plates, 132 b. & w. illus., £35.00

This is an enjoyable and stimulating book, albeit not entirely convincing. Mary Vidal's argument can be summarized as follows: (i) Watteau's paintings show conversations; (ii) from the mid-seventeenth century in France conversation was seen as a form of art distinctive of the aristocracy and those aspiring to it; (iii) the open-endedness of Watteau's paintings mirrors the open structure of conversation and conversation as process, rather than product, is represented by Watteau's loose technique; (iv) these characteristics of the artist, in which he linked conversational and pictorial aesthetics, were conscious attempts to enhance the status of the artist, firstly by liberating painting from dominance by the written word, and secondly by identifying the artist with the aristocratic amateur.

Crucially, Vidal's argument depends upon her analysis of Watteau's paintings, and this is sometimes stretched. It is not difficult to concede that most of the paintings are about social exchange of one kind or another, and that some show conversation, but many do not and in those that do, conversation is not always central. It is important to distinguish between conversation on the one hand, involving the spoken word, and other types of social exchange which may involve only silent gesture or expression, not least because, as Vidal herself shows, the art of conversation consisted of polite speech. It did not consist of longing looks and vacuous stares as in the Thyssen *Pierrot content*, or of physical struggle as in the Louvre's *Le Faux-pas*, or of the kind of conversation occurring in the Wallace Collection *Voulez-vous triompher des belles?* Regarding *Le Faux-pas*, Vidal argues that like some other paintings by Watteau, the refusal of physical embrace is paradigmatic of the artist's conversational rhetoric, the intention of which is to show the viewer that 'the source of civility and art lies precisely in the tension between powerful natural impulses and their displacement in or through social rituals . . .'. In other words, just because *Le Faux-pas* is not a conventional conversation does not mean it does not have a conversational message, and as readers of Hoffmann's *Struwelpeter* may remember, representations of inappropriate behaviour can be more powerful (and more fun) than sermonizing.

The problem for Vidal is that to make conversation central to Watteau's art, to show, as she puts it, the artist's preoccupation with the subject, she is forced into fascinating, but nevertheless personal, interpretations of the paintings, of the artist's intentions and of the reception of the pictures by his contemporaries, interpretations for which there is little evidence. While Vidal shows the importance of conversation amongst the nobility and the higher bourgeoisie, and that the conversation or '*entretien*' became a fashionable mode of didactic writing, the connections with Watteau are conjectural. She assumes conversation around 1700 to have been spontaneous, informal and non-specific (p. 19), and sees this as characteristic of Watteau's art, but does not note that the books on the art of conversation written then were none of these, as the pedestrian dialogue quoted by Vidal from Vaumorière's *L'Art de plaire dans la conversation* (1688) makes clear. Given Watteau's known interest in the theatre, it might have been more fruitful to analyse dialogue in comic plays of the period, but this has not been done.

Equally suspect are the arguments that Watteau's paintings were attempts to advance artistic status through linked conversational and pictorial aesthetics. These are partly based on the claim that 'the rarity of Watteau's self-portraits should be linked . . . with [the] aristocratic notion of propriety, whereby the successful display of self can never be "eager"' (p. 157). To speak of rarity, however, assumes that Watteau's contemporaries frequently portrayed themselves, and had aristocrats really been restrained in self-display, then Rigaud and Nattier, to name but two portraitists of the period, would have starved.

Vidal has clearly looked closely and thought hard about Watteau's paintings (often profitably). But she is prone to overstate her case. A more modest proposal, comprehending some only of the paintings, might have been more persuasive.

Humphrey Wine
The National Gallery, London

CORRESPONDENCE

From Barbara Maria Stafford, University of Chicago

To the Editor:

The review of *Body Criticism*[1] by Ludmilla Jordanova is sufficiently biased and inaccurate that a response is called for.[2] The book's arguments were caricatured by the systematic excision of sentences from their context and gratuitously distorted in the recounting. Further, the contents of entire chapters remained unmentioned for whose absence *Body Criticism* was then discredited as being 'ahistorical' or, conversely, falsely periodizing. While I urge the readers of your journal to consult the real thing not the prejudiced retelling, the record needs to be set straight on a number of key points.

Professor Jordanova's review dismissed the book as intellectual 'bricolage'. The review claims it says 'little about medicine', 'very little about pictures', and is actually three books 'trapped' unsuccessfully in one. The review further distorts the message of *Body Criticism* to be 'that art historians, and other specialist image interpreters, do not have the status they deserve because Western philosophical traditions are mistrustful of pictures.' According to the review, therefore, the book is concerned only with 'the kinds of claims art historians are entitled to promulgate'. A laundry list of *ex cathedra* pronouncements follows. I shall deal with these unsubstantiated statements, first as they relate to two general issues, and then point by point, in chapter order.

How can one take seriously a review that lifts out a small segment of chapter one (completely ignoring the physiognomy/pathognomy debates and the growing split between theory and practice across a number of key disciplines)? In addition, the reviewer omits to mention chapter two, except for a grudging approval of the discussion of marbling (but ignores the entire social construction of knowledge through dictionaries, encyclopedias, epitomizing manuals and compressive caricatures). Chapter three is passed over in silence, as is chapter four on the museum of the Hôpital Saint-Louis, the rise of dermatology, the production and reception of proper and improper pigmented or chromatic skin in human beings, and works of art.

To the major issue of silence or misrepresentation, however, must be added the implication that art historians should stick to their own territory. Consequently, this review seems to find most objectionable the fact that the book draws parallels between early modernism and postmodernism. Yet the past embeddedness of the image/word debate in an elite aniconic social and cultural order is depressingly recapitulated in the current linguistic hierarchies obtaining in the humanities and the social sciences. Although the history and philosophy of science and the history of medicine may combine rational analyses with visual perception, the historiography of these fields has not. Why is it that scholars in other disciplines fearlessly appropriate art history, but when art historians venture into visual studies engaged with another knowledge base, they are taken to task for over-extending themselves intellectually and not blending 'historical detail, conceptual sophistication and the development of big bold themes' with 'the right approach'? I believe this is at the heart of Jordanova's own discomfort.

Beyond these central concerns, the record needs to be corrected on key issues. The reviewer asserts that *Body Criticism* 'bizarrely' compared polychrome wax sculpture to automata. In fact, the book speaks of the *nesting* construction of removable anatomical parts. This desire for *lifelikeness* (also found in the related invention of triple-plate colour mezzotints) was fundamentally connected to the ideal of an organic mechanism or artificial person. Further, the review finds the body as machine to be a 'dated' notion by the end of the eighteenth century. This typically uncorroborated assertion would not only have amazed the novelty vendors in the boutiques of the Palais-Royal, but Galvani, Kleist, Coleridge and Mary Shelley as well. As to the remark that 'physic and surgery were less distinct than professional structures suggest', the review ignores Garengeot's perceptive history of the progressive disjunction between intellect and knack in medicine and fails to detail how the 'theoretical and practical were closely related'. Recall that this was an era when the teaching of medicine was separated from its clinical practice.

Turning to the use of the term 'materialist' which the review claims is placed within a 'rigid mind-body duality', it is significant that it does not refer to the extended discussions of this durable dichotomy throughout the book. The assertion that 'in general' *Body Criticism* does not ask how and to what ends these dualisms were constructed is unfounded since this is precisely one of its major tasks. In alleging the ignorance of the complexities of materialism, the review is silent about the contents of chapter three. In it is demonstrated how preformationism, based on a late theurgic Neoplatonism, and epigenesis, specifically conditioned by certain strands of French and British materialist thought, informed not only medical but gendered aesthetic theories of maternal reproduction and paternal creation.

This review fails to engage with the claim in chapter five that microscopy fundamentally called into question the long-standing Western construction of a coherent body by exploding it into monstrous fragments unrelated to their looks. Instead of dealing with the chapter's thesis that the logical connection between invisible depth and visible surface had been broken, thus permitting the construction of the modern grotesque, the review states: 'Many naturalists' [who?] 'considered microscopy irrelevant to the understanding of life.' This *non-sequitur* means that the review again deals neither with the argument nor the evidence presented.

Nor is the discussion of the horrible practice of vivisection accurately represented. The book is said to 'tick off' (*sic*) Haller for carrying out experiments on living animals. What chapter six — unmentioned except for this literal bit on Haller — does is situate the problem of voluntary and involuntary motions within the larger strategy of making visible the invisible. These macabre experiments, which are connected to mesmerism and galvanism, used the manifest signs of pain to demonstrate somatic functions that otherwise remained unapparent. Moreover, vivisection had been controversial at least since the time of Newton, who was nauseated by the virtuosi's attempts at blood transfusion, and Hogarth, who offered a commentary on the ghoulish practice in his *Four Stages of Cruelty*.

Most deceptive, however, is the review's assertion that 'so much excellent scholarship' has been ignored. It mentions Simon Schaffer [and Steven Shapin] (whose fine work on mid-seventeenth century British science, especially Boyle's air pump, I admire and respect) to imply that the issues raised in *Body Criticism* are old hat. Indeed, Shapin and Schaffer, writing principally about the seventeenth century, dismantle the assumption that experimentation and the use of instruments is an inevitable and unassailable programme for learning nature. They write about the political and religious polemics shaping the experimental programme of the Royal Society in the fraught years following its foundation. *Body Criticism*, however, is concerned neither with the Royal Society *per se*, nor with the seventeenth century. I should add that after the publication of *Body Criticism*, Simon Schaffer turned to investigate eighteenth-century experimental science, and this work is certainly central to my current project. *Body Criticism* also engages other perceptive and thoughtful historians of science including Roy Porter, G. S. Rousseau and Richard Toellner. But this is not accurately presented, just as the extensive, critical bibliography is dismissed as merely 'plenty' of references.

In sum: *Body Criticism* looked at the pivotal moments and concrete historical instantiations when a Baroque oral-visual culture shifted towards high Enlightenment logocentric forms of communication. Let me reiterate the book's conclusion that we must remetaphorize the debased and degraded image-as-simulation, just as we need to reconceptualize the vertical relation between phenomenal and noumenal experience. The acceptance of the cognitive importance of optical modes of knowing, as well as of the existence of a 'body in the mind', will require a transformation in entrenched values. It was this conviction that compelled me to construct an alternative, metaphorical method for organizing information along pictorial, not textual, lines. But this point, clearly made in the book, is ignored. Jordanova states that the development and use of twentieth-century technology (all of it?) is 'imperialistic'. This is her privilege. But taking quotations out of context, delivering unsupported judgemental assertions, relying on *ad feminum* uses of terms such as 'wacky' or 'half-baked', and engaging a relentlessly sneering tone, is not.

Barbara Maria Stafford
Department of Art History, Cochrane-Woods Art Center
University of Chicago
5540 S. Greenwood Ave
Chicago IL 60637

NOTES

1 Barbara Maria Stafford, *Body Criticism: Imaging the Unseen in Enlightenment Art and Medicine*, Cambridge, MA: MIT Press, 1991.

2 Ludmillla Jordanova, 'Body Images', in *Art History*, vol. 15 (December 1992), pp. 537–41.

Ludmilla Jordanova, University of Essex, replies:

I was most interested to read Professor Stafford's denunciation of my recent review of her book. And, of course, I warmly endorse her invitation to readers of *Art History* to judge for themselves. Yet there is a piquant contradiction in Stafford's request, since she refuses to accept a reviewer doing just this. Professor Stafford's main outrage seems to focus on my taking items 'out of context', but in a sense this is not just inevitable but essential in a short review of a very long book. The point is surely that by giving page numbers, readers can go to the volume and see that quotations have been used responsibly. The review in fact makes, without any sneering at all, serious points about scholarship to which I hope readers of this journal will give due consideration. The condition of authorship is a curious one; it involves the need to accept multiple readings of one's work in the knowledge that some will be uncongenial. This applies to reviewers too! Yet mature scholarship can only be built on acceptance of this condition. Thus, I stand by the arguments of the review and affirm the sustained engagement with a difficult book that they represent.

*Yale*Art

The Royal Palaces of Tudor England

Architecture and Court Life, 1460-1547

Simon Thurley

In a book which provides a fascinating architectural and social history of the court of Henry VIII, Simon Thurley examines the development of royal Tudor palaces and the public and private activities of their occupants.

Published for the Paul Mellon Centre for Studies in British Art

288pp. 200 b/w illus. + 158 colour plates £29.95

Rodin: The Shape of Genius

Ruth Butler

In this major reinterpretation of Rodin's life and times, an accomplished Rodin scholar draws for the first time on closely guarded archives and letters to reveal the facts of this legendary artist's life and provide new interpretations of the motivations, execution and reception of his extraordinary artistic creations.

October 608pp. 200 b/w illus. £19.95

Paris: An Architectural History

Anthony Sutcliffe

In this lavishly illustrated book one of the city's leading historians traces the main features of the development of Parisian building and architecture since Roman times, explaining the interaction of continuity and innovation and relating it to power, social structure, the property market, fashion and the creativity of its architects.

October 232pp. 70 b/w illus. + 180 colour plates £25.00

African Zion

The Sacred Art of Ethiopia

Marilyn Heldman et al

Written by leading scholars in Ethiopian and Byzantine art, this handsome book is the first comprehensive introduction to Ethiopian Christian art of the fourth to the eighteenth centuries, and the first to address the function of art within Ethiopian society.

October 304pp. 30 b/w illus. + 120 colour plates £40.00

Piranesi as Architect and Designer

John Wilton-Ely

Although Piranesi (1720-1778) is widely recognized as a graphic artist of genius, this book is the first to examine his activities, theories and influence as a trained architect and to consider his impact on the decorative arts, particularly his influential role in the formation of the neoclassical style.

October 192pp. 132 b/w illus. + 8 colour plates £30.00

Judith Leyster

A Dutch Master and Her World

Edited by James A. Welu and Pieter Biesboer

Judith Leyster (1609-1660) was the most famous woman painter of the Dutch golden age. Written by a team of scholars including art historians, economic historians and painting conservators, this book gives new insight into Leyster's world — her life, her art, and the society in which she lived.

390pp. 200 b/w illus. + 45 colour plates £45.00

The Age of the Baroque in Portugal

Edited by Jay Levenson

The eighteenth century was a true golden age for the visual arts in Portugal. This handsome volume is the first major work in English to be devoted to this period of Portuguese art and history.

October 288pp. 25 b/w illus. + 140 colour plates £40.00